THE BYZANTINE PATRIARCHATE
451—1204

THE BYZANTINE PATRIARCHATE
451—1204

BY

GEORGE EVERY, S.S.M.

LONDON

S·P·C·K

1962

First published in 1947
Second edition, revised, 1962
S.P.C.K.
Holy Trinity Church
Marylebone Road
London N.W.1

Printed in Great Britain by
Billing & Sons Ltd., Guildford and London

DEDICATED TO
WLADIMIR WEIDLÉ

PREFACE TO FIRST EDITION

THE CHRISTIAN East disappears from the field of vision of most English students, both of European history and of general church history, after the reign of Justinian (527–65). Yet the influence of the East upon the West in the five centuries following was more continuous than is commonly supposed. This is most obvious in the field of art, where Western styles continued to be variants upon Byzantine models until the twelfth century, but like conclusions could be drawn from the study of other subjects.

The first object of this book is to fill up a gap in the library of the English theological student who wants an introduction to Eastern church history after the Council of Chalcedon; but I hope it may be useful to others as an introduction to the ecclesiastical and theological aspects of Byzantine civilization. At the present time the Byzantines are likely to interest us more and more, for three main reasons. Firstly, their empire was an early example of a Christian society ruled by an educated lay bureaucracy. Secondly, Byzantine art had symbolic and decorative aims that we now find sympathetic, in contrast with the naturalistic aims of Hellenistic and Renaissance sculpture. Thirdly, those European peoples who were most thoroughly Byzantinized now form together the most powerful practical force in Europe and Asia. It is necessary for us to understand their background, especially where it diverges most from the mediaeval background of post-Renaissance Western Europe.

The first eleven chapters of this book make no claim to originality. They are concerned with the Byzantine church in its relations with other churches, especially, but not exclusively, in the West, from the middle of the fifth to the beginning of the eleventh century. In this period differences between East and West were real and important, and sometimes led to schisms;

vii

but these were healed because they were regarded, at least on the Byzantine side, as schisms within the one Catholic and Orthodox church. The last three chapters call for a special note, since two of them derive material from original sources in a greater degree than the rest of the book. This is because I have been driven to depart from what has been the normal view of the final divergence between East and West.

It used to be supposed that the two churches were at enmity from the time of Photius (858–86), and in schism from the year 1054, when Papal legates excommunicated the Patriarch Michael Cerularius. But recent research has reduced the significance of both these crises.

So long as the transition was ascribed to the tenth century, the responsibility could be laid upon Byzantine self-sufficiency at a time when Rome's prestige was admittedly at a very low ebb. But if it be transferred to the eleventh and twelfth a larger share of the responsibility must be attributed to the reformed Papacy. The transformation of the Papal primacy into a central government for the universal church could not but offend the deepest feelings of the Eastern churches, who were ready to acknowledge the Pope as the first among equals, but not to submit to his sovereign instructions.

The Byzantine objection to this was political in a deep and serious sense. Considerations of immediate policy often favoured an alliance with Rome, but the structure of Byzantine society would be endangered by the acknowledgment of a supreme ecclesiastical authority independent of the emperor. In the Byzantine world there was no rigid distinction between two societies: the monks and the married clergy on the one hand, and the laity on the other. All had their office in the church, and all were equally interested in theology. The emperor appointed and at times deposed Patriarchs, but the custody of dogma belonged to the whole people. The Eastern Patriarchs, who inherit this tradition, wrote to Pius IX in 1848: "For us the guardianship of religion rests with the whole body of the church, that is with the people itself, which desires that religious dogma should remain unchanging and conformed to that of the

Fathers." [1] This is the clue to the failure of emperors and Popes to bring about a reunion of East and West by political means. The Byzantine people, and those peoples who inherit their tradition, stubbornly remain responsible for the maintenance of dogma, of a mystery which they understand through the order of the liturgy and the pattern of the icons on their church walls. Dogma with them is not only an intellectual system apprehended by the clergy and expounded to the laity, but a field of vision wherein all things on earth are seen in their relation to things in heaven, first and foremost through liturgical celebration. Therefore they can endure political changes that would gravely embarrass Western churches, because the power of the clergy to speak their own mind matters little, if the rite is preserved. Religious freedom in the East is freedom for the liturgy, not for preaching, or education, or youth organizations. Yet "all these shall be added", for the Church is a sermon, a school, and a family.

The Reverend Thomas Smith, a somewhat severe critic of the Greek clergy in the days of their degrading subservience to the Turkish government, paid eloquent tribute to the influence of liturgical observance upon the laity:

> Next to the miraculous and gracious providence of *God*, I ascribe the preservation of *Christianity* among them to the strict and religious observation of the *Festivals* and *Fasts* of the Church. . . . For Children and those of the most ordinary capacities know the meaning of these holy Solemnities, at which times they flock to church in great companies, and thereby retain the memory of our *Blessed Saviour's* Birth, dying upon the Cross, Resurrection, and Ascension, and keep up the constant profession of their acknowledgment of the necessary and fundamental points of Faith, as of the doctrine of the *Blessed Trinity* and the like. And while they celebrate the sufferings and martyrdoms of the *Apostles* of our Lord and Saviour Jesus Christ, and other great Saints, who laid down their lives most joyfully for His name, and underwent with unwearied and invincible patience all the torments and cruelties of their *Heathen* Persecutors, they take courage from such glorious examples, and are the better

---

[1] Cf. the letter of Alexis Khomiakoff to William Palmer in W. J. Birkbeck, *Russia and the English Church*, vol. i, London, 1895, p. 94.

enabled to endure with less trouble and regret the miseries and hardships they daily struggle with.[1]

My own knowledge of Orthodox church life in the modern world is very limited. I have never actually visited an Orthodox country; and most of my Orthodox friends, though not all, are of the Russian emigration. But I have received much help in the understanding of Byzantine history from my brother, the Reverend E. Every, who has lived in the neighbourhood of Constantinople, and has stayed among Orthodox surroundings in Jerusalem and Alexandria, Greece and Cyprus. Dr Zernov has given me much encouragement, and in particular matters I have been able to rely on the assistance and criticism of Miss Avrilea Vlachou, Dr Eugene Lampert, M. Methodie Kusseff, the Reverend Alexis van der Mensbrugghe, and two Armenian priests, the Reverend Tiran Nersoyan and the Reverend S. Kalloustian.

Two English authorities on Byzantine history, Dr Norman Baynes and Dr Joan Hussey, have helped me a great deal with advice and criticism, though they must not be reckoned responsible for any of my errors. Among others who have assisted me with the loan of books and in the verification of references I must mention in particular Sir Eric Maclagan of the Victoria and Albert Museum, Professor R. M. Dawkins of Oxford, the Metropolitan Germanos of Thyateira, Dr Otto Demus, the Reverend D. J. Chitty, the Reverend J. Perret, the Reverend T. F. Taylor, the Reverend T. M. Parker of the Pusey House, Oxford, and the authorities at St Deiniol's Library, Hawarden, Dr Williams's Library in London, and the National Central Library.

For criticism of particular chapters I have to thank Fr Lionel Thornton and two other members of the Community of the Resurrection at Mirfield, Dr F. J. E. Raby, and members of my own community, especially Fr Victor Ranford, at whose instigation the book was written. Acknowledgments for assistance in connection with the illustrations will be found in the notes on

[1] From *An Account of the Greek Church*, by Thos. Smith, B.D., London, 1680, pp. 18–19.

the illustrations, and so far as possible my obligations to books are acknowledged in the footnotes. Details for some of those that I have used frequently will be found under abbreviations.

GEORGE EVERY, S.S.M.

KELHAM, *August* 1945.

PREFACE TO SECOND EDITION

SINCE THIS book was written I have looked up into the cupola at Daphni, and with a pack on my back and Helicon in front of me climbed up to the monastery and church of Hosios Loukas in Stiris. I have clambered from church to church on the holy mountain of Aegina. I have seen Gratchanitsa, and the Holy Sepulchre. I should like to write a different kind of book, but since this is still required and deserves revision, I have kept as close as I can to my text, except in the last chapters, where it is no longer necessary to apologize for discarding traditional views, and where my task has been assisted by the publication not only of Professor Dvornik's full-length study of Photius,[1] but also by Mr Runciman's *History of the Crusades* [2] and his *Eastern Schism.* [3] The change in the situation is perhaps most aptly illustrated by the *Festschrift* for Dom Lambert Beauduin, *L'Église et les églises.* [4] This was published in commemoration of "neuf siècles de douloureuse separation", 1054–1954, but it begins with a masterly essay by Père Yves Congar analysing the effect on the idea of schism of the discovery that "the Great Schism" cannot be precisely dated. Two earlier books that were not available in England during the Second World War have been very useful. They are Ostrogorsky's *History of the Byzantine State,* [5] and Père Martin Jugie's *Le Schisme Byzantin.* [6] They too have made a difference to the general acceptance of new views on the schism, and perhaps the first edition of this book has not been entirely without effect.

G. E.

[1] *The Photian Schism, History and Legend,* Cambridge, 1948.
[2] In three volumes, Cambridge, 1951–4.   [3] Oxford, 1955.
[4] Chevetogne, Belgium (*Irénikon*), 2 vols., 1955.
[5] Cited in English translation by Professor J. M. Hussey, Oxford, 1956.
[6] Paris, 1941.

CONTENTS

There was no general schism in or before 1089, but a conflict in Italy and Constantinople, where the Pope was no longer commemorated in the diptychs. This did not affect Antioch in 1054–60, or Jerusalem before 1187. The schism at Antioch in 1100 was local, and the general schism grew gradually with the exercise and rejection of Papal claims. These were met by theological objections to the *filioque*, and to Latin eucharistic doctrine and practice.

ILLUSTRATIONS

facing page

Cassino and Constantinople at that time see pp. 188-9. The church was the property of the Abbey. The atrium was injured in the campaign of 1944.)

Photograph by S. B. Anderson.

8 Miniature of the Descent from the Cross in Egerton MSS. 1139, a psalter made in the Latin kingdom of Jerusalem in the second half of the twelfth century, after designs resembling those at Bethlehem (p. 184), and others in a Jacobite psalter made in Mesopotamia in about 1220   119

   (See T. S. R. Boase in *Journal of the Warburg Institute*, ii (1938), pp. 14–15; and Hugo Buchthal in *Syria*, Paris, 1939, p. 138.)

   Photograph by courtesy of the British Museum, crown copyright reserved.

Acknowledgments for assistance in the collection and selection of these illustrations are also due to M. Wladimir Weidlé, Mr T. S. Eliot, Mr Rudolph Wallfried, Dr Otto Demus, Miss Muriel Bentley, and others.

MAPS

ABBREVIATIONS USED IN THE NOTES

Alexiad: *The Alexiad of the Princess Anna Comnena*, Greek test in CB, PG 131, and elsewhere, Eng. trans. by E. A. S. Dawes, London, 1928.

Bettenson: *Documents of the Christian Church*, ed. H. Bettenson, Oxford, 1943.

Bindley: *Oecumenical documents of the Faith*, ed. T. H. Bindley, revised by F. H. Green, London, 1950.

B.O.:   *Bibliotheca Orientalis*, ed. J. Assemanus, Rome, 1719–28.

Bury, E.R.E.:   *History of the Eastern Roman Empire from Irene to Basil I*, by J. B. Bury, London, 1912.

Bury-Gibbon: *The Decline and Fall of the Roman Empire*, by Edward Gibbon, ed. J. B. Bury, illustrations selected by O. M. Dalton, 7 vols., London, 1926–9.

B: *Byzantion*, Brussels and Boston, U.S.A., 1924 *ff*.

BZ: *Byzantinische Zeitschrift*, Leipzig, 1892 *ff*.

C.A.H.:   *Cambridge Ancient History*, 1923–39.

C.B.:   *Corpus scriptorum historiae Byzantinae*, Bonn, 1826–97.

C.H.J.:   *Cambridge Historical Journal, 1923 ff*.

Chron. Eccles.:   *Chronicon Ecclesiasticon* by Gregory Bar-Hebraeus, Syriac with Latin trans. by J. B. Abbeloos and T. J. Lamy, 3 vols., Louvain, 1872–8.

C.J.C.:   *Corpus Juris Civilis*, ed. P. Kruger, T. Mommsen, R. Schöll, G. Kröll, 3 vols., Berlin, 1906–12.

C.Med.H.:   *Cambridge Mediaeval History*, 1911–36.

C.Q.R.:   *Church Quarterly Review*.

D.A.C.:   *Dictionnaire d'archéologie chrétienne et de liturgie*, ed. F. Cabrol and H. Leclerq, Paris, 1907–52.

Diehl, *Manuel*:   *Manuel d'art Byzantin*, by Charles Diehl, 2 vols., Paris, 1925–6.

Dölger: *Regesten der Kaiserkunden des Oströmischen Reiches*, ed. F. Dölger, 3 vols., Munich and Berlin, 1924–32.

D.T.C.:   *Dictionnaire de théologie catholique*, ed. P. Vacant and others, Paris, 1899–1950.

Eastern Schism: *The Eastern Schism*, by S. Runciman, Oxford, 1955.

E.C.Q.:   *Eastern Churches Quarterly*, Ramsgate, 1937 *ff*.

E.H.R.:   *English Historical Review*, London, 1885 *ff*.

E.O.:   *Echos d'orient*, Paris, 1897 *ff*.

First Bulgarian Empire: *A History of the First Bulgarian Empire*, by S. Runciman, London, 1930.

Gay: *L'Italie méridionale et l'empire Byzantin*, by J. Gay, Paris, 1904.

H-L: *Conciliengeschichte*, by C. J. Hefele, French trans. by H. Leclerq, Paris, 1907–14.

Hist. Hier.:   *Historia Hierosolymitana*, by Fulcher of Chartres, ed. H. Hagenmeyer, Heidelberg, 1913.

Jaffé: *Regesta Pontificum Romanorum to 1198*, ed. P. Jaffé, G. Kaltenbrunner and others, 2 vols., Leipzig, 1885–8.

J. M. Hussey, Ch. and Learning: *Church and Learning in the Byzantine Empire, 867-1185*, by J. M. Hussey, Oxford, 1937.

J.T.S.:   *Journal of Theological Studies*, Oxford, 1900 *ff.*

Kidd, *Documents*: *Documents illustrating the history of the Church*, ed. B. J. Kidd, vols. ii and iii, London, 1923–41.

Lib. Pont.:   *Liber Pontificalis*, ed. L. Duchesne, 2 vols., Paris, 1886–92.

Mansi: *Sacrorum conciliorum . . . collectio*, ed. J. D. Mansi, 31 vols., reprint, Paris and Leipzig, 1901–12.

MGH epp ss sgus: *Monumenta Germaniae Historica*, ed. G. Pertz and others, Hanover, 1826 *ff.*, *epistolae, scriptores, scriptores rerum Germanicarum in usum scholarum.*

Mich. Syr.:   *Chronicle of Michael the Syrian*, ed. with French trans. by J. B. Chabot, 3 vols., Paris, 1899–1910.

Michel: *Humbert und Kerullarios*, ed. A. Michel, 2 vols., Paderborn, 1924–30.

Ostrogorsky: *History of the Byzantine State*, by G. Ostrogorsky, Eng. trans. by J. M. Hussey, Oxford, 1956.

P.G.:   *Patrologia Graeco-Latina*, Paris, 1857–66.

Photian Schism: *The Photian Schism, History and Legend*, by F. Dvornik, Cambridge, 1948.

P.L.:   *Patrologia Latina*, Paris, 1844–55.

P.O.:   *Patrologia Orientalis*, Paris, 1907 *ff.*

Potthast: *Regesta Pontificum Romanorum 1198-1304*, ed. A. Potthast, 2 vols., Berlin, 1873–4.

PPTS: *Palestine Pilgrims' Text Society*, Eng. trans. of pilgrim texts, 34 nos. in 13 vols., London, 1884–97.

Premier temps: *Les premier temps de l'état pontifical*, by L. Duchesne, Paris, 1904.

REB: *Revue des études Byzantines*, Paris, 1943 *ff.*

REG: *Revue des études Grecques*, Paris, 1888 *ff.*

ROL: *Revue de l'orient Latin*, Paris, 1894–1911.

Runciman, *Crusades*:   *History of the Crusades*, by S. Runciman, 3 vols., Cambridge, 1951–4.

Schisme Byzantin: *Le Schisme Byzantin*, by M. Jugie, Paris, 1941.

Tellenbach: *Church, State, and Christian Society in the Investiture Contest*, by G. Tellenbach, Eng. trans. by H. F. Bennett, Oxford, 1940.

Tixeront: *History of Dogmas* by J. Tixeront, Eng. trans. St Louis and London, vol. iii, 1916.

Vasiliev: *History of the Byzantine Empire*, by A. A. Vasiliev, 2nd English edition, Madison, 1952.

VIème siècle: *L'église au sixième siècle*, by L. Duchesne, Paris, 1925.

I

BYZANTINE CIVILIZATION

GIBBON's *The Decline and Fall of the Roman Empire*,[1] a master-piece of literature and a landmark in the history of historical research, belongs to an age that had no doubts of any kind about the meaning of civilization. The civilized way of life came down from Hellas, enshrined in Greek and Latin literature, Hellenistic and Roman sculpture, declined into the Dark Ages, and emerged at the Renaissance into the enlightenment of modern times. Four volumes of the seven in Bury's edition are given to the decay of Rome from Diocletian (284–304) to Justinian (527–65), and one to the last agony of the fall of Constantinople and the dispersion of Greek culture in the West. Only two deal summarily with the eight hundred years from 565 to 1350, which are in this way forcibly assimilated to the periods of decay before and after. In England they are still neglected, for although J. B. Bury's *History of the Later Roman Empire from Arcadius to Irene* [2] was continued in another *History of the Eastern Roman Empire from the Fall of Irene to the Accession of Basil I* (867),[3] the second edition of the first of these two books, published in 1923,[4] did not go beyond 565.

Bury's titles show his special emphasis on the continuity of the Roman empire from Augustus to 1453. This is justified by the continued use of the Roman name by the Byzantines, who called their country Romania, and by the modern Greeks, who call their language Romaic. But this language is Greek, not

---

[1] The original edition in six volumes was published in London, 1775–88. All citations in this book are from the illustrated edition by J. B. Bury, 1926–9.

[2] 2 vols., London, 1889.   [3] 1 vol., London, 1912.

[4] 2 vols., London, 1923.

Latin. The Byzantines knew no Latin poetry, history, or theology. Virgil, Livy, and St Augustine were no part of their
tradition. The Latin element in their civilization was legal,
political, and military. The Greek classics made a deeper impression upon them, for they always remained an essential element in their higher education. The Hellenes, as the Byzantines
called the pagan Greeks, were unbelievers, but ancestors. Every
educated Byzantine could catch an allusion to Homer, and
many were familiar with Plato, Aristotle, and Pindar.

Byzantine civilization was the result of a development in
Greek culture within the carapace of Roman administration,
assimilating many oriental elements, pagan, Persian, Jewish,
and Christian, until this syncretism affected not only the culture, but the framework of administration and government.
The empire of Diocletian and Constantine, which lasted until
the time of Justinian, used a system of taxation and compulsory
service that was borrowed from the immemorial usages of
ancient Egypt.[1] The law of the Theodosian Code (438) and the
Code of Justinian (529–34), the civil law which was studied in
the Middle Ages (when Dante regarded Justinian [2] as the
typical Roman emperor), was not the law of Cicero and
Augustus, but a product of the transition from Roman to
Byzantine. Later Byzantine developments, which have had less
influence on the West, led the law of the East farther away from
Rome, especially after the dissolution of the administrative
system of Diocletian and the rise of a new model of Byzantine
government, sketched in the eighth, elaborated in the ninth,[3]
and formalized in the tenth century.

The new society has been called oriental, especially by
Professor Charles Diehl, whose various works [4] will be fre-

[1] See M. J. Rostovtzeff, *Social and Economic History of the Roman Empire*,
Oxford, 1926, pp. 461–6.

[2] *Paradiso*, canto v, 115–vii, 8, *passim*.

[3] See J. B. Bury, *The Imperial Administrative System in the Ninth Century*,
London, 1910.

[4] See also *Histoire de l'empire Byzantin*, Paris, 1919; Eng. trans., Princeton,
1925; and *Byzance, grandeur et decadence*, Paris, 1920. For the history of the
Byzantine empire see A. A. Vasiliev, *History of the Byzantine Empire*, 2nd
English edition, Madison, 1952, pp. 3–39, and Ostrogorsky, pp. 1–20.

quently cited in these pages. It is true that it revolved round a sacred palace, where water issued from a throne beside which mechanical lions roared and musical birds sang. "By such means", wrote the Emperor Constantine Porphyrogenitus in his *Book of Ceremonies*, "we shadow the harmonious movement of God the creator around this universe, while the imperial power is preserved in proportion and order." [1] But the Byzantine sacred monarchy was set in a city, exposed at times to the hissings of an angry mob around the racecourse at the Hippodrome, to demonstrations in St Sophia against heresy or heavy taxation, and to the risks of rebellion in the army, the navy, and even the *scrinia* or secretarial bureaux. No Byzantine dynasty sat long upon the throne.[2] Several rose from the ranks, for Justin I was an itinerant rope-seller, Leo III a Syrian sheep-drover, Michael the Amorian an obscure Phrygian, Basil "the Macedonian" an Armenian adventurer who first distinguished himself by his skill in taming horses. Others sprang from the official aristocracy of generals and administrators. Though the frequency of revolutions in Byzantine history can be exaggerated, in all periods the danger of insurrection was real; and this sets limits to a sovereign power that was theoretically uncircumscribed. Revolutions might begin in the administration and the army; or in the city *demes*, the blue and green factions in the Hippodrome at Constantinople, who concerned themselves, not only with racing, but with police and the management of minor public services, under the leadership of *demarchs* or *democrats* from the class of skilled craftsmen and shopkeepers.

After the beginning of the seventh century the *demes* became formal divisions. The Senate of great officials had some political significance, especially in the reign of Constans (641–68), who spent much of his time at a distance from the capital, leaving

---

[1] CB, p. 5. For the throne of Solomon, cf. bk. ii, c. 15, p. 569. For the textual problems of the *De ceremoniis*, which incorporates much earlier material, see J. B. Bury in EHR XXII (1907), pp. 209–27, 417–39; and for the running water Ibn Batouta in B. Trapier, *Les voyageurs Arabes au moyen age*, Paris, 1937, pp. 154–8.

[2] The Macedonian dynasty (867–1056) is an apparent exception, but its tenure was interrupted by long regencies in 913–45, 963–76, and after 1028.

the senators in charge.[1] F. Dvornik has argued that the Oecumenical Councils of the church were meetings of the senate in its ecclesiastical aspect under the presidency of the emperor's representatives.[2] Several such councils were held besides the few that appear in both Eastern and Western lists. Ecclesiastical business of less moment was transacted at the *synodos endemousa* or permanent synod of bishops present in Constantinople, corresponding to the *consistorium* or imperial council of civil officers. In no branch of public business was the conscience of the empire more sensitive, for orthodoxy was in effect its constitution.

Theoretically the sole legislator, in practice the emperor, was hedged about on every side by powerful orders devoted to precedents, and open to the sway of voices from the marketplace, not only in Constantinople, but in the other Greek cities and colonies from Naples in Campania and Reggio in Calabria to Antioch in Syria and Cherson on the north coast of the Black Sea. Monks were especially formidable critics, for persecution made them martyrs. The only effective way of dealing with them was to move them to an unsympathetic monastery, and even then they might exercise too great an influence over their hosts. The Greek monk was often a politician, like the Greek citizen. It must never be forgotten that the Greek cities were the heart of the empire. Those on the coasts of Italy and Asia remained loyal when the highlands in the interior were conquered by the Lombards and the Turks. The oriental element in Byzantine culture and art was always kept in check by the Greek tradition.

The strength of this tradition was proved in the iconoclast controversy of the eighth and ninth centuries, when the influence of Greece and the islands defeated an Asiatic attempt to make all ecclesiastical art symbolic and abstract, and won the day for a religious art that could retain the Greek interest in the representation and interpretation of the human body.

---

[1] See C. Diehl, *Le Senate et le peuple Byzantin au viième et viiième siècles* in B i (1924), pp. 201–13, and Ostrogorsky, p. 124.
[2] *The General Councils of the Church*, London, 1961, pp. 14–16.

Byzantine mosaic and mural painting sacrifice bodily proportion to answer problems of human destiny beyond the normal range of classical enquiry. For these they found a surer medium than sculpture [1] in the play of light on coloured surfaces, revealing rhythmical movement or reposeful rest. But decorative aims were always subordinated to the revelation of the soul through garments of flesh.

The luxury of Byzantine decoration can be exaggerated. For instance, the mosaics of the Holy Family that once belonged to the oratory of the Greek Pope John VII in Old St Peter's at Rome [2] show the same tenderness for women and children, for the poor and for labour, that we discover with the same surprise in Byzantine legislation. In the later developments of Byzantine law [3] women were practically on an equality with men in respect of property and the guardianship of minors. The Byzantine law of divorce is remarkable for an attempt to strike a qualitative balance between the claims of wife and husband. The grounds for divorce were not the same for each, but every advantage to him was compensated by some corresponding advantage for her. The church frowned on all marriages after the first, but did not refuse a second or even a third chance to the divorced, unless the grounds were considered altogether insufficient. Such marriages were performed with maimed rites, and entailed a period of penance. [4] Similar penances were imposed on widowers and widows who re-

[1] The difficulty of using classical busts for Byzantine ends can be seen in some of the opening plates of H. Peirce and R. Tylor's *Byzantine Art*, London, 1926, showing imperial portraits of the third and fourth centuries. For another view of the transition see C. Rodenwalt in *C.A.H.* xii, pp. 561-70.

[2] See Paul Muratoff, *Peinture Byzantine*, Paris, 1928, plates lv, lvi.

[3] See especially G. D. Buckler, *Women in Byzantine Law about 1100*, in B, xi, 2 (1936), pp. 391-416; Bury-Gibbon, v, pp. 557-9; *Nomocanon*, PG 104, c. 892 (tenth century), with *scholia*, ibid., c. 1167-94; Matthaeus Monachus, *Quaestiones et causae matrimoniales*, PG 119, c. 1275-82.

[4] Rules in the *Nomocanon*, PG 104, c. 907-8, with comment from Balsamon and others (twelfth century), ibid., c. 1193-4, provide for seven years of graduated penance. In mediaeval Byzantium divorce was an affair of the civil law. The church was not directly involved until the question of remarriage arose. Only in Russia did cases of divorce come before ecclesiastical courts.

married. Fourth marriages were altogether forbidden, alike to
the divorced, the widower, and the widow. The theory was that
the first marriage created a bond that should survive death. It is
interesting to observe that where there were children remarriage
of any kind was made more difficult.

The place of the mother in the Byzantine family is illustrated
in three remarkable sketches in Charles Diehl's *Figures Byzantines* [1] of the three mothers of Theodore the Studite (*d.* 826),
Michael Psellos (eleventh century), and Alexius Comnenus
(*d.* 1118). The last, Anna Dalassena, was the matriarch of the
Comnenoi, and the real founder of the fortunes of the family.
Other women distinguished themselves by their skill in government, from Pulcheria, the sister of Theodosius II, in the middle
of the fifth century, to Theophano, the sister of Basil II, who
acquitted herself well in the difficult task of ruling Germany
at the end of the tenth century. The narrative of Anna Comnena [2] is interesting evidence of a woman's learning. She refers
to her mother's intellectual and mystical interests that carried
her out of her depth and gave her "a kind of vertigo" [3] when
she was a young girl. Other princesses wrote poetry, like
Eudocia Athenais, the wife of Theodosius II. [4] The daughters
of Constantine Porphyrogenitus did secretarial work for their
learned father. The Comnenoi in their foundations made provision for choirs of male and female voices, [5] and for a lady
doctor [6] as a regular member of the staff of a hospital.

Another remarkable difference between classical and Christian times is in the status given to labour. The classical aristo-
crat was a gentleman of leisure, who did political work in his
spare time. The Byzantine bureaucrat was a hard-working
administrator, accomplishing his "liturgy" in accordance with

[1] 2 vols., Paris, 1906–13, Eng. trans. by Harold Bell, *Byzantine Portraits*,
1 vol., London and New York, 1927, pp. 105–25, 276–326.
[2] *The Alexiad of the Princess Anna Comnena*, Eng. trans. by E. A. S. Dawes,
London, 1928; also in CB and PG 131.
[3] *Alexiad*, v, c. 9.
[4] S. Runciman, *Byzantine Civilization*, London, 1933, p. 249. One of her
poems is in PG 85, c. 827–64.
[5] *Alexiad*, xv, c. 7.
[6] J. M. Hussey, *Church and Learning in the Byzantine Empire*, Oxford, 1936,
p. 185.

instructions laid down in books on procedure, like the *De administrando imperio* of Constantine Porphyrogenitus. The soldiers worked to similar drill books, *The Strategicon* of the Emperor Maurice and the *Established Tactics* of Leo VI.[1] The biographers of some emperors boast their skill in calligraphy, in handwriting and diplomatic forms, their mastery of the art of administration. A like passion for exact craftsmanship runs through the whole of Byzantine society, and probably under-lies the success of Byzantine citizens in the minor arts, especially ivories, enamels and jewellery.[2] Few textiles survive, but travellers' tales testify to a universal impression that by Italian standards everyone in Constantinople was magnificently dressed.[3] The government took every care, perhaps too much care, to preserve the standards and secrets of craftsmanship, and to regulate prices, hours, and wages. The silk industry was a state monopoly, and we do not hear of large fortunes made by private persons in legitimate commerce. Usury, on the other hand, though very strictly regulated, was never so completely forbidden as in the West.[4] Byzantine trade remained prosperous, and a safe source of revenue for the government, until the loss of Asia Minor, that sure source of men and supplies, sapped the economic strength of the empire,[5] and bestowed decisive ad-vantages upon the Italian cities, whose trading colonies in Constantinople were able to evade the ordinary controls. J. B. Bury [6] argued, from the standpoint of the nineteenth century, that Byzantine commerce was ruined by over-severe government supervision and the absence of a satisfactory credit system. It certainly did not suffer, as Western commerce suffered in the Middle Ages, from the indifference of a landed aristocracy. The Emperor Theophilus in the ninth century

---

[1] See Sir C. Oman, *A History of the Art of War in the Middle Ages*, London, 1898, pp. 169–215.

[2] Examples in H. Peirce and R. Tylor, *Byzantine Art, passim.*

[3] See the narrative of Benjamin of Tudela, a Jew (about 1162), in T. Wright, *Early Travels in Palestine*, London, 1848, pp. 74–6.

[4] See Ostrogorsky, p. 168.

[5] See *idem*, pp. 318, 325, 335, 345.

[6] Bury-Gibbon, v, appendices 12–13, pp. 561–6; see also Ostrogorsky, pp. 224, 255–6.

personally investigated the quality and price of the goods in the bazaars, especially the food, though he objected to his own empress investing in commercial ventures.[1] In the thirteenth century John Vatatzes bought his empress a new crown, called "eggy", from the proceeds of her chickens.[2]

In theory at least no one might be or remain in Constantinople except on business.[3] Idlers, aristocratic or plebeian, had no encouragement. The able-bodied unemployed were set to work at street cleaning, weeding the public gardens, or working in the bakeries, which were public property like the silk factory. The infirm were cared for in hospitals, founded in every period for old and young. The *Orphanotrophos*, or minister of orphanages, was an official of standing, who might rise to the first place in the hierarchy. Hospital trains accompanied the Byzantine armies. Alexius Comnenus brought his column to a halt every time a woman in the company was taken in the pains of childbirth,[4] and then, after a trumpet-blast, moved on.

A like consideration for the weak is to be found in Byzantine agrarian legislation, even if we have to admit that it was not finally successful. The long struggle of Byzantine governments to prevent the growth of a feudal class,[5] and to preserve the free village of independent peasant proprietors in Macedonia, Thrace and Greece, has left behind a certain impress on the traditions of peasant life in those countries, where a Christian feudal aristocracy has seldom, if ever, established itself against the tradition of the free commune, so long supported by the Byzantine government. Even the criminal gained by the reluctance of the Byzantines to kill in cold blood. Their economy in the use of their small professional armies shocked Western observers, trained in the dare-devil ways of feudalism.[6] The

[1] Theophanes Continuatus, CB, pp. 87–9.
[2] Gregoras, CB, vol. i, p. 43.
[3] *Corpus Juris Civilis*, vol. iii, ed. R. Schöll, G. Kröll, Berlin, 1912, pp. 482–3 (novel 99); J. B. Bury, *Later Roman Empire* (1889), vol. ii, pp. 527–8.
[4] *Alexiad*, xv, c. 7.
[5] See Ostrogorsky, pp. 120–1, 241–4, 248–50, Vasiliev, pp. 345–9, and the article by A. M. Andréades in *Byzantium*, ed. N. H. Baynes and H. St L. B. Moss, Oxford, 1948, pp. 55–60.
[6] For Byzantine military ethics see Sir C. Oman, op. cit., pp. 199–201; and G. D. Buckler, *Anna Comnena*, Oxford, 1929, pp. 97–105.

same observers were often horrified at the use of mutilation as a substitute for death. The amputation of a finger or a slit in the nose revolts our susceptibilities, but the intention was humane: to humiliate, and then to provide an opportunity for penitence. J. B. Bury saw no reason to doubt contemporary testimony that in the reign of John Comnenus (1118–43) no one was put to death.[1] Even unsuccessful revolutionaries were more often interned in monasteries, from which they might emerge at the next swing of the political pendulum.

It is not easy to form a picture of the humbler classes in the Byzantine empire, but the style of some chronicles and many lives of the saints suggests that they were written for a popular audience, who took pleasure in vivid colour, and wanted to know the personal appearance of the heroes of the Trojan war. Dr Norman Baynes can compare the *Chronicle of John Malalas* to a modern Sunday newspaper.[2] If this argument is valid, literacy may have been common, at least in the capital. More evidence points to continuous excitement on religious themes. In the fourth century St Gregory of Nyssa complained that the baker and the bath-keeper would argue about Arianism.[3] As early as the sixth century this popular interest veered from theological to liturgical issues, for

> theology is . . . always the professional preserve of the clergy and the interest of a comparatively small educated *élite* of the laity. Liturgy is a . . . universal Christian activity, and so a *popular* interest.[4]

Rival versions [5] of the *Trisagion* were sung by rival parties in the choir at Antioch and at Constantinople. Later on popular excitement raged over images or animal designs on the walls of churches, over the ceremonial veneration of icons of the saints, the use or omission of Alleluia in Lent, the right day to begin

[1] *C. Med. H.*, iv, preface, p. xiii.
[2] *The Byzantine Empire*, London, 1925, pp. 35–6.
[3] B. J. Kidd, *Documents Illustrating the History of the Church*, vol. ii, London, 1923, no. 105.
[4] Gregory Dix, o.s.b., *The Shape of the Liturgy*, London, 1945, p. 7.
[5] *Infra*, p. 34.

fasting, and the use of leavened or unleavened bread in the Eucharist. These issues are reflected in hagiography,[1] the journalism of the Byzantine church. A hagiographical war between rival parties in the ninth century [2] has done much to complicate the history of the schism between East and West.

To understand the part played by the Byzantine laity in liturgical controversies it is necessary to understand the meaning of liturgy in the East. In the Greek city state the word was used of any kind of public service, from building a battleship to providing a chorus at the festival of Dionysus. In the early church bishops, presbyters, deacons, and laity all had their accustomed services,[3] especially in the celebration of the Mass. In the West we have become accustomed to think of the Mass as something performed by the clergy for the congregation, since the usual form is a Low Mass with one priest and one server. In the East, on the other hand, every celebration of *The Divine Liturgy* is a High Mass performed with full ceremonial by priest and deacon, reader and acolytes, choir and people. The icons in the roof and on the screen, the image of Christ in the cupola, the Virgin Mother over the altar, the saints and angels in the upper story, are actors in the same drama with the clergy in the sanctuary and the people in the nave. In modern times the high iconostasis divides the normal Eastern church into two halves, and excludes the laity from direct participation in the action that takes place within the sanctuary, except at two dramatic moments when the Royal Doors swing open for the Great Entrance, and for the final revelation of the Body and Blood at the communion; but Byzantine screens, like the one in St Mark's, Venice, were low and open. Many descriptions imply that the images in the roof of the sanctuary, and the incense rising towards them from the altar, could be seen from the nave. The Emperor Justinian commanded that all the words of the liturgy

[1] See H. Delehaye, *Les legendes hagiographiques*, Brussels, 1906.
[2] See E. v. Dobschutz, *Methodius und die Studiten*, BZ, xviii (1909), pp. 41–105.
[3] See *The First Epistle of Clement to the Corinthians*, c. 40.

should be said in a loud voice,[1] audible to the people. Even after considerations of time made it necessary to allow two parts of the over-elaborated rite to proceed simultaneously inside and outside the iconostasis, the sense of a common action remained strong. This underlies the very interesting history of vernacular liturgies in the East. From very early days the Mass was constantly being translated into new languages, Abasgian, Avar, Old Slavonic in the early Middle Ages, Zyriane in the fourteenth century, Rumanian in the seventeenth, Kalmuck and Japanese in the nineteenth.[2] Through these vernacular liturgies Ukrainian and Arabian peasants acquired a fanatical devotion to the letter of the ritual. In the seventeenth century opposition to reforms and corrections in the Russian liturgy produced the schism of the "Old Believers".[3] To-day a like antagonism to the reform of the calendar has led to similar conflicts on Mount Athos and in other parts of Greece.[4]

The peasants were more sensitive to liturgical issues than the citizens, for in village churches the whole congregation joined in those parts of the service which a city church could leave to a professional choir. In the country, choristers and acolytes learnt by heart their gestures, words, and music. Sometimes they rose in middle life to be readers, deacons, and priests. In most ages and regions this may have been the normal method of recruitment for the village clergy, who were almost invariably married before ordination, and lived in matrimony, though they were not allowed to marry afterwards, or to marry a second wife. Bishops, on the other hand, were required to live in celibacy. They were generally chosen from the monasteries, seldom from the parish clergy; but to important sees the appointment of a civil servant with administrative experience, unmarried or a widower, was by no means uncommon. Such appointments puzzled and shocked Western critics, but in this way the

---

[1] *C.J.C.*, iii, p. 699 (novel 137, c. 6); J. Pargoire, *L'église Byzantine*, 3rd ed., Paris, 1923, p. 100; N. H. Baynes, *Byzantine Studies*, London, 1955, pp. 263–4; P. Trembelas in *L'église et les églises*, ii, pp. 207–20.

[2] See *infra*, p. 128, and references.

[3] See *Life of the Archpriest Avvakum*, Eng. trans., London, 1924.

[4] See R. M. Dawkins, *The Monks of Athos*, London, 1936, pp. 199–200.

Byzantine church gained the services of some distinguished theologians and more capable administrators.[1]

Byzantine laymen and women knew their theology, not only through the liturgy, but through the liturgical scheme of church decoration,[2] constant in style and subject, continually re-interpreted by painters of real though anonymous genius from the sixth century to the seventeenth. This pattern formed a frame on which scattered fragments of knowledge, derived from the lives of the saints, from sermons, from prayer, and from mystical reading, could combine and cohere.[3] Many Byzantines made too much of trivial issues of a ritualistic kind on which their feelings played too easily. Few were as ignorant as those Western clerks who had never proceeded beyond the painful preliminaries of a Latin education.

The laity never became a purely passive element in the Byzantine church community. This is the real clue to the relations between church and state in the East. In the monasteries most of the monks were laymen. It was not uncommon for lay monks to assume functions that were properly reserved for the priesthood, especially absolution. The very ancient custom, dating from the times of persecution, whereby the laity were allowed to reserve the Eucharist in their own houses to communicate themselves during the week, was forbidden by the council in Trullo (691–2) for fear of abuse,[4] but revived during

[1] John of Damascus left the Arabian civil service to become a monk, c. 735. Former Byzantine civil servants include Maximus Confessor (d. 662), Photius, Patriarch of Constantinople (d. 891), and another Patriarch, John Xiphilinus (d. 1075). All these were remarkable as theological thinkers. The administrators stretch from Ephrem of Antioch (d. 545) to Nicholas Mysticus (d. 925).

[2] The Byzantine Guide to Painting, as used on Mount Athos, was printed in an Eng. trans. (from the French of M. Paul Durand) as an appendix in the English edition of A. N. Didron, Christian Iconography, vol. ii, London, 1886, pp. 265–399. The pages on the distribution of subjects (cf. C. Diehl, Manuel d'art Byzantin, vol. ii, Paris, 1926, pp. 484–92) are probably older than the detailed directions. It is significant that three-quarters of these last are concerned with scriptural material.

[3] See Nicolas Cabalisas, Explanation of the Divine Liturgy, in PG 150, c. 368–492, the work of a layman of the fourteenth century (French trans., Paris, 1943; English, London, 1960).

[4] Canon 101: communicants may not receive the sacramental elements in vessels. For the use of these vessels in the seventh century, and again in the

the iconoclast troubles. Other evidence [1] can be cited to show that weekly or even daily communion was not uncommon in the seventh, or even in the ninth century. The disciples of Theodore of Tarsus, the Greek missionary who became Archbishop of Canterbury from 668 to 690, recalling his *obiter dicta* on Greek and Latin customs,[2] say that the Greeks communicate every Sunday, and put to penance those who miss three Sundays in succession "according to the canons". In the West annual communion was already becoming usual. In the East, too, it eventually became customary, but the communion of clergy and people remained the climax of the Mass, since a Mass where the celebrant alone communicated was almost unknown. The people came to communicate in the prayers, not to see the priest perform an action for them. They could not see all that passed in the sanctuary. They were intent upon their own liturgy, the responses and the chants.

Many of them left the church to perform other liturgies in the sacred palace, where:

> The logothetes run down the porphyry stair
> bearing their missives through the area of empire.[3]

---

ninth, see J. Pargoire, *L'église Byzantine*, pp. 228, 339–40; Anastasius the Sinaite in PG 89, c. 765; Theodore the Studite in PG 99, c. 1116, 1661; H. Delehaye in *Les saints stylites*, Paris and Brussels, 1923, p. clxxii. Stylite hermits used to draw them up to the top of their pillars on the end of a string.

[1] Especially Anastasius the Sinaite, ibid., c. 753; Theodore the Studite, ibid., c. 1668.

[2] In the compilation known as the *Penitentiale* of Theodore, printed in A. W. Haddan and W. Stubbs, *Councils and Ecclesiastical Documents relating to Great Britain and Ireland*, vol. iii, Oxford, 1871, p. 186. The canons referred to are certainly the second canon of the council of Antioch and the ninth (or tenth) in the collection called *The Apostolic Canons*. Of the Greek commentators on these canons in the twelfth century, printed by W. Beveridge in his *Syntagma canonum*, Oxford, 1672, reprinted in PG 137, c. 53–4, 1279–84, Zonaras agrees with Theodore's disciples, while the others take a laxer view of the obligation in accordance with the custom of their own time. There is a discussion in the article, "The Canonists on Non-Communicating Attendance," by J. W. L., in *The Union Review*, London, 1873, pp. 257–86.

St John Chrysostom refers to wide varieties in frequency of communion on his seventeenth *Homily* on Hebrews, PG 63, c. 131–2; cf. also his fifth *Homily* on 1 Timothy, PG 62, c. 529–30 (end of the fourth century).

[3] *Taliessin through Logres*, by Charles Williams, Oxford, 1938, p. 6.

Byzantine labourers sowing seed, building houses, and digging wells obeyed rituals that are still preserved in the *Euchologion*, the book of occasional offices of the Eastern Orthodox church.[1] The difference between church and state was that the church was larger in space and time. She had an upper story for angels and archangels, prophets and martyrs and saints, with the Blessed Virgin at their head, and Christ in glory reigning over all from the cupola. In the diptychs of the dead all Orthodox Patriarchs were commemorated, in the diptychs of the living the heads of all Orthodox churches outside as well as inside the bounds of the empire. The church was too old and too vast to be turned into a department of the palace, but the emperor was in supreme control of all the outward ordering of church affairs. He regulated the disposition of benefices, and the election of bishops, metropolitans, and Patriarchs. His place in the church has been compared with that of the deacon in the liturgy,[2] who from the point of view of the people seems far more active than the priest. To a Western reader a better parallel might be with the choirmaster, who is more important in an Eastern church than the organist is in the West, since the selection of such parts of the service as can be sung aloud and in full is, in practice, in his hands. The emperor was not a layman, no less a person than Pope St Leo the Great could write of his "royal power and sacerdotal vigilance".[3] In the constitutional theory of the empire, expressed in the *Ecloga* and the *Epanagoge*, emperor and Patriarch are the two chief organs of the body politic, and harmony between them was essential for the health of the empire. Some later commentators, such as Theodore Balsamon [4] in the twelfth century, found a theoretical justification for the superiority of the emperor in the Patriarch's detachment from bodily affairs. Many Patriarchs, however, had been civil servants, and wielded great political

[1] See *infra*, p. 80.
[2] By Alexis van der Mensbrugghe in *Sobornost*, Oxford, Dec., 1944, p. 10.
[3] PL 54, c. 1034, cited, with other references, by P. Dabin in *La sacerdoce royale des fidèles*, Brussels, 1950, pp. 126–7.
[4] Cited in Vasiliev, p. 470. See extracts from the *Ecloga* in J. B. Bury, *Later Roman Empire*, vol. ii (1889), p. 415; and the *Epanagoge* in PG 119, c. 909–10.

influence, especially in the period of the Macedonian dynasty (867–1056). Western scholars have debated whether the Patriarch, when he crowned the emperor, represented the church or the people. I do not think that the Byzantines would have attached much meaning to this question, which has its bearings on Western history because the Pope imitated him when he crowned a rival "Roman emperor" at Rome in A.D. 800. At that time he represented the "republic of the Romans", the citizens of the Byzantine empire in Italy, not only the clergy of the Roman church. The idea of the spiritual independence of the clergy never took root at Byzantium. When bishops, priests, and monks engaged in administrative work, as they often did, it was in the employ of the sacred monarchy that protected all alike from famine, disease, and heresy. It seemed perfectly natural that administration, in religious as well as in secular matters, should normally be in the hands of the civil bureaucracy at the sacred palace, who combined administrative experience with theological learning and devotion to accepted standards of orthodoxy. The church in the Byzantine empire never developed a bureaucracy of its own.

Byzantine monasteries remained private institutions. They were never associated in great orders like the Cluniacs, the Cistercians, and the Premonstratensians of the West. Many were so small that they easily died out, and left ruined buildings to be used again by fresh enthusiasts.[1] Individually monks might be politicians, but monasticism was never a political power. No Eastern order "ever conceived of itself as an instrument for reshaping secular life".[2] Though Byzantine bishops were normally monks, the constructive statesmen of the Byzantine church came from the civil bureaucracy, and were ordained comparatively late in life.

The moral effects are exceedingly interesting. It does seem true to say that in the Byzantine church promotion and esteem depended more upon spiritual and intellectual qualities than on that political and legal skill that gradually became the one

[1] See J. M. Hussey, *Ch. and Learning*, p. 165.
[2] F. Borkenau in *Horizon*, London, September, 1944.

thing necessary for a Western archbishop, or for a cardinal of the Roman church. At all times there were disorders and abuses, especially in the monasteries; Byzantine monks and hermits wandered about far too easily in the course of their spiritual pilgrimage. A strange restlessness led them from Mount Athos to Campania or Jerusalem and back again. By Benedictine standards they lacked stability. But sanctity was comparatively common [1] and self-indulgence remarkably rare, even in the sacred palace. Of all the heretical emperors between the fifth and ninth centuries, only one was accused of sexual vice by his Orthodox opponents. Despite the apparent laxity of Byzantine divorce legislation, in comparison with the West, very few Byzantine emperors divorced their wives. Second and third marriages at court were the occasion of much scandal. In this as in so much else our picture of Byzantium has been distorted by the interests of Gibbon. In fact, the scandalous periods in Byzantine court history were few and short, and all ended in violent purges.

The moral weakness of the Byzantines was on the side of truth, not chastity. To play barbarians against one another was a necessary part of the diplomatic ritual, essential for the defence of the frontier against enemies who were formidable in arms but ponderous in wit. The use of stratagems against Franks and Normans gave the "subtle Greekling" a reputation for guile that was not undeserved. Anna Comnena wrote with intense pride of her father's achievements at the time of the Latin occupation of Constantinople during the first Crusade:

> He gave orders that all the Franks should come in freely every day, partly because he wished them to state their requests, and partly too because he was manoeuvring by arguments of various kinds to bring them to accede to his own wishes. . . . One came after the other . . . always preferring one excuse after another for further talk, whilst he stood unmoved in the midst of the Franks, quietly hearing their endless chatter. . . . If any one of his ministers tried to cut them short, the Emperor prevented him. For knowing

---

[1] The Byzantine Acta Sanctorum made in the tenth century by Simeon Metaphrastes is in PG 114-16. See also "Les stylites à travers les ages" in H. Delehaye, Les saints stylites, pp. cxvii–cxliii.

the Franks' natural irritability he was afraid lest for some trifling pretext a great fire of scandal should be lighted. . . . Like a hammer-wrought statue, made perhaps of bronze or cold iron, he would sit the whole night through, from the evening until midnight perhaps, and often until the third cock-crow, and very occasionally almost till the sun's rays were bright. All his attendants were dead tired and would retire and rest and then come back again grumbling. . . . The emperor alone presented an unyielding front to all this labour. And what words could properly describe his patience? For in this babel of tongues each one spoke at length and "wrangled on unbridled of tongue", as Homer says; then he would stand aside for another and give him the opportunity of speaking, and he passed it on to another, and so on from one to the other. And they only stood at intervals, but he had to retain his position unceasingly.[1]

Alexius was the hero of the *Alexiad* as Odysseus "of many wiles" was the hero of the *Odyssey*. Both were Greeks in their subtlety, but the patience of Alexius as Anna describes it had a quality unknown to the pagan world.

And from that time on to his death the rheumatism visited him at periodic intervals, and caused him exquisite agony. But he endured it so patiently without ever uttering a word of complaint, but only said, "I deserve the pain; it comes upon me justly because of the multitude of my sins." If perchance a word of despondency had escaped his lips, he at once made the sign of the cross against the miscreant demon, and said, "Away from me, thou wicked one! Perdition to thee and thy machinations against Christians."[2]

A civilization that combines respect for intelligence with loyalty to dogmatic standards, asceticism with respect for the family, chastity with subtlety and patience, ought not to be dismissed as mean or decadent. Nor is it just to say that Byzantine culture was arrested in its development by a dead weight of administrative machinery,[3] for it reached maturity long before the corresponding Christian civilization of the Western Middle Ages. Byzantium was old when the West was still

[1] *Alexiad*, xiv, c. 4. [2] Ibid.
[3] See A. J. Toynbee, *The Study of History, passim,* but especially vol. iv, Oxford, 1939, pp. 340–405.

young, but it had as long a course in history, and perished by violence in the first stages of decay;[1] while Western mediaevalism died naturally within a millennium, a short space for a civilization. A modern critic finds in Byzantine art "one of the most deeply moving manifestations of the human spirit",[2] the one point at which East and West really meet. To the present writer Byzantium offers a proof of the possibility of continuity, that a new life is possible without a descent into darkness and disorder. In one corner of the earth at least a Christian culture was born within an empire, and this may be so again.

No one would claim that Byzantine civilization is the only Christian one. For us in the West it is not on the line of our own ancestry. We can learn from it only as we learn from more exotic cultures, Indian, Malayan, and Chinese. Englishmen will never decorate their churches with mosaics, or talk metaphysical theology on the way home from the baths. They can learn from the plurality of Christian cultures that it is not necessary to be Latin in order to be Christian, and that it is necessary for every Christian civilization to grow a culture of its own.

[1] The quality of Byzantine art in the eleventh and twelfth centuries is very imperfectly illustrated by plates 4–8 in this book. M. Paul Muratoff in the introduction to his *Peinture Byzantine* endeavours to trace the course of an important artistic revival from the twelfth to the fourteenth century. The literary culture of the same period was by no means lacking in quality. Economic decline may be explained by the loss of granaries in Asia Minor and the rise of Italian, especially Venetian, sea-borne trade. But the Byzantine empire could still subsidize its allies in the reign of Manuel (1143–80). See *infra*, pp. 167–8.

[2] Eric Newton, *European Painting and Sculpture*, London, 1941, p. 66.

2

HERESY AND CHURCH ORDER

To the Byzantine Greek Orthodoxy meant not only right belief, but right worship and right reason. Heresy was idolatry and perversity of spirit, the worship of a false image of God, contrary to the whole wisdom transmitted in the Scriptures and in the definitions and traditions of the church. To ascertain the Orthodox answer to a question was never easy, for the hierarchy might speak with various voices. The tradition must be found through the consent of all the authorities, and ratified by the voice of the whole church, laity and clergy, bishops and the emperor. A general council was a normal way of discovering the voice of the church on an important issue, but general councils attended by many bishops might fail to commend themselves to the whole church as interpreters of the Holy Tradition. So the Arian councils of the fourth century fell to the ground despite their impressive numbers. The Second Council of Ephesus in 449 was regarded as the *Latrocinium*, the robber synod, outside Monophysite circles. The Iconoclast General Council of 754 was rejected by Rome and the Eastern Patriarchates, and in course of time by the church within the empire. No synod could finally determine Orthodoxy. The true doctrine would in the end be recognized by its harmony with the past, by its own intrinsic balance, and its place in the course of history. "If this thing be a counsel or work of men, it will be overthrown: but if it is of God, ye will not be able to overthrow them."[1]

This conception of Orthodoxy explains the provisional acceptance of imperial edicts on dogmatic matters. These were generally drawn up with the counsel and consent of the *synodos*

[1] Acts 5. 38-9.

endemousa, but the emperor himself was universally regarded as
an officer of the church from the day when Constantine the
Great was hailed as a thirteenth apostle. Gratitude to him for
his gifts on the morrow of the persecutions may do something
to explain the hold that the empire acquired over the organization of the church at the moment when she came to the surface,
and ceased to be an illegal, though grudgingly tolerated society.
But in the fourth and fifth centuries no government could have
stood neutral in theological controversy.

Theological excitement may be explained partly by the
Greek passion for theory, which from the third century onwards
played mostly on religious questions, and partly by the place
of the church in civic society. The city councils never regained
the prestige that they inevitably lost in the last days of the
undivided Roman empire. In the third and fourth centuries
they became almost entirely agents for the collection of taxes.
Their members were bound to their houses and lands by the
most stringent regulations; what had been an honour became
a terrible burden. The *curiales* dragged out some kind of an
existence until the sixth century, when their remaining powers
were transferred to other councils,[1] but the centre of civic life
left the curia for ever, and more and more came to reside in the
Christian cathedral, where the bishop and his clergy dispensed
charity, not only to their own flock. The membership of the
clergy, the number and nature of the diocesan officers, and the
choice of a bishop, all became matters of absorbing interest to
the citizens who thronged the market-place. Party conflicts
between groups in a city, or between the citizens and peasants
in the surrounding country, might arise for many reasons,
social, linguistic, or economic, but they very easily took an
ecclesiastical and theological colour. A bishop who was disliked
as a Greek or a Syrian, a haughty aristocratic or a pushing
plebeian, a friend of corn-merchants or a friend of peasants,
would be denounced for some form of heterodoxy. By this I do
not mean that heresy was merely a blind for social and
economic conflicts. It would be much nearer the truth to say

[1] See A. H. M. Jones, *The Greek City*, Oxford, 1940, pp. 209–10.

that it was in the detection of heresy that the Byzantines were interested. The rival theological doctrines, especially conflicting images of the perfected human nature of Christ, expressed distinct conceptions of the final destiny of man.[1]

Most Greek cities had a bishop before the conversion of Constantine to the Christian faith. In those days the individual diocese was necessarily autocephalous for all normal purposes. Bishops sometimes met in council, and the bishops of the chief sees had a certain authority, especially Rome, in southern Italy and Sicily, Alexandria in Egypt, and Antioch in "the hollow Syria". But there was nothing in the way of permanent organization over and above the diocese in most parts of the Roman world before the coming of the Christian empire. Ecclesiastical provinces were the first contribution of the Christian empire to the organization of the church. At the Council of Nicaea in 325 it was laid down that all bishops should be consecrated at the capital of the civil province in which their see was situated, except the bishops of Egypt, who were accustomed to resort to Alexandria; and those of the "suburbican" dioceses of southern Italy, Sicily, Sardinia and Corsica. These formed the metropolitan province of Rome. The larger Patriarchates of Rome and Constantinople came into existence soon afterwards, when rules for "appeals to Rome" from all parts of the Western church were laid down at the Council of Sardica (343).[2] Rescripts from two Roman emperors, Gratian in 382 and Valentinian III in 445,[3] gave legal authority to Roman decisions. The First Council of Constantinople in 381 assigned to the church in the new capital "equal rights of seniority" with the elder Rome; and an imperial law of 421[4] gave to its archbishop authority to judge disputes in the large civil "dioceses" of Thrace, Pontus, and Asia in the Prefecture of the East, and in the whole of the Prefecture of Illyricum (Greece and "Dacia", the modern Albania and Serbia). But the boundaries of the Patriarchate of Constantinople at the

---

[1] Cf. 1 Corinthians 15. 22: "So in Christ shall all be made alive"; and *infra*, pp. 25–6, 29.

[2] H. Bettenson, *Documents of the Christian Church*, Oxford, 1943, pp. 112–13.

[3] Ibid., pp. 29–30, 32–3.   [4] *C.J.C.*, ii, p. 12.

time of the Council of Chalcedon (451)[1] were limited to the Eastern "dioceses" of Pontus, Asia and Thrace. Illyricum, which was disputed between the Eastern and Western halves of the empire, was assigned to the Patriarchate of Rome. Nevertheless, the church of Rome objected to this twenty-eighth canon of Chalcedon,[2] partly because the Patriarch of Constantinople was given so large a Patriarchate, at the expense of the "Exarchs" of Asia and Pontus, at Ephesus and Trebizond, to whom the like authority had been assigned in 381; but even more because of the implications latent in the grounds given for setting Constantinople on an equality with Rome. The council said that "the Fathers gave privileges to the throne of Old Rome with good reason, because it was the imperial city". Therefore the new capital might claim "the like rights of seniority". The church of Rome, on the other hand, claimed seniority as the see of St Peter and St Paul, the shrine of the Apostles and martyrs.

The Roman church was still a revolutionary minority in a largely pagan city. The Christian empire was never firmly established in the Western provinces, for pagan opposition in the "city" *par excellence*, as well as in remote country districts in Africa and Gaul, was still strong when the empire tottered to its fall. The prestige of the church grew with the decline of the empire. St Leo, the first Pope to play a great part in politics, saw the Vandal sack of the city in 455. The rescripts of Gratian and Valentinian never had an important place in the Roman tradition, though they are the historical foundation upon which later Romans reared the fabulous *Donation of Constantine*.[3]

Constantinople, on the other hand, was refounded by Constantine the Great in 330 to be the capital of the Christian empire. Though pagan shrines were plundered to set up their monuments there, it had no new pagan temples of its own. The historical associations of the city were Christian, but

[1] Bettenson, pp. 116–17.
[2] See C. J. Hefele, *Conciliengeschichte*, French trans. by Dom H. Leclerq, vol. ii, pt. ii, Paris, 1907, pp. 815–26.
[3] Bettenson, pp. 135–40; *infra*, p. 106.

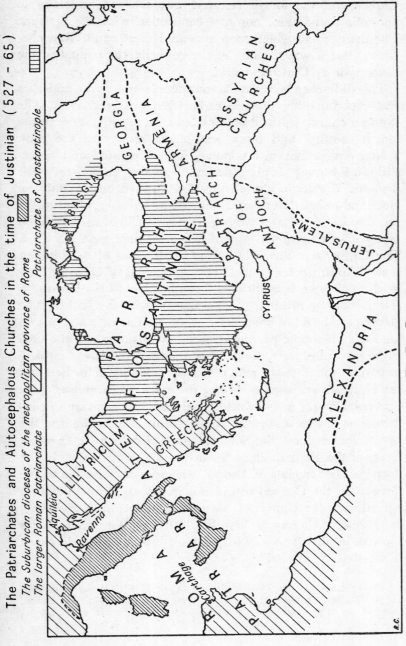

The Patriarchates and Autocephalous Churches in the time of Justinian (527 - 65)

The Suburbican dioceses of the metropolitan province of Rome

Patriarchate of Constantinople

The larger Roman Patriarchate

Patriarchate of Rome

THE FIVE PATRIARCHATES

ABASGIA

GEORGIA

ARMENIA

ASSYRIAN CHURCHES

PATRIARCH OF CONSTANTINOPLE

PATRIARCH OF ANTIOCH

JERUSALEM

CYPRUS

ALEXANDRIA

ILLYRICUM

GREECE

MARE

PATRI

Aquileia

Ravenna

Carthage

R.G.

Christian of the fourth century. The see had no claim to apostolic foundation, nor any connection with the martyrs. The many relics which soon appeared there came from elsewhere. But it was the city of the councils, the capital of the contemporary Christian world.

This difference between Constantinople and Rome underlies and explains other differences between East and West. The Western church was still surrounded by a pagan society in the fourth century, and by a semi-pagan society in the fifth. Western paganism was popular, unsophisticated and superstitious. For most people it was still a matter of demi-gods and demons. The Latin church therefore insisted on the unity of God, and resisted every tendency in Greek theology that might possibly lead men and women to regard Christ as some kind of a semi-divine, super-human person, neither man nor God. The Latins were intensely hostile to all forms of Arianism or semi-Arianism before and after the Council of Nicaea. They stuck to their own traditional formula, that Christ is consubstantial, of one substance, *una substantia*, with the Father. The Greeks, on the other hand, were more familiar with an abstract kind of philosophic paganism, Neo-Platonism, where the One is the ground of everything. They thought that it was equally important to affirm the real, distinct personality of the Son and the Holy Ghost, who have come down from heaven and done particular works in the world. The Latins were ready to condemn the cruder and more absurd forms of Sabellianism, the heresy that reduces the Son and the Spirit to mere forms or facets of the Father. They did not easily scent danger in the doctrine of Marcellus of Ancyra, who seemed Sabellian to the Greeks. At the Council of Ephesus in 431 the Roman church agreed with the church of Alexandria that God "was born", as against the heresy of Nestorius. But for a long time Latins showed, by their very careful qualifications, a great reluctance to say that "God died".[1]

---

[1] For instance, in the *Tome* of St Leo (449); Kidd, *Documents*, ii, 209; T. H. Bindley, *Oecumenical Documents of the Faith*, ed. by F. H. Green, London, 1950, pp. 159–80; Bettenson, pp. 70–2. Cf. also *infra*, pp. 43–6.

Among the Egyptians and some of the Syrians the emphasis was almost exactly opposite. The nature of God was to them a dark mystery that might well be left in the dark. Salvation was a present necessity, and their traditions led them to seek salvation through physical union with a dying and rising God. Christ was a far more real and intimate God than Adonis or Osiris, since He had walked upon their hills and beside their streams, and they themselves might go on a pilgrimage to the land where He had lived and died. Still He was first and foremost a saviour-God, a means to reunion with the earth in the spring festival. Their religious ideas lead them to look forward to the transfiguration of the body into something wholly impalpable, utterly absorbed in God. This process seemed to them to be beginning in the bodies of some of their own ascetics, who lived in complete detachment from ordinary human necessities in the desert or on pillars. The nearer they could get to such an absorption in the stream of deity the better it would be for them. Surely then Christ's human body must be lost in God as a drop of oil or fresh water is lost in the sea.

St Athanasius, the first great Egyptian Patriarch of Alexandria, taught how "God became man that man might become God". In Christ our human nature is made one with the Word of God; with the Logos or plan behind the world; with the order of nature, winter and spring, summer and autumn. Our alienation from this order is abolished when we enter into all the benefits which He has won for us, and especially when we are united to Him in the life-giving sacrament of His body and blood. The Incarnation is the atonement, and the atonement can only be complete if the Incarnation is complete, if the union of the two natures is actual. According to St Cyril of Alexandria, the second great Patriarch of the Alexandrian church, who died in 444, "One is the enfleshed nature of the Word".[1] He never denied that Jesus Christ was human as well as divine; but he insisted so strongly on the union of the two natures that his teaching might seem to imperil the truth that Christ remains man, even in His ascended body.

[1] μία φύσις του λόγου σεσαρκωμένη.

The critics of the Alexandrians are commonly called "the School of Antioch", but their real home and centre was in inner Syria, and over the border in Persian Mesopotamia. They were also found in Palestine, as might be expected, for they were especially devoted to the scenes and sites of the two Testaments, and therefore to the historical and literal interpretation of Scripture. They feared any doctrine that might reduce the divine drama to a puppet show, and therefore emphasized the humanity of Christ and the freedom of His human will. Their great master was Theodore, a very able exponent of the literal meaning of Scripture, who was Bishop of Mopsuestia in Cilicia when he died there in 428. The most notorious representative and leader of the school was the Patriarch of Constantinople, Nestorius, who was deposed at the First Council of Ephesus in 431, because he raised a scandal in his own city by preaching that Mary cannot be called the Mother of God, nor can the Word of God be called three months old; since all the human actions and sufferings of the Word should be ascribed, not to the Word Himself, but to the Son of Man in whom He tabernacled.

This teaching was condemned at Egypt and at Rome, and in its more extreme forms almost everywhere. In 433 the Syrian followers of the school of Antioch, led by Theodoret of Cyrrhus, agreed with St Cyril of Alexandria in a formula of peace.[1] They all confessed that the Word of God "united with Himself from the very moment of conception the temple which He took" from the Virgin Mary. Mary might rightly be called "Mother of God", and Nestorius had been justifiably condemned. The conflict flared up again after St Cyril's death in 444, when a more headstrong Patriarch, Dioscorus, came to the throne of Alexandria. In 449 the Patriarch of Constantinople was attacked for his treatment of Eutyches, a Byzantine archimandrite, who seemed to him to have gone too far in the opposite direction from Nestorius, since he denied that Christ's human nature was of the same substance as our own. The Egyptians flocked to Ephesus in the train of their Patriarch,

[1] Bindley, pp. 138–48.

and there (as they thought) renewed the anti-Nestorian decisions of the First Council in 431. They excommunicated not only the Syrian followers of the school of Antioch, but the great Pope, St Leo of Rome, who had written to the Patriarch of Constantinople a dogmatic letter, the *Tome* of Leo, which substantially supported him in his attitude to Eutyches. In the disorder at Ephesus the Patriarch was murdered.

The excesses of Dioscorus and the Egyptians produced a not unnatural reaction in Constantinople. Many Byzantines had disapproved the methods of St Cyril in 431, at the time of his attack on Nestorius. They were too reminiscent of similar methods that had been used by an earlier Patriarch of Alexandria, an uncle of St Cyril, against the great Byzantine preacher St John Chrysostom. Dioscorus carried violence even further; and his theology was extreme in that he and his Second Council of Ephesus committed themselves, most unwisely, to the defence of Eutyches, a muddle-headed person, who said that there were "two natures in Christ before their union, one afterwards". It is more than likely that he himself did not know what he meant. The Egyptian attack on St Leo of Rome was also unpopular. When in the next year, 450, the Emperor Theodosius died, and his sister, the Princess Pulcheria, raised to the throne a Macedonian soldier, Marcian, from the Latin-speaking province of Illyricum, public opinion in the capital was ready to support a change of policy, a reconciliation with the Pope and the Western empire, and an alliance of the old and the new Rome against Egypt. But the Byzantines were not prepared to accept the *Tome* of St Leo as the only authoritative settlement of the controversy. The Emperor Marcian insisted that the Roman church should send representatives to a new council at Chalcedon in 451.

At Chalcedon the *Tome* was approved, and a new definition of doctrine was framed.[1] This contained the controversial expression "in two natures", which was in line with the traditions of Latin theology. In the West theologians had long insisted that Christ was perfect God and perfect man "without

---

[1] Kidd, *Documents*, ii, 214; Bindley, pp. 183–99; Bettenson, p. 73.

any confusion". In the East the idea of two natures in Christ was associated with Theodore of Mopsuestia and Nestorius, whose friends and followers in Syria and Palestine were restored to their bishoprics by the Council of Chalcedon, though Nestorius himself was condemned by name. The ex-Patriarch in his distant exile heard and approved the Chalcedonian decisions. He would not write a letter to the Pope, lest this should cause him acute embarrassment:

> that I might not hinder from his running him who was running fairly because of the prejudice against my person.[1]

But he saw in the definition of Chalcedon the victory of his own theology.

Others shared the same impression, that there could be no harmony between St Cyril's "one enfleshed nature of the Word" and St Leo's "in two natures". Nevertheless, the Byzantines struggled to remain loyal to both. The idea of deification as it was developed by St Athanasius and St Cyril continued to be central to their theology. It is the very foundation of Byzantine mystical piety as it is found, for instance, in the writings of St Simeon, the new theologian, in the tenth century.[2] But between Byzantium and Egypt there was a difference of emphasis that is best illustrated in Byzantine icons of Christ and the saints. The Byzantines did not desire to disappear into the abyss of mystery, but to grow in God and with God into a richer, fuller and more completely personal life. They knew that the redemption of the body is not to be transformed into spirit, but to be "made like unto His glorious body, according to the working whereby He is able to subdue all things unto Himself".[3]

The more extreme Monophysites in Egypt and parts of Syria taught that the flesh of Christ had become incorruptible, so that He suffered only in appearance, even before His resurrection. Others allowed that He really suffered, but maintained

---

[1] *The Bazaar of Heracleides*, ed. by G. R. Driver and L. Hodgson, Oxford, 1925, p. 378.
[2] See J. M. Hussey, *Ch. and Learning*, p. 223.
[3] Philippians 3. 21.

that each separate suffering was a miracle, an act of condescension to the low estate of humanity, for the God-Man could not be subject to necessity. These were the extreme and moderate *Aphthartodocetae* or Julianists, called after their leader, Julian of Halicarnassus. Most Monophysites were more cautious, and in condemning Julianism moved into positions [1] not easily distinguishable from Chalcedonianism. They would not say "in two natures", but they could say "two ousiae", or kinds of being, since they insisted that Christ was of one substance with the Father and with us. The real difference between them and the Orthodox was not about the reality of His human nature, but about its permanence. The obstinate persistence of disagreement on this matter reveals the real centre of the controversy.

The real quarrel was about the perfection of human nature. If Christ's manhood is made of one nature with God, then it is the final destiny of humanity to become divine, and in so doing to cease from being human. If, on the contrary, the flesh of Christ, though deified, remains human within divinity, the man in perfect obedience to God will be perfect man. The struggle against Monophysitism was a battle for Christian humanism.

As we shall see, the battle in the East was much confused with other issues, social, political, and national. Still both sides had the same concerns. Both were intensely interested in the deification of humanity, though different groups conceived deification in a variety of ways. On the Chalcedonian side the descendants of the school of Theodore of Mopsuestia, who remained influential at Edessa until 489, and after that continued to control the church in Persia and farther east, thought primarily in terms of the exaltation of the Son of Man to the right hand of God. Others in Constantinople, Thrace, and Syria were much nearer in spirit to the Egyptians.

The West was not deeply stirred, because the deification of man had never yet become part of her theology. To the Latins Monophysitism was simply a heresy, a rebellion against the

[1] See especially J. Lebon, *Le Monophysisme Severien*, Louvain, 1909.

D

traditional teaching of the *Tome* of St Leo. Because the *Tome* was directed to the particular case of Eutyches, who had been so rashly defended by Dioscorus and the Second Council of Ephesus, they were inclined to class all Monophysites as Eutychians. They were too far away to discriminate between those who were near to Chalcedon and *Aphthartodocetae* whose doctrine approached the very old Gnostic heresies condemned in the First Epistle of St John.

Monophysites, on the other hand, classed all Chalcedonians as Nestorians. They had some justification, since Nestorius as well as Theodoret approved Chalcedon. Moreover, the Latins had a blind eye for some of the errors of the school of Antioch, as in the Arian controversy they missed the objections to the Sabellianism of Marcellus of Ancyra. Nestorius was condemned because he could not say that God was born. For a long time the Roman church feared to say "One of the Trinity suffered in the flesh".[1]

[1] *Infra*, pp. 43–5.

3

ALEXANDRIA, CONSTANTINOPLE, AND ROME

MONOPHYSITES WERE chiefly found in Egypt and Armenia and in the inland parts of Syria, Asia Minor and Illyricum. In all these regions there was some tension between the Greek cities founded after the conquests of Alexander the Great, and other cities, towns, and country villages that had retained or, regained their own languages and customs. The Christian church had spanned this gulf more successfully than any pagan cultural agency. Sir William Ramsay brings evidence [1] from inscriptions to show that in Lycaonia and Isauria Christianity and the Greek language grew together. But it was no part of the church's business to spread Hellenism, and in Egypt and Armenia, as well as in Syria and Palestine, the language of the people in the villages was used in Christian worship from the very first. In Alexandria and in Syria the same diocese contained churches where the liturgy was celebrated in two or three languages. In Armenia, which was an independent Christian kingdom until it was annexed to the Persian empire in 428, colonies of Greek and Syrian Christians had bishops of their own. [2] The Syrian Christians in Armenia belonged to the church of Persian Mesopotamia, whose teachers came from the school of the Persians at Edessa, and followed the doctrine of Theodore of Mopsuestia; while the national church of Armenia was open to the influence of the extremer forms of Mono-

[1] In *Luke the Physician*, London, 1908, p. 146, with references to other works.
[2] See the references cited in F. Dvornik, *National Churches and the Church Universal*, London, 1944, pp. 14–15.

physitism. In the Armenian kingdom, therefore, rival theological tendencies were already represented by distinct churches before the Councils of Ephesus and Chalcedon; but the fissures were national as well as theological.

In Egypt the social cleavage was older and more bitter, for the ancient pattern of social life had continued in its accustomed channels since the days of the Pharaohs, mastered, but little influenced, by the Greek and cosmopolitan culture of the great port and university city of Alexandria.[1] The rise and fall of the Nile determined the system of irrigation, and made the establishment of the autonomous Greek city impossible. Alexandria was not a city in the Greek sense, but rather quarters for government officials and commercial magnates, who exploited the countryside in the interests of the empire as a whole. The *fellahin* had no means of resistance except the "anachoresis",[2] the flight to the desert, where they met other anchorites, Christian hermits who did not live by robbery, and need not return to their masters for fear of starvation; for they had learnt to support a life of contemplation on the pittance provided by the desert itself. Naturally these hermits [3] became heroes. As hermitages gave place to communities which lived a common life, manufactured baskets, and even planted gardens in the desert, and *parabolani* or hospital monks performed corporal works of mercy in the poorer quarters of Alexandria, popular support for Christian asceticism increased. In his conflicts with the government at the time of the Arian controversy St Athanasius was able to rely on the enthusiastic sympathy of rural Egypt, where the hermits and the *fellahin* hid him from his enemies, the Arian Greek officials in the government offices at Alexandria. The stubborn loyalty of the Egyptians to their own gods and temples, that had so long presented an unyielding front to Greek penetration, transferred itself to

---

[1] See M. J. Rostovtzeff, *The Social and Economic History of the Roman Empire*, pp. 253–74.

[2] Ibid., pp. 256, 437.

[3] See especially the life of St Antony, translated by Sir E. A. Wallis Budge, in *The Paradise of the Fathers*, vol. i, Oxford, 1907, pp. 1–73. The Greek text, ascribed to St Athanasius, is in PG 26, c. 835–975.

the new religion in the person of the Patriarch of Alexandria, who became to Egypt as Pharaoh.

The same loyalty that was given to St Athanasius was retained by St Cyril and Dioscorus. The Council of Chalcedon had few defenders outside the Greek quarter of Alexandria and Tanis. This, the ancient capital of the Hyksos or "Shepherd kings", was Egypt's Ulster.[1] In 457, when the Emperor Marcian died, the Egyptians rose and murdered the Chalcedonian Patriarch. They elected a successor to Dioscorus, one Timothy Aelurus.[2] The new emperor consulted the bishops of the empire, who all replied that this election must be treated as void, though some [3] recommended a revision of the decisions of Chalcedon.

The government therefore arrested Timothy Aelurus, and confined him at Cherson, on the north coast of the Black Sea. The new Patriarch of Alexandria, who was also called Timothy, did his best to conciliate the Monophysites by commemorating Dioscorus in the diptychs or intercessions with all the previous Patriarchs. St Leo of Rome wrote a letter of explanation, the so-called *Second Tome*,[4] in which he took care to quote St Cyril at length and avoid the expression "in two natures". The Egyptians remained obstinate in their loyalty to their own choice. They would not communicate with the new Patriarch, who in their view was in communion with Chalcedonians in Rome, Palestine, and Edessa who were practically Nestorian. As their leaders were monks and hermits who would have welcomed enthusiastically any physical form of martyrdom, the government and church authorities could do very little against them.

After a time the battle spread to Armenia, Mesopotamia, and Syria, where the Monophysites found a leader in Peter the

---

[1] According to W. A. Wigram, *The Separation of the Monophysites*, London, 1923, p. 41, Tanis then remained obstinately Chalcedonian.

[2] The weasel, or perhaps the cat.

[3] See L. Duchesne, *The Early History of the Christian Church*, Eng. trans., vol. iii, London, 1924, pp. 334–5. The objectors were the Metropolitans of Side and Perga, with their comprovincial bishops. Both these provinces are in Pamphylia, southern Asia Minor.

[4] Epistle 165 in PL 54, c. 1155–90.

Fuller, who added to the traditional *Trisagion*, "Holy God, Holy and Almighty, Holy and Immortal, have mercy upon us", the words "Who was crucified for us". The old and new forms became watchwords of the rival schools of Edessa and Alexandria, for while the followers of Theodore of Mopsuestia still hesitated to say "God was born", the Monophysites reiterated, "God died".

In 475–7 the struggle came to a head during a civil war between two claimants to the imperial throne. Basiliscus sought to conciliate the Monophysites by recognizing Peter the Fuller as Patriarch of Antioch and Timothy Aelurus as Patriarch of Alexandria. He gave them an *Encyclical* letter [1] in support of their views, which were imposed on all the churches by his imperial decree. The other claimant, Zeno, won the support of the Patriarch Acacius of Constantinople, whose authority was threatened when Timothy Aelurus held a council at Ephesus [2] and restored the autonomy of the Exarchate of Asia, assigned by the Council of Chalcedon to the Patriarchate of Constantinople, Basiliscus soon found that he had under-estimated the strength of Greek sentiment in favour of the Chalcedonian definition. Popular feeling in the capital mani-fested itself in demonstrations, during which St Daniel the stylite descended from his pillar to defend the threatened faith. Basiliscus capitulated, and issued an *Anti-encyclical* [3] in direct contradiction to his previous measures, but it was too late. In September, 476, Zeno entered Constantinople in triumph.

It was another matter to impose the Council of Chalcedon on Antioch and Alexandria. Peter the Fuller was arrested, but Timothy Aelurus was allowed to die in peace. The Mono-physites found him a successor in a certain Peter Mongus (the "stammerer"), who remained at large in the desert, sheltered by the *fellahin* and the hermits, like another Athanasius; while in Alexandria the Chalcedonian Timothy presided over empty churches, for only Greeks and officials would come.

[1] In Evagrius, *Historia Ecclesiastica*, bk. iii, c. 4.
[2] See L. Duchesne, *Early History of the Christian Church*, iii, p. 339.
[3] Evagrius, op. cit., bk. iii, c. 7.

When he died in 482 his party gave him a successor in a monk of Tanis, John Talaia; but the government and the Patriarch of Constantinople gave up the battle, and offered to Peter Mongus an *Henoticon* or formula of union.[1] In this they confessed that Christ is "one and not two", gave special authority to the twelve "chapters" [2] which St Cyril, "of holy memory", had written in 430 against Nestorius, and condemned any contrary doctrine that might have been taught, "whether at Chalcedon or in any synod whatever". Peter Mongus accepted these terms, to the distress of some of his followers, who would be satisfied with nothing less than an open anathema upon Chalcedon and the *Tome*. A year later Peter the Fuller also accepted them, and returned to the see of Antioch. The Syrian supporters of the tradition of Theodore of Mopsuestia withdrew across the frontier from Edessa to Nisibis in 489. They had a rival formula,[3] drawn up in 486 at the Council of Seleucia, but they did not at this time deny the orthodoxy of the Byzantine church.

The *Henoticon* condemned no one but Nestorius and Eutyches. It exalted a controversial letter of St Cyril, and did not mention the *Tome* of St Leo. This silence did not commend it to Egypt, where the *Acephali* or "headless party" broke off communion with Peter Mongus because he would not explicitly condemn those who approved the Council of Chalcedon. At Rome resentment was more serious. Though Roman legates came to Constantinople in 483, and consented to appear at a liturgy in St Sophia, where the name of Peter Mongus was read in the diptychs, in July, 484, Pope Felix III excommunicated them for their compliance. He went further, and deposed the Patriarch of Constantinople.

The church of Rome derived her information about Eastern affairs partly from John Talaia, who claimed to be the lawfully elected Orthodox Patriarch of Alexandria; and partly from the *Acoimeti* or "sleepless monks", who preserved in

---

[1] Kidd, *Documents*, ii, 235; also iii (1941), 3; Bettenson, pp. 123-6.

[2] Bindley, pp. 124-37, and Bettenson, pp. 65-6.

[3] Kidd, *Documents*, ii, 236; J. Labourt, *Le Christianisme dans l'empire Perse*, Paris, 1904, pp. 147-8, 262-3.

Constantinople the traditions of the school of Antioch. Felix
III and Gelasius (492–6) maintained an attitude of unyielding
protest towards those who tampered with the *Tome* of St Leo.
The government could do very little about it, for their power
in Italy was limited. The real rulers of the country were two
German masters of the Soldiers, Odovacer, and Theodoric,
king of the Ostrogoths (493–526). Theodoric ruled Italy in
the name of Anastasius, who reigned in the East from 491 to
518. He preserved the Roman methods of government, and
collaborated with the Senate and the Roman church, though
he himself was an Arian. Most Christians of his race had
received their religion from an Arian missionary called Ulphilas,
who gave them their Gothic liturgy and Gothic Bible in the
middle of the fourth century. Theodoric himself wished to be
on good terms with the court of Constantinople, and he almost
certainly favoured overtures for religious peace that were made
by Pope Anastasius II in 498 to the Patriarch Macedonius.
But it was obviously not in his interest to alienate any strong
party in Italy in order to restore harmony between Constantinople and Rome. On the contrary, he had something to gain
by continued discord, that would cause Roman Christians to
prefer the rule of an Arian king to the reunion of the Western
provinces with the Roman empire under a Monophysite
emperor.

Between the senators and the king of the Ostrogoths the
clergy held the balance of political power. It is significant that
at this moment Pope Gelasius developed, in a letter to the
Emperor Anastasius in 494, the theory of two distinct and
independent spheres of church and state.[1] This theory corresponded to the actual condition of things in Italy, where an
Arian military commander and senators whose traditions were
still those of philosophic paganism, though most of them were
now personally Catholics, allowed the church of Rome to
develop on its own lines, and to exercise considerable authority
over all other Catholic churches of Italy. The independence of
the Roman church was tested by the crisis that followed the

[1] Kidd, *Documents*, iii, 4.

death of Pope Anastasius II in 498. Before his death a considerable party had withdrawn from his communion, in the belief that he was wavering in his resistance to the *Henoticon*.[1] It seems that though his legates in Constantinople insisted that the name of Acacius must be removed from the diptychs, they were more tolerant of subsequent Patriarchs whose personal sympathies were Chalcedonian. They were attacked by the *Acoimeti*, and by their special friends in Rome, who elected Symmachus to succeed the "heretical" [2] Anastasius II, while the majority of the senators, and others of the party of peace, chose the archpriest Laurentius. Theodoric decided in favour of Symmachus, and at first it seemed that this would be decisive; Laurentius himself gave way. But some headstrong acts of Symmachus and his party led in their turn to renewed strife, which lasted at least until the election of Pope Hormisdas in 514. In 507 Theodoric again intervened in favour of Symmachus, and assigned the churches to his party, but for some time at the beginning of the sixth century he stood aside and let events take their own course.

This controversy produced a fertile crop of propaganda, relevant to our purpose in so far as it was one of the principal objects of the Symmachian party to justify the sentence of Felix III in the matter of Acacius, where he might seem to have exceeded his powers in deposing another Patriarch unheard. It was also important to insist that the Pope is "judged of none". Neither the Emperor Anastasius, nor King Theodoric, nor the senate, nor any synod of bishops could pronounce a verdict on the claims of Symmachus, or on his behaviour during the controversy. To sustain these theses, a copious supply of records were either enlarged from very slender materials, or quite simply fabricated.[3] No doubt the chief object of the forgers was to impress Theodoric and his Ostrogoths. This Symmachian literature includes the *Vita Silvestri*, an important source of the later *Donation of Constantine*. This explicitly states

---

[1] See L. Duchesne, *L'église au sixième siècle*, Paris, 1925, pp. 14–16, 113–28.
[2] Dante placed him in hell, *Inferno*, xi, 8–9.
[3] See L. Duchesne's introduction to his edition of the *Liber Pontificalis*, vol. i, Paris, 1886, pp. cii–cxl; *VIème siècle*, p. 124

the theory of the universal episcopacy of Rome, that the Pope was to the other Patriarchs and to the bishops as the emperor was to the Praetorian Prefects, provincial governors, and local authorities. Evidently this was primarily intended to defend the deposition of Acacius.

The same Symmachian party were theologically extreme in their hostility to Monophysitism. They never quote any writings of St Cyril [1] except those that were included in the acts of the First Council of Ephesus, where Rome and Alexandria combined to condemn Nestorius. In Rome, after the death of St Leo, St Cyril was regarded as a semi-Monophysite. In this we can see the influence of John Talaia and the Alexandrian Chalcedonians, and also of the *Acoimeti*, who revered Theodore of Mopsuestia. While these influences gained ground in Italy at the expense of Laurentius and his friends, who were in communion with Macedonius of Constantinople, the pure Monophysites gained ground in the East, where they had much influence with the emperor. In 511 Macedonius was exiled, and replaced by a Monophysite. In 512 Severus, the ablest of the moderate Monophysite leaders, replaced a Chalcedonian follower of the *Henoticon* on the throne of the Patriarchate of Antioch. Constantinople, Antioch, and Alexandria, all the key positions in the East, were in the hands of bishops personally hostile to the decisions of Chalcedon. In Egypt they were openly anathematized for the satisfaction of the *Acephali*, though it seems that not all were contented. Some believed that the Patriarch of Alexandria was in communion with Greeks who were tainted with the heresy of Chalcedon, and so with the errors of Nestorius.

So from both sides the *Henoticon* was undermined: by those who believed that it was Monophysite, and by those who considered it a feeble compromise with the "Nestorianism" of the Chalcedonian definition and the *Tome*. In Constantinople itself Chalcedonian sympathies revealed themselves in the Blue faction, who demonstrated at the games against the Emperor Anastasius. In Thrace and Illyricum, where Latin was spoken,

[1] *VIème siècle*, p. 59.

the bishops made their own terms with Rome. Pope Hormisdas offered them a formula,[1] the so-called creed of Hormisdas, containing the famous sentence, "The Catholic faith is always kept inviolate in the Apostolic see". They had to remove from their diptychs not only Acacius, but all the subsequent Patriarchs of Constantinople, including Macedonius. This was the real obstacle to peace negotiations, which were again attempted in 515, for in Constantinople Macedonius was the saint of the Chalcedonian party. In Rome he was associated with Laurentius and Pope Anastasius II.

In 518 an Illyrian from Macedonia mounted the throne of the Byzantine empire. Justin had risen from the ranks, and was almost illiterate, but he was well served by his nephew Justinian, who had received an excellent education in Roman law and Latin theology. Their first acts were those of partisans of Latin influence in the East. Henceforth the Latin provinces, so long abandoned to the invasions of Vandals, Goths, Franks, and Huns, were to receive their share of attention from the government at Constantinople.

Immediately after the succession of Justin the congregation in St Sophia clamoured for the proclamation of four councils, including Chalcedon, and the restoration of the names of Macedonius and Pope St Leo to the diptychs. Severus could no longer be commemorated, and the Patriarch John was pressed to send his "systatic letter" to Rome, but the place given to Macedonius and his predecessor Euphemius in the popular demands shows that the formula of Hormisdas was not quite what was wanted in Constantinople. Eventually, under the influence of Justin and Justinian the names of all the Patriarchs since Acacius were removed from the diptychs at St Sophia for the time being. The Patriarch John smoothed things over with an open letter, in which he declared that the old and the new Rome were now at one, and "one Apostolic see".[2]

For a brief time in Constantinople and in Syria the old

[1] Kidd, *Documents*, iii, 8.
[2] PL 63, c. 444 (in Latin); for a later Byzantine view of this affair see Photius in PG 104, c. 1219–22.

theology of Antioch had a new lease of life. The *Acoimeti* were powerful in the capital. At Cyrrhos, the see of Theodoret, the memory of Nestorius was revived.[1] In Egypt, on the other hand, it was so clearly impossible to shake the supremacy of the Monophysite party that, despite some Roman protests, nothing was attempted. The *Henoticon* remained in force, and Monophysite Patriarchs continued to be recognized not only by the government, but by the Alexandrians and the men of Tanis, whose sympathies were Chalcedonian, until 536. Many Monophysite bishops from Syria took refuge in the Patriarchate of Alexandria, where they carried on vigorous controversies among themselves on points of theology, after the manner of exiles. It was at this time that the cleavage developed between Julian of Halicarnassus, the leader of the *Aphthartodocetae*, and Severus of Antioch, whose theology could not easily be distinguished from the Chalcedonian definition, as it was interpreted by those who wished to reconcile St Leo with St Cyril.

The position in 518–36 resembled the *Henoticon* in reverse, for while before 518 all the four Eastern Patriarchs were in communion with one another and not with Rome, now four of the five Patriarchs were in communion with one another and not with Alexandria. It does not therefore follow that all individuals who went to Egypt refused the communion of the church, or that all Egyptians were refused communion at Jerusalem or Constantinople. These schisms had not the same rigidity as modern denominational differences. Western pilgrims who came to Jerusalem at the time of the *Henoticon* seem to have communicated with the Patriarchs, whose sympathies were Chalcedonian. So did Persians and Armenians, who at home might be semi-Nestorians or advanced Monophysites. Only the extreme *Acephali* and the most ardent Symmachians and *Acoimeti* refused communion for opposite reasons to all who were tainted with the *Henoticon*. In the eyes of Orthodox Eastern Christians most Monophysites were not heretics but *diacrinomenoi*, "distinguishers". They were ready to condemn Eutyches and Julian of Halicarnassus as well as Nestorius, but they drew

---

[1] *VIème siècle*, p. 68.

a distinction between St Cyril and St Leo. It was the vocation of the church of Constantinople to make a further attempt to reconcile the apparent contradictions in the teaching of these Fathers, both of whom were equally authoritative for her. The *Henoticon* had failed, but it was scarcely buried when monks from Scythia began to agitate for another formula, not very far removed from it.

4

JUSTINIAN AND ALL
THE CHURCHES

JUSTINIAN, WHO succeeded his uncle Justin in 527, and reigned until 565, was in many respects the most Roman of the Byzantine emperors. His *Code* and his *Digest* of Roman law have made his name familiar to every student of legal and constitutional history. He was probably [1] the only emperor between Theodosius I (377–95) and Manuel Comnenus (1143–80) to attempt the recovery of the Western provinces of the Roman empire. His success was more superficial than real, for the war of liberation that destroyed the kingdom of the Ostrogoths wrought more havoc in Italy than any of the earlier barbarian invasions, and prepared the way for the coming of the Lombards. As the emperor grew older an increasing interest in the administrative problems of the Eastern half of the empire made him more sensitive to Greek and Syrian opinion. Defensive wars against the Persians drew his attention away from his original plans in Italy and Spain, until at the end of his reign the Latin provinces of Italy, Pannonia, and Illyricum were the most neglected. After his death they fell prey to new barbarian invasions.

The theological interests of Justinian show a similar evolution. In the reign of his uncle Justin he was a defender of Latin theology, and an ally of the *Acoimeti* against the monks from Scythia, who came to Constantinople in 518 and accused them of concealed Nestorianism. These Scythians, John

---

[1] Constans (641–68) visited Rome and died at Syracuse, but his objects were probably defensive rather than offensive.

Maxentius, Leontius, and others, came from Tomi, a Greek city at the mouth of the Danube, where the language of the hinterland was Latin. They desired to reconcile St Leo with St Cyril in a new formula, "One of the Trinity suffered in the flesh". This was derived from the letter of St Cyril to Nestorius, with the twelve anathemas, or "twelve chapters",[1] honoured in the *Henoticon* in place of the *Tome*. The immediate source of the expression seems to have been a letter [2] of Proclus, Patriarch of Constantinople, to the Armenians in 437, in the aftermath of the Nestorian controversy. Proclus had an unblemished reputation for Orthodoxy, but in the suspicious eyes of the *Acoimeti* and of the Roman legates, especially Dioscorus, a Chalcedonian exile from Alexandria, "One of the Trinity suffered in the flesh" seemed far too near Peter the Fuller's addition to the hymn *Trisagion*, "Holy God . . . who was crucified for us". Both expressions seemed equally inconsistent with the language of St Leo's *Tome*:

> It belongs not to the same nature to . . . hang upon the cross, and changing light to darkness, to make all the elements tremble. . . . On account of the unity of the person . . . the Son of God is said to have suffered these things, not in the divine nature in which He is the only begotten of the Father . . . but in the weakness of human nature.

In 519 the Scythians themselves paid a visit to Rome, where Pope Hormisdas gave them a chilling reception, though some African theologians were more sympathetic. In 520 the Pope turned them out of the city and wrote a letter against them to a friend in Constantinople. But he hesitated to condemn them as heretics, for in their absence they had found a new friend in Justinian. His letter to the Pope in their defence marks the first beginning of an evolution that left him at the end of his life under a suspicion of Aphthartodocetism.

One cause of this evolution was his affection for Theodora, who became his wife at the very beginning of his reign, though they had been lovers in the reign of Justin. The personality of this remarkable woman reveals itself in clear outline through

---

[1] *Supra*, p. 35.　　　　　　[2] PG 65, c. 856–73.

the mists of legend, gossip, and caricature that in her own time gathered round her name. That she had a dubious past is probable enough, though no one seriously accused her of unfaithfulness to her husband after their marriage. On the contrary, she appears as a stern moralist, a staunch and bitter defender of neglected wives against their erring husbands, and a pioneer in preventive and rescue work; though Procopius, her most malignant detractor, says that she made the lives of her rescued prostitutes so miserable in the convent called Metanoia that "some of them threw themselves down from a height . . . and in this way escaped the compulsory change".[1]

Theodora also collected monks of Monophysite inclinations, who were always certain of a refuge and a welcome within the walls of her palaces. The discrepancy between her patronage of suspected heretics and her husband's orthodoxy puzzled contemporaries, and led Procopius to the conclusion that the two were in collusion, and pursued opposite policies to puzzle their adversaries; but he was not only an embittered critic, but at least half a pagan. Monophysite theologians, who in their correspondence with one another did not fear to criticize theological aberrations in their "divine empress", do not charge her with insincerity, though they realize that her success in protecting them depended on a very accurate knowledge of the exact limits of her power. She could give them sanctuary in her own quarters, and help them to establish churches and even monasteries in Constantinople, but in Syria she could not protect them from the vigilance of the Chalcedonian Patriarch of Antioch and the imperial police. Only within limits could she hope to modify the emperor's ecclesiastical policy.

Justinian and Theodora, though they differed in theology, had fundamentally the same aim: to reconcile the Chalcedonians and Monophysite parties in an overriding unity. Neither of them believed the other party to be heretical in the sense in which Arians or Eutychians were heretical. Both were anxious to avoid the establishment of another church, like the

---

[1] Procopius, *Historia quae dicitur Arcana*, ed. J. Haury, Leipzig, 1906, xvii, 5, pp. 105–6.

Montanist church in the highlands of Asia Minor, which preserved from the second to the eighth century the ancient heresy
of the Paraclete. From this point of view it was most important
to keep the Monophysite bishops where they could be under no
temptation to perpetuate their hierarchy. Monasteries and
individual priests were less dangerous, and were seldom
molested except in districts where there might be reason to
fear disturbance; but bishops who remained in Syria were
hunted by the police. Many fled to Egypt or Armenia, or
across the border into Persian Mesopotamia. Others found a
sanctuary under the protection of Theodora, where they were
accessible to argument, in an atmosphere of comparative
comfort, away from their fanatical followers in the Syrian and
Egyptian deserts. Especially after 533 conversations between
Orthodox and Monophysite theologians played an increasingly
important part in Justinian's plans. They had some hope of
success if Rome could be persuaded to recognize the authority
of the "twelve chapters" of St Cyril, and of the Scythian
formula, "One of the Trinity suffered", which was included by
Justinian in the definition of the orthodoxy in the second edition
of his *Code*.[1]

In this sense another approach was made to Rome in 533–4
by two of the bishops who had played a part in the conversations
between Chalcedonians and Monophysites in 533. This time
Pope John II [2] admitted the orthodoxy of the formula, and
condemned the *Acoimeti*, who had now gone so far as to object
to the term *Theotokos*, Mother of God. They had in their
antagonism to Monophysitism returned to the exact position
occupied by Nestorius. This does something to explain the
changed sympathies of Rome, but something too must be
allowed for the effect of resumed relations between Rome and
the East since 518. The visit of the Scythians had not been
altogether useless. Their discussions with Latin theologians had
led to the translation of Greek works into Latin, notably the
"twelve chapters" of St Cyril. The political situation had also

---

[1] *VIème siècle*, pp. 89–90; *Codex Justinianus*, i, c. i; *C.J.C.*, ii, pp. 8–11.
[2] See his letter to Cassiodorus and others in PL 66, c. 20–4.

E

changed since the time of Pope Hormisdas. Byzantine armies had already invaded North Africa, and the kingdom of the Ostrogoths, rent by internal dissensions since the death of Theodoric in 526, might well seem to be tottering to its fall. The authority of Justinian in the elder Rome was far greater in 534 than in 519.

In 536 Pope Agapetus came to Constantinople with authority from the Ostrogoths to negotiate for the surrender of their kingdom, or at least for its submission to the imperial protection. There he was drawn into negotiations which had already begun between Anthimus, a new Patriarch of Constantinople, translated from Trebizond the year before; Theodosius, the moderate Monophysite Patriarch of Alexandria, whom the government were supporting against the fierce opposition of the *Aphthartodocetae*; and Severus, the ex-Patriarch of Antioch, who had lately been brought to Constantinople to take part in further theological conversations.[1]

Agapetus was warned in time by the Patriarch Ephrem of Antioch. As soon as he arrived in Constantinople he objected to the election of Anthimus on the ground that he was bishop of Trebizond, and that translations were not permitted. When Justinian insisted, he put the Patriarch through his theological paces, and exposed Monophysite sympathies. The emperor's Italian campaign was already under way, and meeting with unexpectedly stiff resistance in some places in the south. It was a bad time to quarrel with the Latin church, and Pope Agapetus won a resounding victory. He consecrated a new Patriarch of Constantinople in place of Anthimus, who took refuge with Theodora. The Pope was about to preside at a General Council of all the Patriarchates when he died suddenly in April, 536. The council was held under the Patriarch Menas, and as a result of its deliberations many of Theodora's Monophysites were removed from Constantinople to be interned at Dercos, thirty miles away. There they were joined soon afterwards by the Patriarch Theodosius of Alexandria. Justinian had at last

---

[1] See their letters to one another in *The Syriac Chronicle known as that of Zachariah of Mitylene*, Eng. trans. by F. J. Hamilton and E. W. Brooks, London, 1899, pp. 271–95 (Monophysite account).

decided to end the immunity of Egypt, and to impose a Chalce-donian Patriarch among the men of Tanis. Henceforth there were three Patriarchs of Alexandria: a Melkite or "king's man", followed only by the Syrians of Tanis and the Alexandrian Greeks; an Aphthartodocete, who at first had the most popular support; and Theodosius, the exiled Monophysite. Theodosius recovered in his exile the popular sympathy that he lost in 535–7, when he was in alliance with the police and the Chalcedonians against his extremist rival. Severus of Antioch, who was sent back to Egypt in 536, died there in 538. It was some years before the Monophysites in his Patriarchate could provide him with a successor.

Justinian and Theodora had not given up their plan for a general reconciliation. These now turned on an explanation of Chalcedon, to harmonize the *Tome* of St Leo with the "twelve chapters" of St Cyril. To this end it was necessary to find a Pope less aggressive than Agapetus. Theodora's candidate was the deacon Vigilius, who had been with him in Constantinople. When the news of the Pope's death reached Rome the Goths were still in possession, and they insisted on the election of Silverius, in whom they hoped to find an anti-Byzantine. He was a son of Pope Hormisdas, presumably born before his father reached the major orders. In this election we may see a revival of the intransigent Symmachians, displeased at the concessions made since 534 to the point of view of Anastasius II and Laurentius. A few months afterwards the Byzantines occupied Rome, and Silverius naturally came under some political suspicion. By the indirect influence of Theodora he was deposed for treason and interned in Lycia, while Vigilius was elected Pope in his place. Silverius found friends in the East, who persuaded Justinian to order an enquiry, but Vigilius and his friends had the ear of Theodora. Silverius was sent back to Rome, found guilty, and confined on the island of Palmaria, where he died of privation and hunger, if his end was not hastened by more violent means.[1]

---

[1] *VIème siècle*, p. 154. The more sensational view is to be found, naturally, in the *Historia arcana*, i, 14, p. 7.

Meanwhile Leontius of Byzantium and Theodore Ascidas, Archbishop of Caesarea in Cappadocia, were working out a new Christology, intended to reconcile the moderate Monophysites with the rest of the church. The most important contribution of Leontius,[1] a monk who belonged to the laura of St Sabbas in Palestine, not far from Jerusalem, was his insistence on the hypostatic, not physical, union of God and man, that the humanity of Christ had no separate *hypostasis* or centre of personal being distinct from the *hypostasis* of God the Word. It was not impersonal (ἀνυπόστατος), but inpersonal (ἐνυπόστατος), in that it found its own centre in the Word of God. All Christ's human actions, including birth, suffering, and death, may therefore be ascribed to one *hypostasis* of the Word, though not to one nature. This doctrine was intended to restate St Cyril's formula, "One enfleshed nature of the Word", in words which clearly conformed to the Chalcedonian definition, "in two natures". It was not far removed from the doctrine of Severus,[2] who in his controversy with Julian and the *Aphthartodocetae* had gone far towards admitting a duality in the one nature of Christ.

A storm naturally arose from the other side, especially from theologians in Syria and Palestine who still cherished the traditions of Theodore of Mopsuestia. Theodore's Christology was under a cloud, and could not easily be invoked, but it was still possible to appeal to his Biblical exegesis. They accused Theodore Ascidas and Leontius, not of Monophysitism, but of the heresy of Origenism. They were tainted with ideas about the ultimate fate of souls derived from the teaching of the great Alexandrian interpreter of Scripture, whose mystical speculations had been constantly abused since he lived and died in the third century.

Origen, in some of his writings, had taught the final absorption of all things in God, including the humanity of Christ and redeemed human souls. The same tendency was latent in

---

[1] See Kidd, *Documents*, iii, 20, summarizing PG 86, pt. i, c. 1275-7; and S. Rees in *Journal of Theological Studies*, xli, Oxford, 1940, pp. 263–80.

[2] See J. Lebon, *Le Monophysisme Severien, passim*.

the Monophysite idea of the absorption of the humanity of Christ in His deity. Some saw it in the Christology of Leontius. Ephrem, the Patriarch of Antioch, held a council in 542 against Origenists; Justinian in 543 published a long edict against them.[1] Theodore Ascidas and Leontius were ready to condemn particular propositions out of Origen, but they insisted that the emperor's anti-Origenist edict ought properly to be balanced by another against the opposite heresies, in Christology and exegesis, of Theodore of Mopsuestia, the master of literal interpretation.

This was no new demand, for at every conference between Monophysites and Chalcedonians someone had asked them for an anathema on Theodore, Theodoret, and Ibas, three friends and counsellors of the heretical Nestorius. To condemn Theodore was not difficult, since most people in the East realized that he was the true author of the heresy called Nestorianism. But Theodoret and Ibas had been accepted as Orthodox at Chalcedon, and an attack on them could be regarded as a flank attack on the authority of the great council. Nevertheless Justinian in an edict in 544, in "Three Chapters",[2] condemned some of their writings, especially letters directed against the "twelve chapters" in St Cyril's third letter to Nestorius.

The letter of Ibas had been read at Chalcedon and apparently approved. For this reason, if for no other, the edict of Justinian aroused great apprehension in the West. Pope Vigilius was brought to Constantinople to consider it in an informed atmosphere, where he could be plied with other extracts from the works of the three theologians. There in 548 he issued his *Judicatum*, in which he expressed agreement with the imperial verdict; but when a great outcry arose in the West, that Chalcedon and the *Tome* of St Leo were being betrayed by a Pope who was suspected of complicity in the death of Silverius, he asked Justinian to summon a general council. The emperor

---

[1] PG 86, pt. i, c. 945–89, quoted in Kidd, *Documents*, iii, 10.
[2] Quotations are collated in J. Tixeront, *History of Dogmas*, Eng. trans., vol. iii, London and St Louis, 1916, pp. 130–1, from Facundus of Hermiane in PL 67, c. 566, 628.

consented, but meanwhile proceeded to enlighten Christendom
upon the issues involved in another edict, the *Homologia*,[1]
which contained an altogether admirable summary of the
doctrine of the hypostatic union, condensed from the writings
of Leontius of Byzantium. This excellent piece of imperial
theology was regarded by Vigilius, not without reason, as an
interference with the proceedings of the council before it took
place. He refused to commit himself to it, and excommunicated
the Patriarch Menas of Constantinople, as well as Theodore
Ascidas. After this he was put under house arrest, but escaped
before Christmas of 551 and took refuge in the basilica of St
Euphemia at Chalcedon, where the great council had given
its decisions a hundred years before. This appealed to Chalcedonian sentiment, always strong in Constantinople, so much so
that the emperor gave way. The edict and the excommunication were alike withdrawn, and all was again referred to the
coming council. There were some further negotiations, de-
signed to minimize the preponderance of Eastern bishops at a
council in the East, but neither the Pope nor the government
would consent to one another's proposals, and so in 553 the
council met in the usual way.

The Pope held himself apart, while Theodore of Mopsuestia
was condemned, and the doctrine of the Incarnation was defined on the lines of Leontius and the *Homologia*.[2] He issued a
Constitutum[3] of his own, in which he condemned sixty propositions from Theodore's writings as against seventy-one condemned by the council; but he refused to pass judgment on
the soul of a bishop who had died in the communion of the
Catholic Church, and so left his person free from the taint of
actual heresy. He would condemn nothing of Theodoret or
Ibas, for fear of a slight upon the Council of Chalcedon, but
in five additional anathemas he accepted the doctrine of the
hypostatic union and freed himself from any suspicion of Nestorianism. The council went further than he did, not only
against the soul of Theodore of Mopsuestia, and "the impious

[1] PG 86, pt. i, c. 993–1035.
[2] H-L, III, i, 105–32.   [3] PL 69, c. 67–114.

writings of Theodoret and Ibas", but in the way of positive statement. To the Fifth General Council we owe more than three anathemas on dead theologians whose influence within the empire was already in decline. We owe the doctrine of the hypostatic union as it is taught to-day in all Orthodox churches in East and West.

The name of Vigilius was removed from the diptychs, though the council did not wish to stress a difference that was more tactical than real, and protested their continued union with the Apostolic see of Rome.[1] At last, when all was over, and the bishops had gone home, Vigilius accepted their decisions in a new statement, his fourth on the matter at issue, and prepared to return to Rome. He died on the way in Sicily in 555. His friend Pelagius, who so far had been more obstinate than he in opposition to the government's policy, made a profession of faith in accordance with the five general councils, a model for future professions of Orthodoxy made by the Popes to the emperor's representatives between their election and their enthronement.[2] A key to the continuity of parties is provided by his use of the Scythian formula of peace, *passibilem carne, eumdem ipsum impassibilem deitate*. On these terms he was allowed to return to Rome as the emperor's candidate for election to the papacy. There he met his critics with assurances of his perfect loyalty to all the Popes from St Leo to Agapetus, and to "the venerable bishops, Theodoret and Ibas",[3] who had not been personally condemned. He was ready to give explanations to any bishop who came to answer them, but chary of public statement.

The prudent dissimulation of Pope Pelagius did not satisfy everyone. Some in the north of Italy made a schism called the schism of Aquileia, after the city where they established a patriarchal see. In 607 the Byzantine government, in an endeavour to recover these dissidents, established another patriarchate of Grado. Some time towards the end of the seventh

---

[1] Mansi ix, c. 367; Tixeront, iii, pp. 139–40.
[2] In A. Hahn, *Bibliothek der Symbol*, Breslau, 1877, pp. 270–2; see *Photian Schism*, pp. 435–47.
[3] PL 69, c. 400.

century the Patriarch of Aquileia was reconciled with Rome, but the rival lines of Patriarchs continued, and were still at strife in the eleventh century. These schisms cannot be considered Christological. The issue in north Italy was simply one of authority. In the view of its critics, the Fifth Council had cast a slur on the *Tome* of St Leo by condemning the letter of Ibas, which was on precisely the same footing. For the theology of Theodore and Theodoret the Latins cared nothing.

It was otherwise at the other end of the Christian world, where the condemnation of the "three Syrian doctors" divided the Syrian Christians of Persian Mesopotamia from the Byzantine church. These Assyrians are often called Nestorians, but it was a long time before this name was commonly applied to them. They accepted Chalcedon, but not Ephesus. In the first part of Justinian's reign they were certainly in communion with the Chalcedonian party in the East. But they were loyal to Theodore of Mopsuestia, whose methods of exegesis were followed at their school at Nisibis. Their loyalty was sharpened by controversy with Monophysites who fled from the imperial police into Persian Mesopotamia, and with *Aphthartodocetae* from Armenia, but they were very slow to condemn the doctrine of the hypostatic union. Whether they ever did so may be a matter of some doubt.[1]

While the "Syrian doctors" were being condemned the Monophysites of Syria and Mesopotamia at last acquired a hierarchy of their own. Justinian was accustomed to allow Monophysite missionaries to proceed to barbarous regions. The Monophysite historian, John of Ephesus, did good work in Asia Minor under the direct supervision of the government, though he had to permit the proclamation of the Council of Chalcedon in the churches of his foundation. It is probable that this elasticity was in the first place responsible for the consecration of Jacob Baradai[2] to be a missionary bishop for

[1] See J. Labourt, *Le christianisme dans l'empire Perse*, pp. 247–87; and for a more sympathetic view W. A. Wigram, *The Assyrian Church*, London, 1910, pp. 265–98.

[2] His life, by John of Ephesus, is in PO, xviii, 4, pp. 690–7, with Eng. trans. by E. W. Brooks.

the Ghassanid tribe of Arabs. Their king, Arethas, brought him from Constantinople in 542. But Jacob did not confine his ministrations to the Ghassanids. He used his extraordinary muscular gifts, and capacity for disguising his form and features under different arrangements of one huge horsecloth, to become absolutely ubiquitous in all parts of Syria, Mesopotamia, Sinai, and even Egypt. Everywhere he ordained priests and consecrated bishops, who in turn ordained and consecrated others, of all shades of Monophysitism.

Though Jacob went to Arabia in 542, it does not appear that he began to ordain on a large scale until about 547, when he provided Severus with a successor in the see of Antioch. At that time Theodora was dying of cancer, and the negotiations that followed Justinian's condemnation of the "Three Chapters" were hanging fire in the face of Western opposition. On both sides of the Byzantine frontier the Monophysites began to form a separate religious community, afterwards called the Jacobites. They themselves claimed to be disciples of St James, the "brother of the Lord". The Orthodox saw their real founder in Jacob Baradai, who remained the real leader of the party until his death in 577, though he was never Patriarch of Antioch in the Monophysite line.

Theologically Jacob was by no means an extremist. He was constantly at war with the *Aphthartodocetae* and other advanced sects, who multiplied as an inevitable consequence of his indiscriminate consecrations. He himself was sometimes prepared to consider terms proposed by the Orthodox—for instance, after the death of Justinian, in 567;[1] but the monks of the Syrian desert, his staunchest supporters, were very obstinate in their resistance to the hated Council of Chalcedon, and won him over to their views. His significance was not theological, but social and national. He became to the Syrians what St Athanasius and St Cyril had been to the Egyptians, a symbol of the revolt of the wilderness against the culture of the Greek city.[2]

---

[1] *VIème siècle*, pp. 347–8.
[2] See W. A. Wigram, *The Separation of the Monophysites*, pp. 133–8, 177–81, for an interpretation of Jacob.

Where Greek influences prevailed, in Asia Minor and northern Syria, the Monophysites were gradually absorbed into the local Orthodox community. In Palestine the theology of Leontius of Byzantium was accepted as an adequate translation of the tradition of St Cyril. There was no Jacobite bishop of Jerusalem before the Arab conquest.[1] But on the borders of the empire, in Istria and northern Italy, Armenia and Mesopotamia, Arabia and Egypt, separated churches came into existence to uphold or to resist the Council of Chalcedon. Within the *Oecumene*, the civilized world of the Roman empire, the policy of Justinian was more successful than is sometimes supposed. His legacy to the Catholic Church in the sphere of theology was probably of equal value with the contributions of St Leo and St Cyril; for without his support the harmonizing work of Leontius of Byzantium could not have been diffused from Palestine to Rome. If at the end of his life he was suspected of Aphthartodocetism, the suspicion probably arose from some oversubtle move of his in his never-ending task of conciliation.[2] He failed in theology as in politics because he attempted too much. The whole Mediterranean world from Spain to Mesopotamia could no longer be comprehended in one culture and one empire. If the nations were to remain in one church, the church must be distinct from the culture as she had not been since before the conversion of Constantine.

[1] See *infra*, p. 182.
[2] Leontius in PG 86, pt. i, c. 1317 disputes with Chalcedonian *Aphthartodocetae*. See S. Rees in JTS xli (1940), pp. 265–6.

5

THE "WATERY UNION"

AFTER THE death of Justinian the Byzantines returned to the caution characteristic of Zeno and Anastasius, who ruled the Western provinces through barbarian princes, and concentrated the regions under their direct rule behind the line of the Dardanelles and the walls of Constantinople. After 568 fresh Lombard invaders were gradually allowed to conquer the interior of Italy, while the Avars, the Bulgars, and their subjects the Slavs spread across the Balkan peninsula, penetrating even into the Peloponnese. In Pannonia, Illyricum, and Thrace their work of destruction was most thorough, for in the course of the seventh and eighth centuries almost all the Latin bishoprics in this region disappeared, except along the coast of Dalmatia and Albania, where Dyrrhacium (Durazzo) and Spalato (Split) long remained Latin sees. In Greece and the Greek cities of the coasts of Macedonia and Thrace the tradition of Hellenism survived every shock, and gradually recovered its ascendancy over new Slavonic and Albanian elements, though the mixture of the races must have been very considerable, and Slavonic tribes in the Peloponnese were semi-independent in the tenth century.[1] The Latin culture of Pannonia and Illyricum was less firmly rooted, and never recovered, though the Latin dialects of this region are represented by Rumanian, which is now spoken chiefly north of the Danube. In Bulgaria, Macedonia, and Thessaly it is spoken by the mountain Vlachs, who were more numerous in the Middle Ages, though they were already a remnant. The older speech of the Illyrians survives in Albanian.

[1] Constantine Porphyrogenitus, *De administrando imperio*, c. 50, CB, iii, pp. 220–4, PG 113, c. 373–84.

Latin remained an official language in the army and the bureaucracy until the remains of the system of Diocletian and Constantine were replaced by a new administration of civil and military affairs, probably in the reign of Constans (641–68). When St Gregory the Great represented the Roman church in Constantinople at the beginning of the reign of Maurice (580–602), he did not find it necessary to acquire a working knowledge of Greek. But as early as the reign of Justinian [1] the neglect of Latin gave rise to difficulties in filling high positions in the bureaucracy. After 602 the language was of little use, except in outposts in Dalmatia and Italy. To a great extent these outposts were left to shift for themselves, and to meet their barbarian enemies as best they could with their own local resources. The government never had many troops to spare for Italy, and these were generally employed either in the Exarchate of Ravenna, the seat of the Byzantine governor, or to protect sea communications around the Greek cities of the south. In this way Rome and Naples, and Grado, the original of Venice, became autonomous if not independent. The local aristocracy were allowed to make their own treaties with Lombard dukes, or even with the Lombard king.

Pope St Gregory the Great (590–604) was a loyal though critical subject of the undivided Roman empire, but he had his own political and spiritual relationships with Lombard kings and queens, the Franks in Gaul, the Anglo-Saxons in Britain, and the Visigoths in Spain, who in 589 turned from Arianism to Catholicism. He corresponded at the same time with the Patriarch Eulogius in Alexandria and with St Augustine in Canterbury. Pope Vitalian (657–72) was able to provide the English church with a Greek Archbishop, Theodore of Tarsus. In his time the conversion of the Lombards to the Catholic faith "abolished the Arian heresy", [2] and strengthened

---

[1] See John Lydus, *De Magistratibus*, ed. R. Wuensch, Leipzig, 1893, bk. iii, c. 68, pp. 158–9.

[2] "Rex Haribertus, pius et catholicus, Arrianorum abolevit haeresem," *Carmen de synodo Ticinensi*, quoted in *VIème siècle*, p. 253. The Arian Bishop of Pavia was converted just in time to succeed his Catholic colleague, and so to become "l'evêque de tout le monde".

the political position of the papacy by providing the Popes with other possibilities of protection. The results are to be seen in the changed situation at Rome between 653, when Pope Martin I was arrested and taken to Constantinople, and 693, when a similar attempt to arrest Pope Sergius I was a total failure. In the interval the Roman nobility had learnt to rely on the Pope as their best protector against the Lombards. His influence could win them help from Constantinople, or forbearance from Pavia and Spoleto. Without him they would have no better chance to avoid being overwhelmed than any other Latin community on the coast of Italy.

The political independence of the papacy came into existence without any particular design on the part of the Popes, the Byzantine emperors, or the Roman nobles. The Popes, on the contrary, wanted more help from the East against the "infamous Lombards". The Byzantines could not afford to take large risks for so distant an outpost. When friction arose between Rome and Constantinople they were reluctant to impose a Pope of their own choice if he would not be obeyed in northern Italy or in the Western kingdoms, for so they would lose the advantage of a diplomatic intermediary, who was useful in negotiations with the Franks or Bavarians. The isolation of the elder Rome at the very edge of the *Oecumene*, the civilized world, did not increase its intellectual influence in the capital of civilization.

At the other end of the Mediterranean Byzantine influence in Armenia increased during a Persian war from 573 to 591, in which the Byzantines and the Armenians were allies. The Armenian church [1] had never been so intransigently anti-Chalcedonian as the Jacobites and the Copts, though it contained some extremist elements. It was outside the frontier of the empire all through the height of the controversy, and therefore subject to no persecution from the Byzantine government.

[1] See John of Ephesus, *Ecclesiastical History*, Eng. trans. by R. Payne Smith, Oxford, 1860, p. 126; and M. Ormanian, *The Church of Armenia*, Eng. trans., London, 1912, p. 41. This Armenian book is useful because it reflects the spirit as well as the letter of its sources, though its point of view is sometimes naïve.

All its troubles came from the Persians and their friends the Assyrian Christians of Nisibis, who stood for the opposite theology of Theodore of Mopsuestia. Under the Catholicos Hovhannes (590–611) a union was arranged that proved impermanent so far as Armenia was concerned, but permanent in Georgia. After the Council of Douine in 609 the Georgians or Iberians had their own Catholicos, and lived as an autocephalus church, with their own liturgy in their own language, in communion with the Orthodox Patriarchates. In 622 the union with Armenia was restored at the Council of Garin. In most parts of the country, if not in all, it seems to have continued until near the end of the century,[1] when the greater part of the country came under Moslem rule. The Armenians have never been in complete unity with the Jacobites. Attempts to settle differences in 726 were not successful.[2] In the ninth and tenth centuries a great part of the Armenian church again resumed commun'on with Byzantium that was not broken until a serious schism among them in 969–71.[3]

This intermittent union with Armenia from 590 to 971 illustrates one possible solution of the problem of diversity of cultures in Catholic Christendom. If the Armenians had lived a little farther from the Byzantines they might have become as Orthodox and as independent as the Georgians, and other Orthodox nations north of the Caucasus, the Abasgians and the Alans, who had national churches in communion with Constantinople. But the boundaries of Armenia had never been clearly defined, and interpenetration increased, bringing new causes of conflict, as Moslem pressure drove the Armenians southward and westward towards Cilicia, where many of them were settled in the eleventh and twelfth centuries.

In 629 the union of Garin was extended to the Jacobites in

---

[1] M. Ormanian, *The Church of Armenia*, p. 44.

[2] Ibid., pp. 45–6; cf. also Bar-Hebraeus, *Chronicon Ecclesiasticon*, vol. i, Louvain, 1872, c. 299–304, and Michael the Syrian, *Chronicle*, vol. ii, Paris, 1904, pp. 492–500.

[3] M. Ormanian, op. cit., p. 49, says that Khatchik I (971–92) was the first Catholicos who "consecrated Armenian bishops for those of his co-religionists who dwelt in Greek dioceses. Until then there had been, in accordance with ancient custom, only one bishop in each diocese."

Syria and Mesopotamia, who had obtained possession of most
of the churches in Syria and Palestine during a Persian occupation of the whole country from 616 to 628. Their diplomatic
Patriarch, Athanasius the Camel-driver, consented to admit
the orthodoxy of Chalcedon, safeguarded as it now was by two
additional formulae, the doctrine of the hypostatic union and
a doctrine of "one new, human-divine operation in Christ"
that the Council of Garin had found in the *Divine Names*,[1]
ascribed to St Paul's companion, Dionysius the Areopagite.
(No one at this time suspected that this was a Syrian compilation of the time of the *Henoticon*, specially suitable for reconciling
moderate Monophysites and moderate Chalcedonians, and
used for this end by the friends of Severus in the conference of
533.) On this condition the Jacobites kept their usages, including the interpolation in the *Trisagion*.

In 630 a further attempt was made to draw in the Assyrians
of Persian Mesopotamia. Their Catholicos of the East paid a
visit to Constantinople, where he was examined, found Orthodox, and received communion. When he returned to his own
people, who soon discovered that he had reconciled them in-
directly to their real rivals, the Mesopotamian Jacobites, there
was a great uproar. He was accused of betraying the "three
lights of the church, Diodore, Theodore, and Nestorius". He
defended himself as best he could and remained Catholicos
until his death in 643. Only after the Arab conquest did controversy flame up again between his successor and Sahdona of
Ariun, who had really been converted to Chalcedonian Orthodoxy during his sojourn in the Byzantine empire.[2] For a time
the heads at least of both the Christian sects in Persia were in
communion with Constantinople and Rome.

An attempt to extend the union to Egypt in 633 met with
more opposition on both sides. The *Tome of Union* [3] in nine

---

[1] Ch. 2, sec. 3.
[2] Bar-Hebraeus, *Chron. Eccles.*, vol. iii, Louvain, 1878, c. 113–16; cf. also
Thomas of Marga, *The Book of the Governors*, Eng. trans., London, 1893,
vol. ii, pp. 125–30; J. Labourt, *Le christianisme dans l'empire Perse*, pp. 243–6;
W. A. Wigram, *The Assyrian Church*, pp. 303–7.
[3] Mansi, xi, c. 564–8; comment in Tixeront, iii, pp. 155–6.

chapters did not satisfy the Monophysites of the desert, who adhered to their own Patriarch Benjamin. On the other hand, it was hotly criticized by the local Chalcedonians, who found in the writings of their own Patriarch Eulogius of Alexandria (580–607) an anti-Monophysite doctrine of two distinct operations or energies in Christ. This was taken up by a monk from Palestine named Sophronius, who in 634 was elected Patriarch of Jerusalem. Palestine, rather than Alexandria or Tanis, was the real stronghold of Chalcedonian doctrine in the East. The Palestinian Christians resented their union with Jacobites who sang Peter the Fuller's version of the *Trisagion*, a watchword of heresy for two hundred years of controversy, but their objections were not all prejudice. Sophronius had a real point behind the somewhat turgid style of the letter that he addressed to the other Patriarchs in 634.[1] He feared lest the humanity of Christ should seem to be no more than a puppet-show of passive attributes, worked from the outside by the divinity of the Word. "One operation", so understood by those in a Monophysite tradition, might prove more Monophysite than Severian Monophysitism.

Before the letter of Sophronius reached Rome Pope Honorius I had received a report on the controversy from the Patriarch Sergius of Constantinople, who had played a large part in all these plans for union since 610. He was an ecclesiastical statesman rather than a theologian, and his great desire was to prevent the ruin of his plans for a general restoration of communion between autonomous churches in the East through a revival of Roman and Western anxiety for the authority of the *Tome* of St Leo. He therefore made haste to anticipate the more precise theological activity of the Patriarch of Jerusalem, and to induce the Pope to support him. He received rather more than he wanted in a dogmatic letter,[2] drafted with the help of Joannes Symponus, who afterwards became Pope John IV. The two Western theologians saw objections to both the two rival doctrines of one or two operations. Both might

---

[1] PG 87, pt. iii, c. 3147–3200.
[2] Kidd, *Documents*, iii, 37; full text in PL 80, c. 470–4.

border on Eutychianism or Nestorianism. They insisted that
the true unity in Christ is a unity of person and of will. What
is said in the scriptures of an apparent conflict in Him is said
"not of a difference of wills but for the economy of the humanity
which He assumed". They were spoken for our example, not
to show a distinction in Him between the will which obeyed
and the will which obtained obedience.

Honorius, like most Westerns, was chiefly interested in moral
issues, in problems of predestination and grace, freewill and
moral effort. It was therefore natural that he should think of
the unity of the will of Christ in these terms, which were equally
acceptable among the Assyrians at Nisibis and Seleucia and
the Syrian Jacobites, but in different senses. The Antiochene
tradition of Theodore of Mopsuestia spoke of a unity of will
between the word of God and the "heavenly man". The opposite tradition of Severus thought of the unity of will as one
relatively uncontentious aspect of the complete unity of hypostasis and nature. To Sergius, therefore, the "one will" formula,
stamped with the high authority of Rome, was an ideal instrument for "reunion all round". In 638 it was embodied in an
imperial *Ecthesis*,[1] which forbade further contention over one
or two operations in Christ.

But all these unions were "watery",[2] as Theophanes said in
about 800. In a surprisingly short time a new gale from the
desert blew them all away. The Arabs began to invade Syria
in 635. In 640–1 they broke into Egypt, where they found the
Copts in rebellion against Cyrus of Phasis, the unhappy author
of the *Tome of Union*, who combined unsuccessfully the functions
of Patriarch and civil governor. Before long he himself came
to terms with them and sailed away, leaving the field free for
his rival Benjamin. A hundred years passed before there was
another Chalcedonian Patriarch of Alexandria, though the
Orthodox community did not die out altogether. For seventy
years no Patriarch could be elected at Jerusalem, where the
Christians were divided between followers of Sophronius and

[1] Mansi, x, c. 991–8; Tixeront, iii, pp. 163–4.
[2] CB, i, p. 507. The word is ὑδροβαφῆ.

adherents of the union of 629. The like divisions rent the subjugated church in northern Syria and in Persian Mesopotamia,
where the conflict between Sahdona of Ariun and his Nestorian
adversaries belongs after 643.

In the West the *Ecthesis* was repudiated by Severinus and
John IV, the successors of Honorius, and withdrawn by the
Emperor Heraclius in 640–1. The next emperor, Constans
(641–68), hesitated to depart from it too completely, lest he
should alienate the Armenians, under their Catholicos Nerses
(641–61), who was a personal friend of his.[1] The Christian
cause in Syria and Cilicia was still being maintained by Mar-
daite and Isaurian mountaineers in Lebanon and the Taurus,
who were followers of Jacob Baradai and Athanasius the
Camel-driver, and still loyal to the union of 629. Constans
therefore published a *Type*,[2] which defined no doctrine at all,
but forbade controversy for or against "one will in Christ".

The ablest adversary of the *Type* was a Byzantine archimandrite named Maximus, who had retired from the civil service
as the last remains of Diocletian's organization of the bureaux
and the army fell crashing to the ground in the Arab wars.
In his work we can see a union of Syrian and Egyptian mysticism (he had a great regard for Origen, the Cappadocian
fathers, and even for the Pseudo-Dionysius, the original author
of "one operation") with the Greek and Roman zeal for the
rule of law, the civil administrator's horror of the centralized,
military government that was imposed upon the empire by the
necessities of the Persian and Arab wars.[3] He and his disciples
were accused of denying the priesthood of the emperor.[4] He
was also asked, "Why do you love the Romans and hate the
Greeks?"[5] In these two charges we see the shadow of later
controversies.

Maximus could not conduct his propaganda in the centre of

[1] M. Ormanian, op. cit., p. 43.
[2] Kidd, *Documents*, iii, 38; Mansi, x, c. 1029–32.
[3] His works are in PG 90–1; summaries of his doctrine may be found in
Tixeront, iii, pp. 180–4, and A. Neander, *General Church History*, Eng. trans.,
vol. v, Edinburgh, 1849, pp. 220–5.
[4] *Acta Maximi* in PG 90, c. 117–18.
[5] Ibid., c. 127–8; comment in *VIème siècle*, p. 455–6.

the empire. He worked his way from Palestine and Egypt to Africa, where he held a disputation with Pyrrhus, an exiled Patriarch of Constantinople, and so by Sicily to Italy. There he informed Pope Martin I of the condition of the East, and caused him to summon a council at the Lateran in 649, where he condemned the emperor's *Type* and broke off communion with the church of Constantinople. The Exarch who was sent to arrest Pope Martin joined his party and began a rebellion. Whatever the degree of his complicity Pope Martin was regarded by the court as the author of this. Another Exarch was sent with superior forces to arrest the Pope and the Archimandrite Maximus, and to carry them by slow stages to Constantinople. There they were tried in 654, not for heresy, but for treason. The government did their best to avoid a discussion of the dogmatic issue that would have aroused Chalcedonian sympathies in the populace of Constantinople, who were in any case disposed to be sympathetic with the imprisoned Pope. His sufferings were great, and ended only with his death from cold and hunger in the Crimea. They were increased by the news that the Romans had deserted him and elected a new Pope, Eugenius, whose envoys at Constantinople acquiesced in a new evasive formula that seemed to restore the harmony of the Patriarchates. It seemed to Maximus that all the world was against him,[1] yet he refused to accept the communion of the church of Constantinople, even though, if he would only have done so, he might have returned to Rome as the emperor's envoy, perhaps as his candidate for the Papacy. He died in exile in the Caucasus in 662.

His theology triumphed soon after his death, because it had never been effectively banned. The evasive formula, which he himself refused, recognized no less than three wills in Christ, one for each nature and one for the hypostasis. A plurality of wills would not appease a Monophysite, nor would an Orthodox theologian find much to blame except a certain meaningless prolixity. In 655 the Roman clergy found ambiguities in the "systatic letter" of the Patriarch Peter of Constantinople,

[1] PG 90, c. 121–2, 131–4.

and persuaded Pope Eugenius I to reject it; but his successor
Vitalian sent a profession of faith to the emperor that was received as satisfactory, and exchanged letters with Peter in 657.
In 663 he received the Emperor Constans in Rome itself.
Though relations were again interrupted from 672 to 679, this
may have been due in part to the power of the Arabs in the
Aegean, who attacked Constantinople by sea in 668 and again in
673–7. It may also be that there was some political distrust, for
the improved relations between the papacy and the Lombards
after they abandoned Arianism can hardly have inspired confidence in Constantinople or Ravenna. Some of the Greek
and Syrian refugees who flocked to Rome at this time may have
been politically suspect. Syrian monks in a Roman convent
were convicted of Nestorianism in 677,[1] when relations with
the East were being resumed.

The restoration of peace was due to the initiative of the
Emperor Constantine IV (668–85). In the East the Patriarch
Macarius of Antioch, an exile in Constantinople, opposed a
move that would certainly alienate some of his Isaurian and
Syrian subjects on both sides of the empire's border. He was
still recognized as Patriarch by the fighting Mardaites on
Mount Lebanon, though in other parts of Syria and Mesopotamia other Jacobites had submitted to the Arabs and repudiated the union of 629. A "Maximist" party repudiated it for
other reasons, following the tradition of Sophronius, which was
naturally stronger in Palestine than in the Lebanon or in
Syria. In the time of the Palestinian Pope Theodore I (642–9)
they had some communications with Rome.[2] These continued
under Martin I, and their resumption through Syrian refugees
may well have served to irritate Macarius. The strength of the
Syrians in Rome is shown by the election of two Syrian Popes
in 685–7, and three more in 708 and 731. Armenian politics
were another argument against abandoning the *Type*; for the
Catholicos Chahak III was still in communion with Constantinople in 689–90, and a Chalcedonian party in Armenia

[1] *Lib. Pont.*, i, p. 348.
[2] Mansi, x, c. 900; cf. J. Pargoire, *L'Église Byzantine*, p. 154.

were denounced to the Caliph by the more Monophysite Catholicos Eghia in 703.[1] The Patriarch Theodore of Constantinople sought to impede the emperor's negotiations with Rome by removing the name of Pope Vitalian from the diptychs, though he wrote a letter, not a "systatic letter", but one of a less formal kind, to Pope Domnus (676–8).

At Rome the imperial overtures were received with some hesitation, for Agatho, who had succeeded Domnus when the letters arrived, feared lest the little learning of Latin ecclesiastics should entangle them in some subtle compromise that later consideration might not be able to sustain against such criticisms as had been launched against Vigilius and Honorius, and others who modified their theology to please a Byzantine emperor. He drew up a careful statement and submitted it to preliminary councils at Rome and Milan, where he collected the signatures of as many Latin bishops as possible to make it seem sufficiently impressive. He waited long before sending his delegation to the East in the hope that Theodore of Tarsus, the Greek Archbishop of Canterbury, might be persuaded to venture on so long a journey for the good of the whole church; but either pressing business in England detained him, or he doubted his ability to act as a champion of the Latins (his views on the remarriage of divorced persons [2] were most decidedly Greek). The other legates had to go without him.

When they arrived at Constantinople they found that the Patriarch Theodore had been replaced by a more sympathetic figure, who restored Vitalian's name to the diptychs. Syrians and Armenians were not popular with the Byzantines, who favoured a union of the old and the new Rome. The Sixth General Council in the winter of 680–1 accepted the *Tome* of Pope Agatho, and condemned the *Ecthesis* and the *Type*, with the doctrines of "one operation" and "one will". Macarius, who refused to submit, was sent into a monastery in Rome. Theodore, on the other hand, accepted the council's decisions,

---

[1] M. Ormanian, op. cit., p. 45.
[2] See his *Penitentiale* in A. W. Haddan and W. Stubbs, *Constitutions and Ecclesiastical Documents relating to Great Britain and Ireland*, vol. iii, pp. 199–201.

and two years later he resumed the Patriarchal throne. The treatment of persons by the Sixth Council is especially interesting, for the issues had been more personal and regional than doctrinal. Four Patriarchs of Constantinople, Sergius, Pyrrhus, Paul, and Peter, had to be sacrificed to Roman objections to their compromising doctrines. To these were added Cyrus of Phasis, the author of the Alexandrian *Tome* of union in 633, Macarius, the present Patriarch of Antioch, one Arabian bishop who had played a part in drawing up the original formulas of union in 622–9, and Honorius of Rome, who had proposed "one will". On the other hand, the three Patriarchs of Constantinople, Thomas, John, and Constantine (667–77), whose "systatic letters" were accounted Orthodox, though the last two did not address them to Rome, remained in the diptychs. They may be compared to the Patriarchs Euphemius and Macedonius, whom the Orthodox in Constantinople wished to spare at the union of 518. In 681 four heretical Patriarchs were balanced against one heretical Pope.

It is curious that the case of Pope Honorius excited little or no attention in the Middle Ages. When the possibility of an heretical Pope was debated, Liberius and Anastasius II were the instances used. The explanation lies in the text of the *Liber Pontificalis*, which names him in the list of condemned Monothelites without calling him a Pope.[1] At the time it does not seem that his condemnation was resented in the West, though Pope John IV, part-author of his letter, had been at pains to defend his orthodoxy. Pope Leo II, reporting the results of the Council to the king of the Visigoths, sets him among the heretics without demur.[2]

That some in the East regretted the Sixth Council was shown by an episode thirty years later, when the Armenian emperor, Philippicus Bardanes, erased a large picture of it from one of the palace walls, and imposed upon the Patriarch and the bishops a formal disavowal of its proceedings. This, however, led to a revolution, a rising of the factions against him. The Monothelite compromise was not a doctrine that could sustain

---

[1] i, p. 359.   [2] See *VIème siècle*, p. 473; H-L, III, i, 515–38.

for long the loyalty of any large party. It left its deepest traces not in Armenia, where the "one operation" formula had its origin, but in the mountains of the Lebanon. There, around the monastery of Beit Marun, a small community maintained the doctrines of Sergius and Macarius against Monophysite and "Maximist" criticism. In about 780 they made an attempt to use the "one will" doctrine as the basis of a union with the Assyrians or Nestorians,[1] who could not admit them unless they abandoned their many Jacobite customs—for instance, Peter the Fuller's version of the *Trisagion*, which was anathema to the disciples of Theodore of Mopsuestia. These Maronites [2] survived as an independent community until 1181, when they submitted to the Latin Patriarch of Antioch. Though they afterwards broke away for a time, they resumed relations with Rome at the end of the fifteenth century, and ever since then have remained a "Uniate" church.[3]

The learned Jacobite historian, Bar-Hebraeus, who was "Maphrian of the East" or primate of the Jacobite church in Mesopotamia from 1264 to 1286, believed that in his time all the churches of the East, Jacobite, Maronite, Greek, Latin, and even Assyrian, "think aright concerning the Trinity and the integrity of the natures of which Christ is formed without conversion or commixture; they fight only about terms".[4] It is not easy to say when the Christological controversies became wholly cultural and verbal. Maximus seems to be struggling with real issues, and the story of Sahdona of Ariun shows that it was still possible to pass from one confession to another for intellectual reasons. But the difference between the Armenians and their neighbours was rather liturgical than intellectual.

[1] See J. Labourt, *De Timotheo I Nestorianorum Patriarcha*, Paris, 1904, pp. 18–19.

[2] See *Mich. Syr.* ii, p. 493.

[3] See J. Labourt, art. "Maronites" in *The Catholic Encyclopaedia*, ix, New York, 1914, pp. 683–8, and J. S. Assemanus in *Bibliotheca Orientalis*, vol. i, Rome, 1719, pp. 496–521.

[4] *Candelabrum sanctorum* in *B.O.*, ii, c. 290–1. This work is in progress in PO, xxii, f. 4, and xxiv, f. 3. For a like view c. 893 see *B.O.*, iii, c. 514–16, a summary of the *Tractatus de concordia fidei inter Syros* of the Assyrian Metran Elias of Damascus.

A Catholicos who objected to union with the Byzantines said that he would not eat "leavened bread or drink hot water" [1] (a reference to the mixed chalice of the Greeks). The same arguments were used against the Jacobites. Both communities might have remained united to the Orthodox Patriarchates if the Arab conquests had not made it preferable that conquered Christians should belong to separated churches, and not suffer the imputation of being Melkites, "the emperor's men".

[1] *VIème siècle*, p. 389, from *Liber de rebus Armeniae*, PG 127, c. 893 (c. 695). See also the tracts against *azymes* attributed to the Jacobite James of Edessa (d. 708) in W. Wright, *Syriac Literature*, London, 1894, p. 146.

6

THE STRUGGLE WITH ISLAM

FROM ONE point of view Islam is the most extreme of the Christological heresies, combining extreme Monophysite and extreme Nestorian elements. Like Theodore of Mopsuestia, Mohammed regarded Christ as the great prophet, the Messiah of the Hebrews, who would return to judge the world at the last day. His inspiration, though unique in degree, was not sufficiently different in kind from the inspiration of any other human leader overshadowed by the Word to make a second Messianic figure inconceivable. The Apostle, the promised Paraclete, was Mohammed himself. The Christ of the Koran was virgin-born, but He did not die, for His true body was spirited away.[1] In this idea of a ghost Christ we see something more like Aphthartodocetism than Nestorianism. Arabia contained Nabataean Arabs evangelized by the Mesopotamian churches, Monophysite Ghassanids, Orthodox Arabs in Transjordania, and also, especially by the Red Sea on the coast of Yemen, unorthodox Jews from Abyssinia. The desert was a refuge for all kinds of extremists rejected by the more Orthodox sects. The Jews in particular seem to have influenced Mohammed, who called his religion a middle way between Christianity and Judaism. But the Judaism of Arabia was the religion of the apocalypses rather than the religion of the Old Testament. From the trance literature of post-Biblical times, more frequently preserved in Abyssinia than elsewhere, and then perhaps equally abundant on both sides of the Red Sea, he derived his idea of revelation as something absolutely direct and immediate in which the human mind does not co-operate at all.

[1] *Koran* iv. 154–end. See R. Bell, *The Origin of Islam in its Christian Environment*, London, 1926.

Islam might be called the most advanced expression of the oriental revolt against Hellenism, rejecting and discarding everything of Judaism or Christianity that concurs in any way with the Greek idea of natural law; in this the Moslems may be compared to other extremists: the Marcionites in the second century, who rejected the Old Testament and three out of the four Gospels; the Manichaeans in the third century, who regarded creation as the work of an inferior deity; and the Paulicians.[1] Those who wholly reject the law as seen by philosophers in the natural order eventually come to reject the law in the Old Testament and to denounce the God of Israel as an imperfect God. The strict Moslem did, in fact, come to reject both science and representative art, because both involve some kind of co-operation with the Creator in His work of creation. Moslem artists were commanded to confine themselves to architectural patterns, arabesques, and scrolls, which may assume plant forms, but not the forms of animals. Likewise the scientific investigation of natural causes is forbidden. The authentic Moslem attitude is expressed in the legendary tale [2] (disbelieved by Gibbon) that the Caliph Omar pronounced this verdict on the library at Alexandria: "If these writings of the Greeks agree with the book of God, they are useless and need not be preserved; if they disagree, they are pernicious and ought to be destroyed."

This fanaticism was soon modified in practice, especially in those regions where the agricultural and trading population became Moslem. But at first Islam was primarily the religion of the desert, where everything happens unexpectedly, and no canon or law is binding on nature. The first Moslem converts outside Arabia were the desert tribes of Syria, Egypt, Libya, and North Africa, and the highland shepherds of Persia and Bactria. For a long time the Arabs did not much desire the conversion of the settled peoples, which would reduce the yield of the poll-tax paid by unbelievers. The army and the

[1] *Infra*, pp. 75-6.
[2] Bar-Hebraeus, *Historia compendiosa dynastiarum*, Oxford, 1663, p. 114, quoted in Bury-Gibbon, v, p. 482.

highest posts in the government were reserved for Moslems, but Christians performed most of the administrative routine. Even in the former Persian empire, where the religion of Zoroaster suffered a fatal blow, Assyrian Christianity spread as rapidly as Islam, and converted a larger proportion of the settled population. The seventh and eighth centuries are a great age in the expansion of the Assyrian church across the oases of Bactria and Turkestan into the Tarim basin, and so into China,[1] following the routes of Syrian traders engaged in the caravan traffic that was further fostered by the size of the Arab empire and the relative ease of communications within it. These Mesopotamian Syrians spread westward as well as eastward, founding colonies in Cyprus and even in Spain, where Assyrian influence probably explains an unexpected reappearance of Nestorian ideas at the end of the eighth century. Syrians served their Arab masters as doctors, lawyers, traders, and administrators. Their translations of Greek and Indian mathematics, and Greek philosophy, laid foundations for the mediaeval culture of Damascus and Bagdad.

In course of time the rigidity of Islam was modified by the inevitable influence of power and wealth. Moslems as well as Christians became interested in poetry, medicine, mathematics, mysticism, and even philosophy. Birds and beasts, hunting and fishing scenes appear in the palace art of Iraq and Iran. All this involved a deviation from the strict tenets of the Koran, which could never be reconciled with the philosophic search. The representative Moslem philosopher is the Spaniard Averroës, who taught them what was true in theology might be false in philosophy, and *vice versa*; but when the rulers did come to share in the culture they inevitably took the lead in its development.[2] As a natural result there was a steady leakage of ambitious young men from the Christian communi-

---

[1] See A. Mingana, *The Early Spread of Christianity in Central Asia and the Far East, John Rylands Library Bulletin,* Manchester, 1925; J. Foster, *The Church of the Tang Dynasty,* London, 1939.

[2] For Islamic culture see C. Dawson, *The Making of Europe,* London, 1932, pp. 148–56; P. K. Hitti, *History of the Arabs,* London, 1949, pp. 240–449.

ties to the dominant religion. The Christians were forbidden
to attempt the conversion of Moslems, and very gradually
their numbers dwindled.[1] They suffered more from famine
and civil war than the ruling classes, but they seldom had to
complain of actual persecution.

Their own ecclesiastical authorities were responsible for their
good behaviour, and judged their own disputes by their own
laws. The Arabs took over the Persian empire the principle of a
"Millet", a separate cultural community that is allowed to continue its own communal life on two conditions: political submission and a very strict abstention from any attempt to pro-
selytize the adherents of the reigning religion.[2] Under these
conditions the Assyrian, Armenian, and Jacobite churches had
continued under the Persian empire, and the various Christian
communities, Assyrian, Monophysite, and Orthodox, continued
under the Arabs. The Orthodox had the most difficult time, for
they were naturally suspected as "Melkites", "emperor's men".
Until the eighth century they were not allowed to choose their
own resident Patriarchs. All communications with Byzantium
were dangerous, but there was not the same objection to
Western pilgrims, who brought alms into the country and had
no direct connection with the Byzantine enemy. Therefore the
Latin monasteries and hospices at Jerusalem became relatively
important.[3] Anglo-Saxon kings might go to die at Jerusalem,

[1] On the connection between the decline of agriculture and the decline
of Christianity in Asia Minor and Syria there are some illuminating passages
in the writings of Sir William Ramsay; see especially *The Thousand and One
Churches*, by Sir W. Ramsay and Miss Gertrude Bell, London, 1907, p. 37;
cf. also *Petra*, by Miss M. Murray, London, 1939, for a picture of an impoverished Bedouin community in a valley that once supported a great
city. Jewish agriculture is now restoring to parts of Palestine the prosperity
that Islam destroyed, not in the seventh century, when the Arabs first
arrived, but in the fourteenth century, when the Christian population began
to be reduced below the level of safety.

[2] For the idea of a "Millet" see a useful discussion in W. A. Wigram, *The
Assyrian Church*, pp. 225–8.

[3] For the Melkite community in Jerusalem in c. 808 see the *Commemoratorium de casis Dei* in *Itinera Hierosolymitana*, ed. T. Tobler and A. Molinier,
vol. i (Latina), Geneva, 1879, pp. 301–5. It contains statistics of hermits
classified by their liturgical languages, thirteen Greek, eight Syriac, five
Latin, five Georgian, and one Arabic. I have discussed the significance of
these classifications in an article in ECQ, vi (1945–6), pp. 363–72.

but envoys from the Eastern Patriarchs rarely and with great difficulty came to Constantinople.

Naturally no more could be done towards union with the Monophysites, except in Armenia, where border princes retained their independence and entered into negotiations from time to time with their Byzantine military allies. Elsewhere the Jacobites and Maronites preferred to stand aloof from the Melkites, from one another, and even from the Armenians, who began to be dispersed in this period, as the Arabs moved them away from the dangerous border regions to Cyprus and Egypt, and Byzantine emperors, equally doubtful of their loyalty, moved refugees and others from Cilicia to Macedonia and Thrace. Sometimes, as at Edessa, they formed one community with the Jacobites. In Jerusalem they seem to have been in communion with the Melkites at the time of the *Commemoratorium*. Elsewhere they would not mix at all, and set up bishops of their own. In this way the Christian nations of the Levant ceased to be associated with particular regions, and became scattered communities more like the Sikhs and Jains in modern India. In and about the holy places were Jacobites and Armenians (later on Copts, Ethiopians, and Assyrians). Even the Melkites were divided by language and associations into Latins, Greeks, Syrians, and Georgians.[1] All these divisions were fostered by Moslem policy.

As the Arabs swept westwards into North Africa (670–700) they won control of the greater part of the Mediterranean. For long periods Cyprus, Rhodes, and Crete were held, and Christian shipping was not safe even in the Aegean, especially during the two great attempts to capture Constantinople in 673–7 and 717–20. In this way the Moslem conquests contributed to the isolation of the Byzantines, not only from the Syrian and Egyptian Christians, but to a large extent from the Latin West. The great Avar invasions, which began in 567–81, cut the land road from Constantinople to Italy. In the seventh and eighth centuries, while Avars, Bulgars, and Slavs roamed unchecked over the Balkan peninsula, and Lombard dukes

[1] *Infra*, pp. 181–2.

and counts isolated Ravenna from Rome, the Arab conquest of North Africa, Spain, and the Balearic islands made the sea route round Sicily dangerous, and Rome became farther and farther from Constantinople. But in the lands that remained to the Byzantine empire there was more homogeneity and a deeper patriotism.

These lands were not all Greek, for in central Asia Minor there were Cappadocians and Paphlagonians, and the non-Greek elements were increased by a large influx of Armenian and Syrian refugees. But it is true to say that the lands where Greek influence was strongest remained most persistently loyal to Byzantium in this time of apparent decline. In Calabria and the heel of Italy, in Sicily and at the entrance to the Adriatic, at the mouth of the Danube and in the Crimea, old Greek colonies remained faithful to the Byzantine version of Greek civilization.

The loyalty of the Greeks to their own traditions was enhanced by the anti-Hellenism of Islam, a non-Christian Monotheism. Greek theologians had always laid more stress on the distinction of persons in the Trinity than most of their Latin brethren.[1] They taught that each of the three persons has His own hypostasis or ground of being, while the Latins taught that all have only one being, substance, and *hypostasis*. In their struggle with Arianism in Spain and Italy the Latin clergy compiled the creed of St Athanasius, so named because the Arians called them Athanasians. When in the hour of their victory they adopted the Greek custom of singing the creed of Constantinople and Chalcedon at Mass, first of all at Toledo in 589 or 653,[2] they brought the two creeds into apparent harmony by inserting from the Western "Athanasian" symbol the Latin word *filioque* into the Eastern Nicene creed at the point of the procession of the Holy Ghost.

This was not an important alteration in itself. The Greeks themselves could say, and sometimes said, that the Holy Ghost

---

[1] For a discussion of this difference, c. 400, see St Augustine, *De Trinitate*, bk. vii, c. 4.

[2] See A. Palmieri, art. "Filioque," in *D.T.C.*, 5, c. 2311–2.

proceeds from the Father *through* the Son. It was important as a symptom of the tendency of Latin theology to make the attributes of the three persons appear as interchangeable as possible at a moment when Eastern Christians, in their struggle with Islam, were more than ever anxious to emphasize the distinct personality of each. In this lay seeds for many future conflicts.

Some Asiatic Christians outside the range of Greek civilization made another response to the Moslem challenge. They accepted the Moslem view that the Christian faith had been perverted by a fusion, not only with Greek art, philosophy, and science, but with the polytheism of Greek religion, especially through the veneration of the icons of the saints. This criticism of Catholic Christianity was pressed in an extreme form by the Paulicians, and in a moderate form by the Iconoclasts.

The Paulicians of the seventh century were chiefly found in eastern Asia Minor, though later on the emperors transplanted them in large numbers to Thrace and Macedonia, partly to break up the heresy, and partly to take advantage of their fighting qualities. There Paulician influence gave birth to the sect of the Bogomiles, whose progress through Bosnia into Italy and the south of France kindled the Albigensian and kindred movements of Western mediaeval heresy. Like the Marcionites, whom they resembled in some important respects, they regarded the God of the Old Testament as an imperfect God, the creator of the world and of matter, the inspirer of Moses and the prophets, but not the God of the Word. The Word was begotten of the ultimate all-Father, and passed through His mother's human body like water through a pipe, taking nothing from her flesh. His death was as unreal as His birth. In this we may see an echo of Aphthartodocetism. The Paulicians made a special point of rejecting all material symbols. They celebrated the Eucharist in water, not in wine, and venerated their own elders or initiates, "perfect men", who were the only images of God.

The "perfect" Paulician was required to abstain from sexual intercourse and from many kinds of meats. The "hearers" or mere adherents of the sect, who had not yet suffered the *endura* or believers' baptism, hoped at the end of the day to reach such standards, and to be admitted for a few months or years to the vexatious but blessed life of an initiate. So they might be purged from the defilement of matter and from the dominion of "the prince of this world".[1]

The Iconoclasts had the same dread of matter, but they were not primarily a theological, but a cultural movement, a response in the field of religious art to Moslem and Paulician criticisms of the materialism of Orthodoxy. Their roots lie deep in the past, in the old Asiatic resistance to Greek culture that had long vanished from the great towns, but lingered in upland regions where Hellenism had always remained a foreign thing. Iconoclasm was another symptom of the revolt of Asia against Greece; it found echoes in the Western world, where the spirals and runes on Celtic crosses show the signature of another culture, driven back to Ireland by Rome, and returning to Gaul and Germany with Irish missionaries.

[1] *The Key of Truth*, ed. by F. C. Coneybeare, Oxford, 1898, is said to be a Paulician text discovered in the Caucasus; but the sect who used it in the eighteenth century had probably modified it very considerably in the course of eleven hundred years. The editor's notes show more enthusiasm than discrimination. Of late critical opinion has become more favourable to an account of the Paulicians written by an Orthodox eye-witness in about 871, the *Historia Manichaeanorum* of Peter the Sicilian, in PG 104, c. 1240–1303. See an article by H. Grégoire, *Autour des Pauliciens*, in B, xi (1936).

7

ICONODULIA

ISLAM WAS the last and the most extreme development in the new movement that began some centuries before Christianity away from polytheism towards a unitary conception of the world. The strict Moslem goes as far towards a complete denial of all secondary causes as any man can go. As Islam rose, Greek paganism as a distinct religion, hostile to Christianity, was finally disappearing from all but the most remote valleys of Epirus and the Peloponnese. Pagan rites still confronted the church in the form of customs practised by professing Christians. To these her attitude was critical, but not invariably hostile. St Gregory the Great advised his missionaries in England to build upon the sites of temples.[1] St Maximus Confessor, the theologian of the Monothelite controversy, revived an idea of the Cappadocian Fathers [2] that the Christian doctrine of God stands between the extremes of pluralism in the Greek worship of a pantheon and monism in Islam and Judaism.

The council "in Trullo",[3] which met in a domed hall in a palace in Constantinople in 691–2, was concerned with pagan customs of four kinds: fertility feasts and rituals; offerings of meat, fruit, honey, and grain in immediate association with the Eucharist; the invocation of classical deities in the law schools; and various kinds of magic and sorcery. Even sorcery was now practised in a Christian connection. The most favoured kinds of charm were made by cutting up liturgical books, so that rules had to be made against their sale, even when out of repair. The church's attitude to offerings of milk and honey

---

[1] PL 77, c. 1215–17, from Bede, *Historia Ecclesiastica*, bk. i, c. 30.
[2] PG 90, c. 891–6.   [3] H-L, III, i, 560–78.

and grapes, and even of animals, was naturally more sympathetic. Rules were made to prevent confusion between such gifts, which might be solemnly blessed, and the Eucharistic elements themselves. The council clearly intended to forbid fertility rites, especially the feasts of Pan and Dionysus, the spring feasts early in March, women's dances, the rioting of men in women's clothes or in "comic, satyric, and tragic masks", and the burning of fires before houses and shops to be trodden out at the new moon or at the midsummer feast. Nevertheless, these customs continued, and many of them are practised in Greece to this day.[1] They were brought into association with saints instead of gods. St George assumed most of the functions of Dionysus at the festival of "the drunken St George". Helios, the sun-god, became the prophet Elijah in his chariot of fire. The midsummer feasts and fires were given to St John the Baptist. The Mother of God, who was honoured above all the saints, acquired the attributes of many goddesses.[2]

It is interesting to compare the Trullan canons against pagan customs with the commentaries of the twelfth-century canonists upon the Christian forms of the same customs.[3] On the whole these are critical. Monastic canonists still frowned upon the law-students' carnival on "the feast of the three holy writers",[4] and congratulated the Patriarch Luke (1156–69) on his effort to put it down. They were even more critical of theatricals in church, and of a feast at which men (even priests) got down on their knees and laid the fire and performed other feminine duties.[5] Yet the dances that they deplore continue to this day. At Megara the women still play the part of fishermen on the Tuesday after Easter, dancing to the rhythm of nets drawn out of the sea.

[1] See Mary Hamilton, *Greek Saints and their Festivals*, Edinburgh, 1910; and *Incubation*, St Andrew's and London, 1906, pp. 173–223.

[2] See H. Delehaye, *Les legendes hagiographiques*, pp. 168–240.

[3] In PG 137, c. 717–36, from the works of Theodore Balsamon, Zonaras, and Aristenus.

[4] St Basil the Great, St Gregory Nazianzen, and St John Chrysostom.

[5] Ibid., c. 729–30; cf. the customs described in Sir James Frazer, *Adonis, Attis, Osiris*, 3rd ed., vol. ii, London, 1914, pp. 253–64.

The most illuminating instance of continuity between ancient fertility ritual and Byzantine Christianity is the agricultural history of the Kara Dagh, or "Black Mountain", as it is described by Sir William Ramsay and Miss Gertrude Bell in *The Thousand and One Churches*.[1] The Kara Dagh was an old Anatolian sacred city, built round a temple enclosure, on land that was cultivated, despite some very formidable natural obstacles, by "an engineering skill . . . which stored up for use in the dry season every drop" of rain that fell. Sir William Ramsay attributes this skill to a religion "whose rules and practices were the annual events" of the agricultural year.

The church did not destroy these practices; on the contrary, throughout the Christian period cultivation grew more intense. The site remained a "Holy Mountain" covered with hermitages, monasteries, and churches. Greek culture, which had missed this part of Lycaonia in pagan times, came with the wider life of the Christian community. From the sixth century to the eleventh Greek inscriptions are common, and all monuments testify to fertility and relative prosperity. In the eleventh century the Turks came, and gradually the Christian agriculturists were killed or fled. The Turks "had not sufficient coherence, or forethought, or education to maintain those works for conserving and supplying water which formed the basis to support civilized life in the Kara Dagh". Moreover, their religion is fundamentally hostile to the observance of natural laws, even for the most purely practical purposes. No good Moslem will keep waterworks in order; only the ruins are left on barren hillsides from Lycaonia to the Persian Gulf.

Fertility ritual is represented in the Greek liturgy by the "great blessing of the waters" on the feast of the Epiphany, a general intercession in the dead of winter for the return of spring, and by the "blessing of the fruits" on 6 August the feast of the Transfiguration. Other offices for particular

[1] Especially pp. 19–38; cf. also Sir W. Ramsay, *Luke the Physician*, London, 1908, pp. 105–98, chapters on *Asia Minor, the Country and its Religion*; *The Orthodox Church in the Byzantine Empire*; *The Peasant God: the Creation, Destruction, and Restoration of Agriculture in Asia Minor*.

occasions—in time of plague and sickness, when children begin
to learn their letters, and "when anything unpleasant has
fallen into the well"—may be found in the Greek *Euchologion*.[1]
They are still increasing at the present day. The Western
church never made the same elaborate provision for the hallow-
ing of home and farm, probably because her clergy were more
exclusively devoted to the ascetic ideal. The mummers' play
and the Plough Monday dance were tolerated horseplay shorn
of their pagan religious meaning, but insulated from immediate
association with the Christmas festival. At Byzantium, on the
other hand, every piece of ritual was brought into its own
appointed place in a liturgical scheme.

Each icon of a saint had its own place on the church walls,
which were decorated in accordance with a cycle liturgically
fixed in an integrated pattern of symbols.[2] In the Byzantine
view the church itself was a symbol, like the Tabernacle and
the Temple as they are described in *Exodus* [3] and the *Second
Book of Chronicles*,[4] for the Byzantines inherited from the early
church an idea of art that is unhellenic. Their pagan borrowings
were in the details; the frame was Biblical, a representation in
earthly, visible materials of an invisible, heavenly pattern,
revealed to the eye of faith upon the mount of God. In some
Rabbinical interpretations, followed by the author of the
Epistle to the Hebrews,[5] the pattern is the plan of the heavenly
temple. Others saw a symbolic representation of the whole
cosmos of "heaven and earth . . . full of Thy glory". The art of
the catacombs continues this symbolic tradition. The early
Christians did not reject human figures from their symbolism.
But instead of idealized representations of the actual human
and historical figures of Christ, the Virgin, and the twelve
apostles, they had the Good Shepherd or Orpheus with his lute
as types of Christ, and the Orans or "the praying lady" as a
type of the church. As late as the sixth century we see in the
apse of St Apollinare in Classe, outside Ravenna, a picture of

---

[1] A Greek edition should be consulted, as translators are apt to expurgate
the agricultural matter.

[2] Cf. C. Diehl, *Manuel*, ii, pp. 484–92.

[3] 24–39.   [4] 3–4.   [5] 8. 5.

the transfiguration of Christ conceived in symbolic terms.[1] Christ Himself is a great patterned cross. Lambs represent the apostles and the heavenly host. A pair of clouds are Moses and Elias. The necessary clues are given in mottoes, but some later artist has painted in the two Old Testament prophets upon their clouds, and broken up the procession of woolly apostles by a human figure of St Apollinaris.

This kind of imagery may also be found in early Christian literature. A passage in a rhythmical sermon of St Ephrem the Syrian,[2] who died about 378, is peculiarly interesting as an example of the same imagery that appears again in the Iconoclast art of Asia in the eighth century:

> In March when the lambs bleat in the wilderness, into the womb the Paschal Lamb entered. Out of the stream whence the fish came up He was baptized and came up who incloseth all things in His net; out of the stream the fish whereof Simon took, out of it the Fisher of men came up and took him. With the cross which catcheth all robbers, He caught up unto life that robber. The living by His death emptied hell; He unloosed from it and let fly multitudes. The publicans and harlots, the impure snares, at the snares of the deceitful fowler did the Holy One catch. The sinful woman, who was a snare for men, He made a mirror for penitent women. The fig that casteth its fruit, that refuseth fruit, offered Zacchaeus as fruit; the fruit of its own nature it yielded not, but it yielded one mystical fruit. . . . As for Iscariot that escaped from His nets, the strangling noose fell upon his neck. His all-quickening net catcheth the living, and he that escapeth from it escapeth from the living.

In a letter [3] of St Nilus, who lived near Ancyra in about A.D. 400, we find evidence of conflict between the supporters of this type of imagery and advocates of another kind of Christian art. The Eparch Olympiodorus, who had written to

---

[1] C. Diehl, *Manuel*, i, p. 221, and an article, *Mosaiques*, by H. Leclerq in *D.A.C.*, xxiii, c. 221–4.

[2] *Rhythm the Third* in *Homilies of St Ephrem*, Eng. trans. by J. B. Morris, Oxford, 1847, pp. 16–7.

[3] PG 79, c. 577–8, translated and quoted in J. Strzygowski, *The Origins of Christian Church Art*, Eng. trans., Oxford, 1923, pp. 144, 163–4. For designs of this character on mosaic pavements see J. W. Crowfoot, *Early Churches in Palestine*, London, 1941, pp. 116–46, and plates xii–xiii, xxi, xxiii. Many of the birds and beasts are from the Nile valley.

consult the saint on a point of church decoration, hesitated between actual representations of martyrs "in the agony of
death" and hunting and fishing scenes. In the nave he was
inclined "to thousands of crosses, and representations of flying,
walking, and creeping beasts, and every kind of plant". St
Nilus, following a newer fashion, wanted plain crosses in the
nave and Bible stories in the choir.

Here we see the shadow of a great conflict. The "deceitful
art of painting" was associated in many Christian minds with
a sentimental idealization of physical human nature, which is
only too common in Hellenistic art under the Roman empire.
The first Christian pictures of miracles and martyrdoms are
done in a narrative style with plenty of gesture and movement.
Of late years this style has been traced back to Syrian exemplars
in a pagan building at Dura Salihiyah in Mesopotamia, first
inspected at the end of the first Great War by F. Cumont and
J. H. Breasted, who found there some wall-paintings of about
A.D. 80 astonishingly like later Byzantine art.[1] Others of the
same kind have since been found in Syria. Of this kind of art
M. J. Rostovtzeff writes that its "most striking peculiarity . . .
is the way in which intense spiritual rather than intellectual
life is reflected, especially in the eyes".[2] From some such Syrian
tradition Byzantine art probably derived its preference for
mural painting and low relief over sculpture in the round.
But by the seventh century Greek sculpture itself had been
transformed by the new spirit. Its own emphasis changed from
the sensual and physical to the spiritual and psychological.
It was ready to be the medium of the new religion. The holy
image of the seventh and eighth centuries is more often a
mosaic or a painting than a statue, but it is recognizably
descended on the one side from Greek images of gods and
goddesses, and on the other from another tradition that goes
back through Syrian pictures to the narrative art of the ancient
East.

[1] See *Oriental Forerunners of Byzantine Painting*, ed. J. H. Breasted, Chicago,
1924; and *C.A.H.*, plates, v, 26–8, 166.
[2] *C.A.H.*, xi, p. 129.

The image or icon is incorporated in a pattern that is neither Greek nor oriental, but Biblical. The Byzantine church, like the Tabernacle and the Temple, was a symbolic copy of the whole cosmos. The dome and the roof over the apse were the heavens spread out over the earth. The sanctuary behind the iconostasis, the great screen, was the Holy Place, the tent of God, where He came down to tabernacle among men. As He stood in the pillar of cloud at the door of the tent of meeting and spoke with Moses,[1] so He stood in the hands of His priest at the "royal doors", between the people and the sanctuary, while clouds of incense were wafted to heaven. It was therefore right that the roof and upper walls of the church should be filled with similitudes of the heavenly host, with Christ reigning among them, as Lord of all, in the splendour of His glorified human body. It was also right that the church should be seen above and behind the altar, either as the Orans, in an attitude of supplication, or enthroned, with Christ enthroned on her. In either instance the church was symbolized by the Blessed Virgin, the God-bearer from the beginning, the root of the church in that the Word tabernacled in her before there were apostles. She represented not only the church, but Israel, Man, and Nature. In her the whole of creation responded to the creator: "Behold the handmaid of the Lord." To the Christ upon her knee angels, prophets, apostles, and martyrs bore witness, each from his own appointed place in the procession on the walls.

The new fashions in religious art were challenged in Asia,[2] where Orthodox Christians were sensitive to Moslem, Paulician, and Assyrian criticisms of "Christian idolatry" or Iconodulia, "the service of icons"; and in parts of the West, where Greek art had never endeared itself to the rural population. The eighty-second canon of the council in Trullo ordered that Christ must be represented in future by a human figure, and not in the form of a lamb. This canon was linked with others

[1] Exodus 33. 9–10.
[2] For controversy in Armenia in c. 560–607 see S. der Nersessian, *Armenia and the Byzantine Empire*, Cambridge (Mass.), 1945, pp. xx, 111, and her article, *Une apologie des images du viième siècle*, in B, xvii (1945), pp. 59–87.

of the same council that censured Armenian, Syrian, African, and Latin customs. The bishops of the Patriarchate of Constantinople sought to impose their own usage as a universal norm in the matter of fasting, the marriage of clergy, and some other disciplinary and liturgical usages. They censured the Armenians for their unmixed chalice, their hereditary priesthood, and certain relics of animal sacrifice. In the ninety-ninth canon the boiling of meat in the sanctuary during the liturgy was forbidden. The Latins, on the other hand, offended by rejecting thirty-five out of the eighty-five canons in the old collection known as "the apostolic canons", probably of the fifth century.[1] One of the rejected rules forbade fasting on Saturdays, except Easter Eve; another the eating of "things strangled" according to the literal interpretation of Acts 15. The sixth apostolic canon forbade priests and deacons to put away their wives "on pretext of religion". The thirtieth canon of the council in Trullo allowed "priests among the barbarians" to do so, according to the Latin rule, adding that "in that case they may not live again with them". Within the empire the Eastern rule must be observed.

The practical effect of this difference must not be exaggerated. Greeks and Latins agreed that bishops should live in celibacy. Another of the Trullan canons is directed against married bishops, especially in Africa. In practice in the Latin West the rule of celibacy was little enforced in the eighth and ninth centuries. In Italy the wives of priests and bishops were consecrated by a special ceremony, and became *presbyterae* and *episcopae*.[2] Whatever the original conditions of their dedication, in practice they generally remained with their husbands. Those in the West who desired to observe a stricter discipline were covered by the exception for "priests among the barbarians". This classification was bound to arouse resentment. It is not surprising that Pope Sergius I refused to sign the canons. An attempt to arrest him in 693 was foiled by the resistance of the Romans, who were much more independent

[1] See a discussion in H-L, I, ii, 1203–21.
[2] L. Duchesne, *Les premiers temps de l'état pontifical*, Paris, 1904, p. 104.

now than in 653 or 546. Political troubles from 695 to 705 postponed any further attempt at coercion. Finally, in 708–9, Pope Constantine came to Nicomedia in Bithynia, and arrived at a compromise with the Emperor Justinian II, who allowed him to sign the canons with some qualifications,[1] presumably reserving the right of the Latin churches to keep their own customs. Henceforth the Greek churches of the Roman Patriarchate in Calabria, Sicily, Greece, and Macedonia were more and more drawn into the orbit of Constantinople, with whom they shared a common discipline. The Greek churches of the Aegean, though not of the West, had been well represented at the council in Trullo.

In Asia antagonism to Byzantine culture was more pronounced. Early in the eighth century it took form in the Iconoclast movement. When the Iconoclasts came into power in the reigns of Leo III (717–41) and Constantine V (741–75), they removed all icons from the churches and substituted hunting and fishing scenes, singing birds, musical instruments, baskets and bunches of fruit, flowers, foliage, scrolls, and many large and small ornamental crosses. These designs do not represent a return to naturalism and realism, though here and there in the palaces the Iconoclast emperors may have favoured a Hellenistic style of secular wall-painting, chariot races and the like, which had persisted almost unaltered from the days of the Roman empire. Byzantine secular painting and secular literature was conservative and classical. To get a clue to the real aims of the Iconoclasts we must turn to accounts of their religious art.

The birds, the musical instruments, the bunches of fruit and flowers all recall the Roman catacombs. The hunting scenes which also scandalized Orthodox controversialists are found, as we have seen, in the sermons of St Ephrem and in the letter of St Nilus to Olympiodorus. Icons of St George and the dragon, of St Michael conquering Satan, and of Christ trampling on the powers of hell, belong to the same tradition. I see no reason to suppose any special connection with the

[1] *Lib. Pont.*, i, 389–91; H-L, III, i, 578–81.

religious art of Zoroasterianism.[1] On the contrary the Armenian evidence suggests that the last Zoroasterians did represent their gods and goddesses in human form.[2] Nevertheless both sides were borrowing from the art of older religions, the Iconoclasts from a religious art that avoids, for magical reasons, any direct representation of particular human forms, the Iconodules from Hellenism. Where the second commandment is interpreted as an anathema on the making of likenesses for magical purposes, the Christian preference for non-representational art is not difficult to explain.

[1] For theories of Mazdaean or Zoroasterian art see J. Strzygowski, *The Origins of Christian Church Art*, pp. 115–26. These are effectively criticized by Professor N. H. Baynes in a lecture on *Idolatry and the Early Church*, printed in *Byzantine Studies* (1955), pp. 116–43, but unknown to me when I wrote these chapters for the first edition.

[2] See S. der Nersessian in B, xvii (1945), pp. 63–4.

8

ICONOCLASM

LEO III, the first Iconoclast emperor, was general of the army of Asia, when in 717 he seized power from the official classes in Constantinople, whose contentions since 695 threatened the military security of the eastern frontier. He won his spurs by defending the city against a great Arab attack in 717–20, and then proceeded to adapt the constitution of the empire to the needs of the situation, as seen from the point of view of a soldier, by a series of legal and administrative reforms, which throw much light on his ecclesiastical aims. His reform of the law, the *Ecloga*,[1] published in 726, is inspired by hostility to the relics of paganism, and by a desire to introduce a more Christian and "philanthropic" spirit into legislation. Divorce was made more difficult, and the position of women was improved. According to Theophanes,[2] the schools of arts and theology in Constantinople were closed. George the Monk [3] goes further, and accuses the Iconoclasts of burning the university, the books, and the professors. Though Theophanes is a partisan, and the unsupported authority of George the Monk (otherwise called George the Sinner) is at no time of much value, some such "burning of the books" would seem to explain the antagonism of the *literati* to the Iconoclasts, as revealed in the repeal of so many of their laws by the classically educated bureaucracy of the age of Photius and Leo VI (877–912).

The bureaucracy probably valued the whole ceremonial scheme of art and liturgy in church and palace as a means to

---

[1] Ostrogorsky, p. 134, n. 6, pp. 140–2.
[2] PG 108, c. 117.   [3] PG 110, c. 919–22.

keep the imperial authority in its context in Orthodox dogma and Roman law. If the Iconoclasts had had their way the emperor's image alone would have received the veneration that had been given to saints and angels. The empire would have been gradually assimilated to the Caliphate of the Moslem Arabs, where the Caliph was the only viceroy of God, and the Koran the only law.

The original authors of Iconoclasm were two Asiatic bishops, Constantine of Nacolia in Phrygia and Thomas of Claudiopolis on the coast of the Black Sea. Their propaganda had much support in the army, which at this time was very largely recruited in Asia; but the very first measures taken by the government in support of their proposals were opposed by riots in Constantinople. In 726 a party of soldiers and workmen demolished the image of Christ enthroned over the Chalke gate of the imperial palace. This was a direct attack on the popular religion of the city, for this particular icon, called "Antiphonetes" or the surety, was a special favourite with mariners, who regarded a prayer towards it as the best form of marine insurance. The first victims of Iconoclast persecution, according to the Orthodox accounts, were women who protested against this violence. Rebellions followed in Greece, the Cyclades, Sicily, and Italy. These may have been directed as much against the political as against the specifically ecclesiastical actions of the government. It was not until January, 730, that the Patriarch Germanus was deposed, and a man of straw, Anastasius, was installed in his place. Protests from Rome against the deposition of Germanus were met, not by anathemas or ecclesiastical censures, but the confiscation of papal property in Apulia, Sicily, and the East, and the annexation of the Greek bishoprics of Calabria, the Terre d'Otranto at the heel of Apulia, Sicily, Greece, and the Cyclades, and of the few remaining Latin sees in Dalmatia, to the Patriarchate of Constantinople, probably in 732.[1] Rome was too far away to be conveniently coerced, when violence might drive the Romans

---

[1] J. Gay, *L'Italie méridionale et l'empire Byzantin*, Paris, 1904, p. 12, argues on slender evidence that no action was taken before 753–4.

into the hands of the Lombards; but she could be deprived of her Patriarchal authority within the *Oecumene*. There was no attempt as yet to condemn the making of icons as heresy, and it is on the whole unlikely that they were formally forbidden by civil law.

From the other side of the Byzantine world to Rome and Italy, in the relative safety of Syria, St John of Damascus, an Orthodox Christian in the service of the Caliph, uttered his three orations in defence of the icons. We now know that there was an earlier controversy between Melkites and Moslems, in 719–20,[1] when the Caliph Omar II attempted to destroy all icons in the Christian churches of his dominions, seven years before the attack upon the "Antiphonetes" in Constantinople. This may have been the occasion which sharpened Asiatic criticism of Greek Iconodulia within the Byzantine world. But St John's three extant orations are all concerned with the Byzantine controversy. At the time when they were given, in 727–33, he was still a layman and a civil servant of a Moslem government. Later, in about 735, he retired to Palestine and entered the monastery of St Sabbas, where he composed his *Fountain of Knowledge*, a summary of Christian doctrine which became classical in the East. Translated into Latin in the twelfth century,[2] it was one of the most important sources of the *Summa Theologica* of St Thomas Aquinas.

St John of Damascus, living right outside the Byzantine state, had unusual opinions about the interference of emperors with ecclesiastical affairs, more natural in a "Millet" than in a Christian society. He wrote words that remind us of later controversies in the West:

> In the ecclesiastical constitution we have our own pastors, who speak the word to us and typify the ecclesiastical pattern. We will not change the bounds which our fathers set for all time, but we will hold fast the traditions as we received them; for if in a small matter we begin to demolish the church's architecture, little by little all will be destroyed.[3]

[1] J. W. Crowfoot, op. cit., pp. 127, 141–6, 162, and plate xxv.
[2] PG 94, c. 789–1228.
[3] *De Imaginibus Oratio*, ii, PG 94, c. 1297–8.

The conservative emphasis is inevitable, for a Millet can change nothing. It is a fossilized civilization, forced to stand still until the day of liberation.

St John made more impression on his Byzantine readers with an argument intended to establish distinctions in degrees of reverence. The respect given to icons no more derogates from the worship of God than the respect given to officials, or to the flag, can injure or insult the emperor. Every Christian understands the difference between the relative veneration paid to the icons and the adoration due to God, to whom the whole liturgy is directed. This argument was probably effective in the atmosphere of court ceremonial that pervaded Byzantine society. The charge of idolatry is repeated by the Iconoclast "General Council" of Hieria in 754, but it is subordinated to other charges, and is not excessively pressed. In 815 it disappears altogether.[1]

St John went on to expound the theory of symbolic art that was common to both parties, with illustrations from the worship of the Tabernacle and the Temple, the instruments of the liturgy, and the sacraments themselves. His object is to convince the Iconoclasts that they, too, use and venerate some material symbols, the book of the Gospels, the Holy Cross, the Eucharistic vessels, and the sacramental elements. All these are matter. The Iconoclast charge, repeated at the Council of Hieria, that

> the deceitful colouring of pictures . . . draws down the spirit of man from the lofty worship of God to the low and material worship of the creature,[2]

implies a Manichaean aversion from the created world; but God looked on His creation, and saw that it was good.

The Iconoclasts objected that the second commandment absolutely forbade Christians to frame "the likeness of any living thing". St John contended that this was composed, like so much else in the Jewish law, in the light of special circumstances.[3] The furniture of the Tabernacle, and especially the

---

[1] *Infra*, p. 98.   [2] H-L, III, ii, 698.   [3] PG 94, c. 1297–1304.

Cherubim, are evidence enough that even under the Old
Covenant all similitudes were not forbidden. Christians have
higher authority for representative art in the example of the
Incarnation. If God took flesh and so became the one "natural
image of God", other images, from the sacraments downwards,
are holy in lesser degree. Because God took flesh, there must be
a place in Christian worship for the image of His flesh.

The reply to these arguments is to be found in the definition
of faith [1] at the Iconoclast Council of Hieria:

> The only admissible figure of the humanity of Christ . . . is
> bread and wine in the Holy Supper. This and no other form, this
> and no other type, has He chosen to represent His humanity.
> Bread He ordered to be brought, but not a representation of His
> human figure, so that idolatry should not arise.

The Fathers of the Church "have not left behind them any
prayer by which an image should be hallowed or made anything else than ordinary matter". The painter of an icon of
Christ "tries to fashion what should be only believed with the
heart and confessed with the mouth". If he portrays the God-
head and the manhood together in fusion, he falls into Monophysitism; if the manhood alone, he separates the two natures
and paints the manhood as something apart from the Deity, a
"fourth person of the Trinity".

This last contention may be compared with Orthodox and
Monophysite arguments against the Christology of Theodore
of Mopsuestia and Nestorius. The Iconoclasts probably shared
with Monophysites of the school of Severus and such "Origenists" as Leontius of Byzantium and Theodore Ascidas a disposition to believe that Christ's humanity is so far absorbed into
His deity that He cannot be represented in human form as He
is in heaven. Some Origenists seem to have believed, with
Origen himself in some of his writings, that all human bodies
will be spherical ($\sigma\varphi\alpha\iota\rho\sigma\varepsilon\iota\delta\eta$) in the resurrection.[2] The
Iconoclasts did not object to human figures in earthly scenes.
They painted chariot races, hunting scenes, and donors in

---

[1] Mansi, xiii, c. 208–356; H-L, III, ii, 700.
[2] See an anathema against this doctrine in PG 86, i, c. 989 (542).

church, and put the emperor's head upon the coinage instead of Christ or the Virgin.[1] They did object to the representation of Christ and His glorified saints in human form and appearance. In this they were at one with other orientals, not only Paulicians and Moslems, but even Assyrians, who have no icons except the cross,[2] probably because they cannot share the Greek reverence for the shape of the human body.

The Iconoclasts used symbols drawn from the traditions of early Christian art in the Roman catacombs and at Alexandria, especially those that had some warrant in the Bible. They found one list of Scriptural symbols in the Pseudo-Dionysian writings, which were at this time almost on a level with Scripture. Dionysius wrote of "oxen, lions, eagles, birds, wheels, thrones, many-coloured horses, and spear-bearing leaders of the host". [3] To these could be added the trees of King Solomon,[4] "from the cedar that is in Lebanon unto the hyssop that springeth out of the wall", his "beasts and fowl, and creeping things, and fishes". The *Physiologus* [5] or bestiary was known to Greek writers of the fourth century, though the first extant manuscript is of the ninth. It was full of stories of mystical and moral animals [6] that probably lay at the base of Iconoclast animal art, just as lore of the same kind lay behind the earlier Christian symbols on the tombstones of Lycaonia,[7]

---

[1] Vasiliev, pp. 289–90.

[2] G. P. Badger, *The Nestorians and their Rituals*, London, 1852, vol. ii, pp. 132–6. Other references in Adrian Fortescue, *The Lesser Eastern Churches*, London, 1913, p. 137. See also L. W. Brown, *The Indian Christians of St Thomas*, Cambridge, 1956, pp. 27, 278–9, for clear evidence that this was true in Malabar before the Portuguese period.

[3] *On the Heavenly Hierarchy*, c. 2, sec. i.

[4] 1 Kings 4. 32–4. The wisdom of Solomon did not consist in natural history, but in proverbs and songs about symbolic animals, birds, and fishes. These multiplied after his time right down to the time of St Basil the Great, who tells in his *Hexaemeron*, PG 29, c. 159–60, of a viper that married a conger eel.

[5] See the article (unsigned) on "Physiologus" in *Encyclopaedia Britannica*, eleventh edition, 1911, vol. xxi, pp. 552–3. Cf. also C. Diehl, *Manuel*, i, p. 383; and A. Karnejev, *Der Physiologus der Moskauer Synodalbibliothek*, in BZ, iii (1894), pp. 26–63.

[6] Like the grifon in *Purgatorio*, canto xxix, 106–14.

[7] See Sir William Ramsay on "The Church of Lycaonia in the Fourth Century" in *Luke the Physician*, pp. 331–410; and Miss Margaret Ramsay in

THE CROSS ON THE SPHERE

THE MYSTICAL HUNT

THEOTOKOS IN IVORY

A ROBE OF GLORY

and the mediaeval monsters on the *tympana* of Norman door-
ways.

This kind of religious art could not become universal. Greece
and the islands, Sicily and Italy, revolted against it in 727–9,
Constantinople in 741. After this revolt the capital was largely
repeopled with fresh settlers from Asia, who were also planted in
military colonies in Macedonia and Thrace, while Slavs were
sent to take their place in Asia Minor. Many civil officials retired from the world with their whole families, not only because
they disapproved of the destruction of icons, but because the
Iconoclasts had changed the secular laws. These defeated statesmen brought into the monasteries of Greece and the Aegean a
new ardour for church politics that did not always commend
itself to monks of an older tradition. They wrote and read books
on the theory of the church, while older monks maintained that
the ideal of a religious was pure contemplation. The older tradition in the end proved stronger, but for a time the monasteries of
Saccudio and St John of Studios, within the very walls of Constantinople, became the centres of a church party, indeed of a
dissident church, out of communion with the defiled Patriarchate.

The Studites, like the *Acoimeti* in the reign of Anastasius,[1]
looked to Rome. Many of their allies in Greece and the islands
ignored the action of the emperors in transferring the dioceses
of Illyricum from the Roman to the Byzantine Patriarchate,
and maintained that Rome alone had authority over them.[2]
Others fled to Rome itself, which was at this time a semi-independent enclave between the empire and the kingdom of the
Lombards. Oriental exiles from Byzantium and Syria, who
filled the Roman monasteries, provided the church with an
Asiatic, five Syrian, and three Greek Popes between 685 and
752. The Romans were intensely interested in Eastern controversies, and hostile to Iconoclasm, which they condemned in

---

Studies in the History and Art of the Eastern Roman Provinces, ed. by Sir W.
Ramsay, London, 1906, pp. 5–92. Lycaonia afterwards became Isauria,
the home of so many Iconoclasts.

[1] *Supra*, pp. 35–7.
[2] But their "Romanism" must not be exaggerated. Theodore the Studite
in PG 99, c. 1161, calls Jerusalem the first of the Patriarchates.

H

local synods in 730 and 769. But they were also reluctant to break with the centre of civilization in the East in order to put themselves under the protection of a barbarous Lombard king. The Iconoclast emperors were almost equally reluctant to proceed to extremes against them. Even in the Italian provinces that they annexed to the Patriarchate of Constantinople, Calabria and the Terre d'Otranto, they only occasionally tried to impose the practice of Iconoclasm. Some attempts were made further afield, but these were even more rare.[1] Calabria remained a refuge for Iconodule partisans, who founded many monasteries there.

It may be that the Byzantine Iconoclasts regarded their legislation against images as primarily a matter for the *Oecumene*. They certainly sought and received some sympathy from the churches of Western Christendom, who were by no means unanimous in the defence of Greek religious art. The Iconoclast schism of 730–86 and 815–43 were not schisms between East and West, but between an Asiatic party at Constantinople and a Greek and Latin party in Greece, Italy, and Rome. On the other hand they led to deeper conflicts within Byzantine society than any that were produced by the Christological controversies.

The extreme Iconodules regarded the beasts and birds of Iconoclast art as diabolical defilements. The extreme Iconoclasts, who were found in the circle of Constantine V, proceeded from antagonism to the icons of the saints to criticisms of the cultus of the saints as such, and especially of the veneration of the *Theotokos*, the Blessed Virgin. According to some accounts they were hostile not only to the numerous Iconodule monks and nuns, but to monasticism. They certainly installed a eunuch and a secular priest as Patriarch of Constantinople in 765. But intermediate parties always existed. The council of 754 professed the Orthodox doctrine that the saints and the Virgin Mother are to be venerated, but not their pictures. The victories of Constantine V over Arab and Bulgarian enemies, by removing immediate dangers, improved the posi-

[1] For an Iconoclast party at Naples see Gay, pp. 17–18.

tion of the more pacific elements in the community, the citizens and the Greeks who were adverse to Asiatic hunting scenes. Under his son Leo IV (775–80) persecution ceased, and icons were tolerated outside the capital. After his death in 780 his widow, an Athenian lady called Irene, who ruled as regent for their young son Constantine VI, visibly inclined towards Iconodulia, but some years passed before any decisive action was taken.

Irene acted through an able group of civil officials, who played a large part in politics for the next thirty years. One of them, Tarasius, who was promoted to the Patriarchate in 784, began a long line of Patriarchs drawn from the civilian hierarchy, who took monastic vows late in life when it was advisable that their administrative experience should be used in the church's service. This custom was never understood in the West. Tarasius was in sincere sympathy with the policy of restoring icons, but it is certain that he had been in communion with the Iconoclast Patriarchs. He did not share the monastic view that Iconoclasm was a form of devil worship; on the contrary, he was anxious to secure the sympathy of those among the existing bishops who were ready to be convinced that it was a political mistake.

His first effort to hold a council was thwarted by the army, who were devoted to the memory of Leo III and Constantine V. The second, at Nicaea in 787, was attended by some representatives of the churches of Syria and Egypt who had no official credentials, and by legates from Rome who had come to Constantinople upon other business, to ask for the restoration of the papal patrimonies. The decisions of Hieria were formally cancelled, and a new definition of doctrine was framed.[1]

This definition sought to distinguish between the relative reverence due to the icons and divine worship, which is proper to God alone. The icons, like the Cross and the book of the Gospels, are to be honoured with incense and lights, but in a defined order of precedence.[2] First comes the icon of Christ,

---

[1] Mansi, xiii, c. 373–80; Kidd, *Documents*, iii, 73.
[2] Cf. G. Dix, *The Shape of the Liturgy*, p. 424.

then His mother, then "the unembodied angels who have appeared to the righteous in human form". Last of all are the holy apostles, martyrs, and other saints. If this definition is read in the light of the whole tradition of Byzantine secular and ecclesiastical ceremonial, as it is given, for instance, in the *De ceremoniis* of Constantine Porphyrogenitus, its constitutional significance will become plain, and with this its appeal to officials like Tarasius. The censing of icons established the authority of a celestial aristocracy over and above the throne. The natural guardians of the tradition of saints and lawyers were monks and bureaucrats. The army had failed to break the fetters of tradition and to establish the emperor in venerable isolation.

But there was soon tension between bureaucrats and monks. The monks rejoiced in canons forbidding the direct appointment of bishops by the lay power, and commanding annual synods in every ecclesiastical province.[1] But some of them distrusted the leniency of Tarasius towards ex-Iconoclasts, who retained their bishoprics without penance. A schism on this head remained unimportant until 795, when it was involved with a new and serious quarrel between the Dowager-empress Irene and the young Emperor Constantine VI. Constantine grew up to be the hope of the discontented Asiatic soldiers, who saw in him the representative of the traditions of Leo III, discarded by his Greek mother and her monastic and civilian friends. His first attempt to break loose from her leading strings were unsuccessful, but in 794–5 he repudiated the wife that she had chosen for him, an Armenian lady called Maria. He accused her of trying to poison him, and immured her in a monastery, where she was compelled to take the veil. He then married one of his mother's ladies-in-waiting, Theodote, a niece of Plato, the Abbot of Saccudio, and a cousin of the great Theodore the Studite,[2] of the monastery of St John of Studios. It would seem that Irene[3] herself was the original author of

---

[1] H-L, III, ii, pp. 778–81.
[2] See A. Gardner, *Theodore of Studium*, London, 1905.
[3] So Theophanes in CB, ii, p. 727, PG 108, c. 944–5.

this change. She was intensely jealous of power and intolerant of any rival influence with her son, but in a very short time she discovered that Theodote was far more obnoxious to her than Maria. Therefore Maria ought not to have been veiled, or Theodote crowned either as bride or as empress. The priest who had performed the marriage service must be sacrificed to her wrath, but he was the steward of the Patriarch Tarasius, who for the time protected him. Irene promptly transferred her patronage to his monastic opponents, who were joined by Plato and Theodore, because they were honestly anxious to dissociate themselves from their young relative's dubious ascent to the dangerous heights of the imperial throne. From 795 the "Moechian schism", or the schism about adultery, grew from strength to strength with the aid of Theodore and Irene, until in 797 Irene deposed her son and put out his eyes.

Tarasius unwillingly surrendered to her power, suspended his steward, and healed the schism. Others showed more sympathy with Theodote and the blinded Constantine. After five years another revolution transferred power to Nicephorus, the Syrian minister of finance, who steered a middle course between the Iconoclasts and the monastic party. On the death of Tarasius in 806 he replaced him by a namesake of his own, another Nicephorus, who was an able ecclesiastical historian, but, like Tarasius, a member of the bureaucracy, lenient to the survivors of Iconoclasm. Theodore the Studite disapproved of him, and revived the Moechian schism in 809 because the offending steward of Tarasius had been restored to the priesthood after twelve years of penance.

In 811 the Emperor Nicephorus was defeated and killed in a battle with the Bulgarians. For the moment Theodore was strong enough to choose his own emperor, Michael Rhangabe, who refused to make peace with Bulgaria because the Studites disapproved of the return of Christian refugees who had fled from the persecution of the Bulgarian king. Archimandrites acted as military advisers, and naturally provoked hostile reactions in the army. In 813 the Asiatics again rose, as in 717, under Leo V the Armenian, who was personally a moderate man, ready to retain Nicephorus in the Patriarchate, and to make a compromise about icons.[1] Images could remain in the upper stories, the Christ in the cupola, the Virgin Mother over the altar, and the host of heaven in the roof. Only no lights or incense must be burnt before them and none might be venerated at the ground level. But the army insisted on an explicit anathema on the council of 787, and to that the Patriarch would not consent. So in 815, after a delay of two years since the revolution, he was expelled from his see and an Iconoclast was installed. In exile he was once again reconciled to the redoubtable Theodore, who had feared his wavering.

A council at Easter, 815, drew up a moderate definition,[2] disclaiming any intention to charge the other party with idolatry. Though the council condemned "the unauthorized and illegal manufacture of pseudonymous images" it does not appear that mural paintings or mosaics were often broken, at least in the roof or in the upper walls. The later Iconoclasts devoted most of their attention to propaganda against the cult of small, portable icons in private houses; where icon tables were used for private celebrations of the Eucharist, the sacramental elements might be received from the hands of an image, the hair of a first tonsure might be offered to an icon, or paint scraped off into the chalice, or into the water of baptism, to bring a special saint into association with the sacraments.[3] Theodore and others who taught that icons were actual channels of divine grace were specially censured. But there was no attack upon monks as such, and it is clear from Theodore's letters that many communicated with the Iconoclast Patriarchs. Those who refused had a good deal of liberty of action, including freedom to correspond. In 820–1 Theodore used this freedom to defeat another attempt by a new emperor to make

[1] J. B. Bury, *History of the Eastern Roman Empire*, London, 1912, p. 62.
[2] H-L, III, ii, 1217–21, not in the German or the English editions.
[3] Mansi, xiv, c. 417–22. See H-L, III, ii, 612.

peace. He was the real centre of opposition until his death in 826.

These efforts towards compromise are symptoms of the exhaustion of the struggle, especially on the Iconoclast side. Iconoclasm began as a Puritan movement against paganism in Christianity. But the Emperor Theophilus (829–42) was an ardent admirer of the luxurious Persian culture of the Bagdad of Haroun al-Raschid, the Caliph of the Arabian Nights. He loved ingenious devices to mystify rustics and ambassadors, such as disappearing thrones and dishes, and lions that really roared. The two Iconoclast leaders of his day were John Hylilas, Patriarch of Constantinople from 832 to 843, who was chiefly famous for his skill in sorcery, and Leo the Philosopher, Metropolitan of Thessalonica, who scandalized the devout by his successful application of astrological learning to the agricultural problems of his diocese.[1] When the Iconoclasts went out of office he was obliged to resign his see, but almost immediately he found fresh preferment as a lecturer in philosophy and mathematics at the revived University of Constantinople, where he educated the principal leaders of Orthodoxy in the next generation. The successor of John Hylilas in the Patriarchate of Constantinople was another man of moderation, the Sicilian monk Methodius, who in the reign of Theophilus had been allowed to live in the palace, despite his Iconodule views, that the emperor might enjoy his learned conversation.

This revival of secular interests was probably a direct result of Iconoclasm itself. The ban on Greek religious art and legal learning encouraged research into other forms of knowledge, into the forbidden wisdom of magic and sorcery, and the luxurious culture of the Moslem East, as at the time of the Renaissance and the Reformation the rejection of Aristotle and the Schoolmen left the ground free for the new science, but also for a revival of astrology. At Byzantium any revival of learning was bound to lead to a renewed interest in the classical past, in Greek literature and Greek art; and this inevitably led to a revival of representative art in a more Greek and sculptural

[1] Bury, E.R.E., p. 442.

style, though sculpture itself, by an unwritten agreement, became rare if not unknown.

Theophilus himself was intensely hostile to Greek painting, which he strove to repress by torturing icon painters, tattooing iambic lines of "not very good" verse upon their faces.[1] Yet his wife Theodora kept icons in her room, and tales were told of how her little daughter, or the court jester, told her husband how she took them out of a drawer and kissed them. She pleaded that they were only mirrors in which the faces of her court ladies were transfigured and transformed.[2] Theophilus, who professed to believe her, must have known that the icons would return when he was dead. In 842 Theodora became regent for their young son Michael III. A year later, with the aid of Methodius, she restored the icons. Her husband's name was spared any formal condemnation, to the disgust of the disciples of Theodore the Studite.

Neither Rome nor the Eastern Patriarchates were represented at these proceedings. After the Second Council of Nicaea Rome played a small part in the controversy, partly because the council was rejected by the churches of Gaul, Germany, and Britain, at the instigation of the kings of the Franks, who favoured a compromise solution, and corresponded with moderate Iconoclasts to that end. In the West the Iconodule definitions were not usually considered authoritative before the eleventh century. But because they represented the mind of Greece and the islands, Sicily and Constantinople, they were in the end accepted as final by Byzantine society, and to-day the Eastern "feast of orthodoxy" is primarily a commemoration of the return of icons.

The issue of the Iconoclast controversy was a second victory for the human image of Christ exalted over the image of salvation through the transformation of humanity into something wholly different, implied in most of the older oriental heresies. The form of the controversy tended to fix Byzantine notions

---

[1] *Vita Theodori Grapti* in PG 116, c. 673.

[2] This tale is translated in R. M. Dawkins, *The Monks of Athos*, pp. 239–40, from *Theophanes Continuatus*, CB, pp. 91–2.

of ritual and church decoration in a more rigid form. This was unfortunate in that it made the Greeks more intolerant, not only of Armenians and Syrians, who might be tainted with older heresies, but of Latins and Franks, who did not venerate icons enough, or venerate the right icons at the right time and in the right way.

9

THE FRANKS, ROME, AND
BYZANTIUM

THE PARTY conflict in the Byzantine church between the
disciples of Theodore the Studite and three Patriarchs of
Constantinople, Tarasius, Nicephorus, and Methodius, was
from time to time involved with another controversy between
the Patriarchates of Constantinople and Rome. Theodore and
his followers did not recognize changes in the ecclesiastical
boundaries made by heretical emperors. The Patriarchs, on the
other hand, maintained their rights of consecration in the
enlarged Byzantine Patriarchate, including Greece, Dalmatia,
Sicily, southern Calabria, and the two Greek dioceses of
Otranto and Gallipoli in the heel of Apulia.[1] They did not try
to extend their authority over the Latin dioceses in this region
which the Iconoclasts had tried to conquer, but doubtless the
numerous Greek churches and monasteries in Naples, Bari, and
Taranto looked for support in any conflicts with the Latins to
the neighbouring Greek dioceses, and through them to the
Patriarchate.

In theory Rome maintained her rights. At the time of the
Second Council of Nicaea Pope Hadrian I protested not only
against the robbery of the papal patrimonies, but against the
consecration of bishops by the Patriarch of Constantinople
even in suburbican dioceses that were part of the metropolitan
province of Rome.[2] In practice in the first half of the ninth

[1] See Gay, pp. 184–91.
[2] H-L, III, ii, 751; P. Jaffé, *Regesta Pontificum Romanorum*, vol. i, Leipzig,
1885, 2448, 2449, 2483. Gay, on p. 13, exaggerates the silence of Rome
from 794–860.

century the attention of the papacy was distracted by other interests. The old Roman Patriarchate had included Greek churches in the inner core, in Naples, Calabria, Sicily, even in Rome, and in the outer fringes from the south of Gaul to Greece. Now the Roman sphere and the Latin world were becoming identical, for the Greek churches of Rome and Naples had the aspect of foreign colonies. The Latin churches in Illyricum, once so rich and flourishing, were now confined to the coasts of Dalmatia and Albania. Behind them one Latin missionary diocese of Nona in Croatia belonged to the Roman Patriarchate.[1] Sooner or later they would be recovered from the Patriarchate of Constantinople, but this was not a matter of immediate urgency. The Greek dioceses in Sicily and Calabria were less desirable, for Greek monks and married Greek clergy were a source of some embarrassment in the Roman Patriarchate in the ninth century, through the differences between their customs and those of the Latins.

The political centre of the Latin world was now at Aachen in western Germany. The house of Pepin of Heristal had been closely linked with the papacy since a Pope sealed with his authority the deposition of the last of the shadowy line of Merovingian kings of the Franks, and the coronation of Pepin the Short in 751. Pepin in his turn had rescued Ravenna from the Lombards in 754, and given it, not to the representatives of the Byzantine emperor, but to the Pope and "the republic of the Romans". Henceforth he appears in papal letters as "patricius Romanorum", the military champion of an ill-defined "Donation of Pepin" between the Byzantine empire and the kingdom of the Lombards. From 774 Pepin's son Charles united the Frankish and the Lombard kingdoms, and so became the suzerain of all France, western Germany, and northern Italy. After December, 781,[2] the Popes ceased to date their documents by the regnal years of the Roman emperor in Constantinople. After Christmas, 800, they had crowned

---

[1] See F. Dvornik, *Les Slaves, Byzance, et Rome*, Paris, 1926, pp. 60–99, for the gradual disappearance of Latin culture in this region.

[2] See Jaffé, *Regesta*, note at the beginning of Hadrian I.

another Roman emperor, more often at Aachen than at Rome, more powerful in Germany than in Italy, the champion of Latin Christianity against the heathen Saxons on the Elbe, and the Moslems in North Africa and Spain, who still strove to invade Italy and Gaul.

It would be a mistake to regard the empire of Charles the Great as a new creation. Charles was at pains to excuse his new title by the femininity and folly of the Greek woman, the Empress Irene. He claimed to be the legitimate successor of Constantine VI, and negotiated with Nicephorus I in 802, and Michael Rhangabe in 812, for the formal recognition of his title as a colleague in the empire.[1] The Byzantines were naturally unwilling to concede this to a Frank, but when it was politically necessary, as in 812, 824, and 867,[2] they swallowed their pride. When relations cooled, the Western emperor became "the King of the Franks". The Franks always wanted to be recognized as lawful partners in that *imperium romanum* for which all Orthodox Christians prayed at Mass, even in Ireland. On the other hand, they feared a revival of good relations between Byzantium and Rome. They feared the Iconodules of Greece, Sicily, and Calabria more than the Iconoclasts of Constantinople and Asia Minor. At the Council of Frankfort in 794[3] the bishops of Gaul and Germany were at pains to anathematize both.

They knew the acts of the Second Council of Nicaea only in a Latin translation,[4] made at Rome by an unpractised hand. His errors illustrate the growing detachment of Rome, as well as of the West as a whole, from Eastern controversies, for he had not even troubled to be consistent in maintaining the distinction (all-important for the argument) between "relative reverence" and "divine worship". The Franks were shocked at the degree of veneration that the Greeks offered to their icons, but we cannot but suspect that they were very ready to be shocked at anything in Greek theology. They were also highly critical of

[1] Gay, p. 57; Bury, E.R.E., pp. 320–1, 325.
[2] *Infra*, p. 120.
[3] H-L, III, ii, 1061–91.   [4] *Idem*, 1070–85.

the confession of faith that came with the acts of the council. In this the Patriarch Tarasius declared, in accordance with the theology of St John of Damascus, that the "Holy Spirit proceeds from the Father through the Son". The Franks in their version of the Nicene Creed, which was sung at Mass in the royal chapel at Aachen, read "from the Father and the Son".

Two Popes, Hadrian I and Leo III, did their best to quieten the controversy. In 809 Leo forwarded to the Emperor Charles a letter that he had received from the Benedictines on Mount Olivet,[1] who had offended the other members of the church of Jerusalem by singing the creed in the version familiar to them in the imperial chapel at Aachen. They wished him to tell them whether they were heretics or not. The Pope took the opportunity to impress on the Franks the dangers to the church's peace in the new custom of singing the creed at Mass that had lately spread through the West from Spain, bringing with it the new clause. He did not object to the theology of the *filioque*, which was in line with the Western tradition, but he did think it important to maintain a common creed for all Christendom.[2] He inscribed the older version on silver shields and had them hung up in St Peter's.[3] There the *filioque* was not officially incorporated in the Nicene Creed until about 1009.[4] In the Stowe missal (Irish of the ninth century) we can see it written into the creed by a later hand.[5]

The Pope did not wish to quarrel with either emperor, at Aachen or at Constantinople. In the same year, 809, he disappointed Theodore the Studite by a polite but firm refusal to take sides in his quarrel with the Patriarch Nicephorus.[6] Nor did he condemn the Franks for their criticism of icons. When the Iconoclasts returned to power in the East in 815 they were not formally condemned by any new Roman council. In 824 the Emperor Louis the Pious, the son of Charles the Great, was

---

[1] PL 129, c. 1257–60, with a covering letter from the Pope.
[2] See Dom B. Capelle in *L'Église et les églises*, ii, pp. 309–22.
[3] *Lib. Pont.*, ii, p. 26.   [4] See *infra*, p. 145.
[5] A facsimile was published by the Henry Bradshaw Society, London, 1906.
[6] Theodore the Studite in PG 99, c. 1021.

even induced by Byzantine diplomacy to favour the compromise that Michael II was vainly trying to impose upon contending parties in the Eastern church.[1] In 825 a council at Paris re-affirmed the decisions of the Council of Frankfort against the breaking and the veneration of images, and representations to this effect were made by a Frankish mission to Rome in 826. So far as we know, no results followed from this combined initiative of the two empires. The Pope could not approve, neither could he condemn. The icons returned in the East without his intervention, as we have already seen.[2] In northern Europe the Seventh General Council was not reckoned Oecu-menical until the eleventh century. Rome, with its Greek churches and Syrian monasteries, remained a border city be-tween Eastern and Western Christendom, equally remote from the centres of either empire; yet the Western empire was Latin as Byzantium was not. Reformers of the church among the Franks sought to commend their ideas as authentically Roman. They saw visions of the whole church organized about the Pope as the whole empire had been, in former days, under the obedience of a single emperor. The idea is found in the last chapter [3] of Walafrid Strabo's *De rebus ecclesiasticis*, a contem-porary treatise on the church and the sacraments. It found support in an older document, *The Donation of Constantine*,[4] probably composed in the eighth century to provide arguments for the real *Donation of Pepin*,[5] out of material partly provided by the older legend of St Silvester in the Symmachian literature of the sixth century.[6] Here we find the Pope placed in the position of an emperor, reigning over the other Patriarchs. The theory was elaborated still further in the *Pseudo-Isidorean decretals*, composed in this period, almost certainly between 847 and 852, and probably in the north of France.[7] These were primarily intended to clip the wings of metropolitans to the

---

[1] See E. Amann, *L'époque carolingienne*, Paris, 1937, pp. 236–9; H-L, III, ii, 612; and Mansi, xiv, c. 417–22.

[2] *Supra*, p. 100.

[3] PL 114, c. 963–6.

[4] Bettenson, pp. 135–40.

[5] *Supra*, p. 103.

[6] *Supra*, pp. 37–8.

[7] See E. Amann, op. cit., pp. 352–6.

advantage of bishops, not of the Pope. Hincmar, the witty Archbishop of Rheims, called them "circumposita omnibus metropolitanis muscipula" (mousetraps).[1] But their form (decretal letters of very early Popes) helped to popularize the idea of the papacy as the original fountain of canon law. From France they made their way to Rome, where Nicholas I (858–67) and Formosus (891–6) probably knew of them and used them.[2] They did not become a regular part of the papal armoury until the time of the German Popes of the eleventh century (1046–58).

Nicholas I reached the papacy through the influence of Louis II, the one member of the Carolingian family who devoted his energies to the affairs of Italy from 844, when he was consecrated king of the Lombards in the lifetime of his father, the Emperor Lothair, until his death in 875. In Rome Louis had trouble with a rival party, who after 843 received encouragement from Byzantium.[3] In 855 in a disputed election to the papacy he supported the claims of Anastasius, afterwards called Anastasius the Librarian,[4] against the pro-Byzantine Benedict III. When the latter died in 858 the matter was compromised by the election of Nicholas, the ex-anti-Pope being absolved. Under Hadrian II (867–72) he took charge of the papal library. In this conflict lay some seeds of many future controversies. The Roman nobility and clergy were much occupied with the immediate problem of repulsing Moorish forays, since the Moslems had occupied the western half of Sicily in 827, and now had strongholds on the coasts of Campania. For this purpose the Byzantine fleet was more useful than the Emperor Louis II, though both might be combined to advantage. Some therefore sought peace and friendship with the Greeks of the south. Other Roman ecclesiastics with a wider horizon saw the future of the Roman church in her leadership of the nations beyond the Alps. They thought of the Greeks as strangers and foreigners, with married clergy and

[1] PL 126, c. 316.
[2] See F. Dvornik, *Photian Schism*, pp. 106, 284–5.
[3] Especially in 853; cf. Gay, p. 80.
[4] Already excommunicated by Leo IV, PL 115, c. 665–7.

strange customs that could be quoted in contempt of discipline by Latins who wished to live with their wives or to preserve the local peculiarities of their own churches.

Nicholas I was in no way subservient to the Carolingian family. On the contrary, he showed great daring in his rebukes to kings and to the Archbishops of the north whenever he suspected them of any act of oppression. Louis II was often urged to act against him, but he could never succeed in driving him from Rome, where the local nobility came to see their best hope of outside help against a Moorish attack in his personal reputation and friendships elsewhere in Italy. His dealings with Byzantium are a good deal more complicated. They arose out of the old conflict [1] between the Studites and their opponents.

When Methodius died in 847 the Empress Theodora sought to propitiate his monastic critics by the appointment of Ignatius, a eunuch son of the Emperor Michael Rhangabe, who had spent all his life since his father's fall in a monastery on an island in the Sea of Marmora. As a Patriarch he was wanting in tact, especially in his dealings with the court circle and the pupils of Leo of Thessalonica, who had great influence in the university. At the very beginning of his reign he antagonized Gregory Asbestas, Metropolitan of Syracuse, and other Sicilian friends of Methodius, who went so far as to make a schism, urging that Ignatius had been uncanonically appointed by the mere will of the Empress Theodora. At first Roman sympathies seem to have been on the Sicilian side, as might have been expected. Leo IV and Benedict III, who were political allies of the Italian Greeks, pestered [2] Ignatius for more information. He in his turn, with a want of tact that seems to have been typical, sent a *pallium superhumerale*, the usual gift of a Patriarch to his metropolitans, to Pope Leo IV, who refused it politely, pointing out that it was his business to send metropolitans their pallium all over Europe. [3] He could not be expected to receive one from elsewhere. Neither Leo nor Benedict took

---

[1] See *supra*, pp. 96–8.
[2] Jaffé, 2629, 2661, 2667.
[3] Ibid., 2647.

sides with Gregory Asbestas, or directly claimed him for their Patriarchate. But there was no reason to believe that Rome would support Ignatius when his quarrel with the Caesar Bardas came to a head in 858. Bardas, who had supplanted his sister Theodora as regent for the young Emperor Michael III in 856, was an able and masterful ruler, a patron of the circle of scholars who followed the lectures of Leo of Thessalonica. He came into conflict with the ascetic Patriarch, who provoked a political crisis by accusing him of incest with his daughter-in-law. The accusation was preposterous, and most probably dictated by party spirit. The compulsory resignation of the Patriarch seems to have been accepted without controversy.[1] He was implicated in a conspiracy to restore Theodora to the regency. The validity of his election was also denied by the partisans of Gregory Asbestas.

The election of his successor was more controversial. Photius was a learned official, a nephew of the Patriarch Tarasius, a man of mature experience, and by all accounts the ablest scholar and theologian of his day. He had already begun his *Myriobiblion* or *Bibliotheca*, an encyclopaedic summary of Greek prose literature in two hundred and eighty articles, containing accounts of many works that have since been lost.[2] His letters[3] reveal him as a real stylist, and his various theological writings bear witness to the subtlety of his intelligence. According to Anastasius the Librarian, a hostile witness, he had lately propounded a theory of two souls in man, one liable to err, the other immune from error, which he afterwards explained as a *jeu d'esprit*, telling his friend Constantine the philosopher, who afterwards evangelized the Moravians, that he wanted to know how Ignatius would deal with it without the aid of logic, a subject which he professed to despise.[4]

Photius announced his election to the other Patriarchs in

[1] *Photian Schism*, pp. 39–69.
[2] The text, ed. by I. Bekker, is in PG 103.
[3] First edited by Richard Montague, Bishop of Chichester, London, 1651; other editions by A. Vallettas, London, 1864, and by J. Hergenröther in PG 102.
[4] PL 129, c. 13–14, but see *Photian Schism*, pp. 33–4.

I

carefully worded "systatic letters" to the Pope and to the church of Antioch, both of which have been preserved.[1] His letter to the Pope was supported by another from the emperor, probably composed by his friend Bardas. But the Studites had a rooted objection to the promotion of learned laymen. The relationship of Photius to Tarasius, and his own intellectual interests, did not tend to propitiate them. After a time Nicholas, the Archimandrite of St John of the Studion, who stood in the place of the great Theodore, Metrophanes, Metropolitan of Smyrna, and others, held a synod in the church of St Irene and withdrew from the communion of Photius, on the double ground that Ignatius had been illegally deposed and that Gregory Asbestas, a schismatic bishop, had been concerned in the consecration of his successor. Ignatius was then required to repeat his resignation. When he refused to do so he was severely maltreated, to the distress of Photius, who wrote to Bardas to protest against acts of violence that compromised his own position.[2]

In 861 legates arrived at Constantinople from Rome bearing replies from Pope Nicholas I to the letters of Photius and the emperor.[3] The Pope took no pains to conceal his suspicion that the official account of the resignation of Ignatius was incomplete. He disapproved of the election of a "neophyte", a mere layman, to be Patriarch. But at the same time he went on to suggest that these and other matters might be overlooked in the interests of "ecclesiastical utility", if he received back the patrimonies of St Peter, confiscated in 732, and some of the many and various dioceses uncanonically transferred at that time from the Roman to the Byzantine Patriarchate. The Roman legates were instructed to report on the situation, but to give no definite decision before their return to Rome.

It used to be said that they were isolated from the friends of Ignatius, and bribed to pronounce a decision in favour of Photius; but recent scholarship [4] has called attention to another

[1] PG 102, c. 585–94, 1017–24.   [2] PG 102, c. 617–22.
[3] PL 119, c. 773–80; also, better arranged, in MGH epp vi (*Karolini aevi*, t. iv), ed. Ernst Perels, 1920, pp. 433–40.
[4] See *Photian Schism*, chapter 3, "The Synod of 861", pp. 70–90. For an

account of their actions, embedded in a collection of canons made in the eleventh century by Cardinal Deusdedit.[1] This records a different kind of bargain. Photius offered to the legates, instead of the dioceses in Italy and Illyricum that the Pope would have wished to receive, an explicit acknowledgment of their authority to judge a dispute at Constantinople on behalf of the apostolic see of Rome. Bishop after bishop of the Photian party rose to say that they were perfectly willing to see the question reopened that the legates of the apostolic see might judge. Ignatius, on the other hand, denied their power on the ground that he had not appealed to Rome. They upbraided him for his behaviour in the matter of Gregory Asbestas, whom he had condemned without informing the Pope, and challenged the regularity of his own election. He did not deny that it had been irregular, but cited precedents in his defence. Eventually he was formally deposed with the assent of the Roman legates, who may well have believed that even if they had exceeded their instructions they had acted in the interests of "ecclesiastical utility".

The Pope was not satisfied, and in March, 862, he annulled their decision,[2] but it was not until Easter, 863, that he held a council at the Lateran and declared Photius an excommunicated layman.[3] His consecration was null, since it had been performed by Gregory Asbestas, a bishop under suspension, and all his acts were void.

The arrival in Rome of Ignatian partisans, bringing their own picture of the state of affairs at Constantinople,[4] may do something to explain the Pope's drastic action, but it is difficult not to connect it with recent events in Moravia, that put an entirely new aspect upon the problem of the disputed provinces.

Eastern Orthodox comment see P. L'Huillier: *Le Saint Patriarch Photius et l'unité chrétienne*, in *Messager de l'Exarchat du Patriarche Russe en Europe occidentale*, 22, Paris, 1955, pp. 98–9.

[1] *Kanonessamlung*, ed. V. Wolf von Glanvell, Paderborn, 1905, bk. iv, c. 428–31, c. 603–10; *Collectio Canonum*, ed. P. Martinucci, Venice, 1865, bk. iv, c. 162. I owe both these references to the Reverend T. M. Parker.

[2] PL 119, c. 785–94; MGH epp vi, pp. 442–51.

[3] PL 119, c. 926–62; MGH epp vi, pp. 454–87.

[4] Mansi, xvi, c. 296–301.

The Moravians were a Slavonic people, who at this time occupied not only Moravia and Bohemia, but Slovakia and large parts of what are now Hungary and Austria. For some time they had been visited by German missionaries of the Latin rite from the dioceses of Salzburg and Passau. In 862 their king, Rastislav, recognizing the growing strength of Christianity, but reasonably fearing German political penetration, asked for a mission from Constantinople with missionaries who could speak Slavonic. In 863 such a mission arrived, led by Constantine the Philosopher, a pupil of Leo of Salonica, a friend of Photius, and an expert, not only in philosophy, but in Slavonic and oriental languages. The choice of a man with diplomatic and missionary experience, who had succeeded Leo as a lecturer in Constantinople, showed how much importance the government and the Patriarchate attached to the mission. Naturally political aims were suspected. From the point of view of the Carolingian sovereigns it was a move towards an alliance of Moravia with Byzantium at the expense of Frankish interests in the Adriatic. From the point of view of Rome it must have been seen as a threat to fill up the whole vacant space between the Adriatic and the Black Sea with dioceses of Byzantine rite and Slavonic speech, stretching north as far as Prague or even farther, and all attached to the Patriarchate of Constantinople. Ecclesiastical Illyricum, which for the last two hundred years had meant a few impoverished sees in Dalmatia and Albania, would in future mean Eastern Europe. The question of boundaries was becoming urgent.

10

BYZANTIUM, THE SLAVS, AND ROME

CONSTANTINE AND his brother Methodius [1] were natives of Salonica. In their own home country of Macedonia they first met the Slavs and first interested themselves in the problem of preaching to them. Philologists believe that the Old Slavonic language, which they constructed to be the literary speech of the Slavonic race, is based upon the dialect spoken in Macedonia, not in Moravia. [2] The liturgical books that they brought with them to Moravia were written for use among the Slavs in the Byzantine empire, and probably used there, for several Slavonic tribes of Thessaly and the Peloponnesus have bishops of their own in Byzantine lists. Constantine was already known as a master of languages. He had been in 860 on a mission to the Khazars, a tribe on the river Don who patronized Jewish teachers, but tolerated a native church. There, and perhaps elsewhere, he had disputed with Jews and Moslems. He knew Hebrew and Samaritan; it has even been argued that he knew Coptic. [3] In fact, he was the kind of person who learns languages very easily, and composes grammars, alphabets, and liturgies out of the most unpromising materials. At the end of his life he changed his name to Cyril, so that in the Slavonic tradition the brothers are St Cyril and St Methodius. Cyril he had better be from the moment of his arrival in Moravia.

[1] See F. Dvornik, *Les Slaves, Byzance, et Rome; Les legendes de Constantin et de Methode vues de Byzance*, Prague, 1933; *National Churches and the Church Universal*.

[2] V. Jagic in *C. Med. H.* iv, pp. 225–6; cf. also Bury, E.R.E., pp. 398–9.

[3] By Snoj in *Staroslovenski Matejev Evangelij*, Ljubljana, 1922, cited by S. Runciman, *The First Bulgarian Empire*, London, 1930, pp. 297–8.

His liturgical books, translated from Greek and Latin, were acceptable to many Moravians. Naturally they were attacked by the German priests already in the country, who knew of no liturgy in their own tongue, except the Gothic liturgy of Ulphilas, received from Eastern sources by the Goths, Vandals, and Lombards, who thereby fell into Arianism.[1] The Arian church had now been extinct for nearly two hundred years, but it had left behind an uncomfortable memory. In the West all Orthodox liturgies were in Latin. To honour Slavonic above German would hurt the racial pride of the Germans without satisfying all Moravians. Rastislav the king favoured the new liturgy, but his relation Svatopulk and other chiefs, who saw in Christianity a means to ascend to a higher level of civilization, preferred the sonorous Latin to a Slavonic dialect which was not even their own, though it was intelligible. The German priests argued that the only lawful liturgical languages were Hebrew, Greek, and Latin, the tongues used in the inscription on the Lord's cross. Cyril and Methodius pointed to many others, not only Armenian, Syriac, and Coptic, but Georgian, Abasgian, Sugdean, Avar, and Khazar.[2] All the tribes north and east of the Black Sea had their own versions of the liturgy of Constantinople. The Germans then added a charge of heresy, accusing the Greeks because they denied the double procession of the Holy Spirit. This was as yet German, not Roman doctrine; the issue was really a political one between Svatopulk, who wished the Moravians to be allies of the Carolingians, and Rastislav, who would have them free from German influence by the distant, diplomatic help of Constantinople.

In 865 this battle spread from Moravia into Bulgaria.[3] The Bulgarians, too, occupied a much larger area than they do at present. Their power extended over the whole of the modern Rumania, much of Serbia, and as far as Ochrida in Macedonia, though at the eastern end of their kingdom Byzantine

---

[1] *Supra*, p. 36.

[2] F. Dvornik, *Les Slaves, Byzance et Rome*, p. 172.

[3] See map on p. 115 and *First Bulgarian Empire*, pp. 99–130, "The auction of souls".

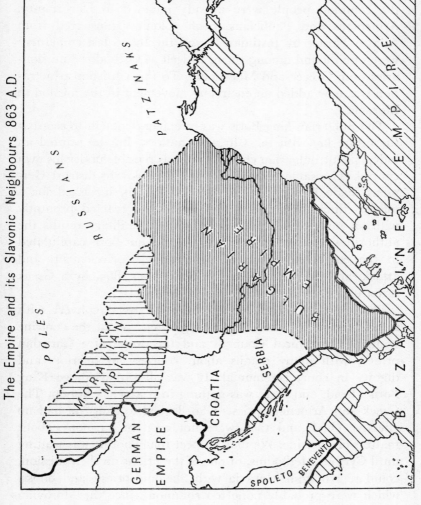

The Empire and its Slavonic Neighbours 863 A.D.

Thrace was larger than the present European Turkey. The nobles were of Hun stock, while the peasants were Slavs, or Vlachs (Rumanians) speaking dialects descended from Latin. Diverse pagan cults were a source of divisions, and many of the common people were already inclined to Christianity. Armenians and Paulicians, from colonies transferred from Asia to Thrace by Justinian II and the Iconoclast emperors,[1] were often found among them, as well as Orthodox [2] missionaries from Greece and Macedonia. To this Christian penetration was now added an encircling movement in the mission to Moravia.

The Bulgarian king Boris was intelligent enough to see that the future lay with the Christian nations. But he wanted an independent Bulgarian church, so far as possible under his own control. The same reasons that led Rastislav to distrust Germans made him critical of Greeks. In 865 he asked for a mission from the Franks. The Byzantines reacted promptly with an invasion of Bulgaria. About the military results the authorities of either nation do not agree, but Boris capitulated to the combined effects of penetration, encirclement, and attack, and he was baptized in September, 865, by a Greek priest under the Byzantine name of Michael.

Photius, however, failed to treat his royal convert with sufficient tact. He wrote him a long letter [3] about the doctrine of the Oecumenical Councils and the duties of a Christian prince, with many details about courtesy to inferiors and dignity in court ceremonial. It was all rather above King Boris's head, and there was nothing in it about a bishop. The Greek and Armenian priests who flocked to Bulgaria had no effective chief, and they were not even in harmony about matters of doctrine. We may suspect that Photius was waiting until Cyril or Methodius, or one of the priests on their mission, could return from Moravia with Slavonic priests and books, which were probably none too common, since the Moravian mission must have drained nearly all the available staff. The

---

[1] *Supra*, pp. 73, 93.   [2] *Supra*, p. 97.
[3] PG 102, c. 627–96.

king saw no immediate prospect of a Slavonic church of his own, and so he turned again to the West, this time taking the precaution of sending a double mission to the Franks and to Rome.

The Franks sent him a bishop and several priests, but they were turned back at the frontier, for before they arrived the Pope had sent him two bishops and very carefully worded answers to a hundred and six questions. In these *Responsa ad Bulgaros* [1] Nicholas appears at his best, as a bishop who could really understand what a barbarian king wanted. His experience fitted the situation better than the scholarship of Photius. He answered the questions as they came, betraying not the slightest impatience at their illogical order and apparent triviality. Some of them were complaints about the Greeks (is all this fasting really necessary?). Others betray a natural anxiety to preserve national customs (may Christians wear trousers?). These gave Nicholas his chance to depreciate the value of Greek culture. In the matter of fasts the Greeks were much too severe. There is no need for a rule against baths on Wednesdays and Fridays, or harm in meat killed by a eunuch. Trousers are permissible, but turbans, like hats, must be removed in church. Monogamy must be strictly observed; no wife may be divorced save for fornication. In matters of civil and criminal law the Pope gave practical advice, again mingled with anti-Byzantine insinuations. He urged the futility of torture and the necessity of sanctuary. At no point did he directly charge the Greeks with heresy, but he implied that they were unsafe persons, much mingled with Armenians and Paulicians. Constantinople should never have been a Patriarchate. Rome was the right place to acquire Orthodox doctrine.

If I am right in my interpretation of his quarrel with Photius, this was the Pope's chance to get all that he really wanted. He was not vitally interested in the wrongs of Ignatius, who had not so far proved,[2] and would not prove in the future,[3] a consistent or reliable champion of the claims of Rome in the East.

---

[1] PL 119, c. 978–1016; MGH epp vi, 568–600.
[2] *Supra*, pp. 108–11. [3] *Infra*, pp. 121–4.

On the question of jurisdiction in a disputed election at Constantinople Photius and his friends had shown themselves accommodating. The Pope was more concerned about the boundaries of the Patriarchates. If the Bulgarian church were once firmly attached to Rome, he would have won the battle for ecclesiastical Illyricum. The plan of attaching Moravia to Byzantium would fall to the ground, and some satisfactory settlement might be reached in Italy and Dalmatia.

The Pope was not altogether fortunate in his choice of agents. One of the two bishops sent to Bulgaria was Formosus of Porto, a stormy petrel in Italian politics for the next thirty years, who could be relied upon not to enter into any arrangement with the Greeks, since he held especially strong views on the procession of the Holy Spirit, on the celibacy of the clergy, and (if we are to believe Photius) on the invalidity of confirmations performed by a priest with oil blessed by a bishop, not by the bishop himself. This was the normal Eastern custom, and it was seldom assailed in the West, but Formosus seems to have been the kind of person who thought any stick good enough to beat a Greek. He also had personal ambitions; before long King Boris wrote to the Pope to ask whether he could be archbishop of Bulgaria, or even Patriarch. Nicholas did not approve. He pointed out that Formosus was bishop of Porto, and that his own diocese needed attention. He recalled him from Bulgaria.[1]

The proceedings of Formosus were the subject of an encyclical letter [2] from Photius to the church of Antioch, and to the Patriarchs of Alexandria and Jerusalem, in which he denounced the Latin missionaries on four main grounds. They draw the faithful away to their uncanonical customs, Saturday fasting, and drinking milk and eating cheese in the first weeks of Lent. They deny the validity of priests' confirmations. They call married priests adulterers, and their children bastards. What is worst of all, they teach a new and strange version of the Nicene Creed. Photius found in the *filioque* two possible

---

[1] Anastasius, *Life of Nicholas I*, PL 128, c. 1375–6.
[2] PG 102, c. 721–42.

FROM MACEDONIA

FROM SAINT SOPHIA

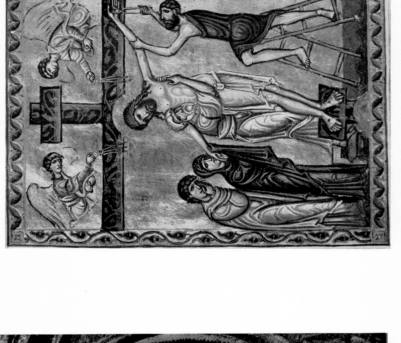

FROM A LATIN PSALTER MADE IN PALESTINE

AT ST ANGELO IN FORMIS, NEAR MONTE CASSINO

heresies. The doctrine of the double procession of the Holy
Ghost must imply either a "Manichaean" division of the god-
head into two sources, out of whom the third agent proceeds;
or a Neo-Platonic scale of being, in which the Holy Spirit is
one degree further removed from the Father than the Son. He
also wrote a more popular attack upon Latin customs in a
letter to Boris of Bulgaria, in which he was at pains to keep on
a level which the king could understand, since his lengthy
treatise in 865 had completely missed the mark. He attacked
the Latins for shaving their beards, to the injury of the image
of God in man, and for bringing a Paschal lamb into church on
Easter day. Boris, who so far preferred bishops with shaven
chins to priests with beards, forwarded the letter to Rome,
where the Pope used it to good effect in his correspondence
with Hincmar of Rheims.[1] Nicholas had also seen the encyclical
of Photius to the Eastern Patriarchs, where he spoke of complaints against the Pope that constantly reached Byzantium
from the West. He feared a combination between the Patriarch
of Constantinople and some French and German archbishops
who objected to his many interventions in the controversies of
their provinces. This he could avert if he did his best to publi-
cize the views of Photius on shaving and the *filioque*, and his
lies about lambs. In this campaign he was successful; for at
least two treatises "against the Greeks" were written at this
time by Ratramnus of Corbie and Aeneas of Paris,[2] and councils
were held at Worms and other places in France and Germany
in the spring of 868 to condemn Greek errors.

These councils have often been taken as replies to a large
council held at Constantinople in the summer of 867, where
representatives of the Eastern Patriarchs joined in the excommunication and deposition of the Pope, who was charged

---

[1] PL 119, c. 1152–61; MGH epp vi, pp. 600–9.
[2] PL 121, c. 225–346, c. 686–762. Ratramnus took a liberal view of
merely disciplinary differences, but argued that the Latins fasted, day for
day, as long and as severely as the Greeks. He was specially ardent in
defence of the *filioque*. Neither notices the basis of Photius's accusation about
a Paschal lamb, in the common Western practice of offering and eating
joints of lamb at Easter, mentioned, with disapproval, by their elder contemporary Walafrid Strabo in *De rebus ecclesiasticis*, PL 114, c. 938–9.

with "excesses" in the interpretation of his powers. But there is no reason to believe that this council condemned any list of Latin errors. On the contrary, a party in the Roman church were represented at it. According to one of the enemies of Photius, he wrote a letter to Engelberta, the consort of the Western Emperor Louis II, in which he hailed her as another Pulcheria, and promised her that she and her husband would be recognized as emperor and empress at Constantinople if they would drive the unjust Pope from Rome.[1] According to another enemy,[2] he at first appeared reluctant to condemn the Pope in his absence, and only gradually yielded to the pressure of his supporters. This would be in line with his own defence against his excommunication at Rome. No acts of the council survive. Before they reached the West Pope Nicholas was dead, Photius was in exile, and the ecclesiastical policy of the Byzantine government had been completely reversed. The Frankish synods of 868 were held in anticipation of an attack that never came. Photius had no quarrel with the Latin church as a whole, but only with a party in the church. In an illuminating passage in his *Replies to Amphilochios* [3] he defended diversity in rites, especially the different icons of Christ made by Romans, Indians, and Ethiopians in their own image and fashion. It is a mistake to imagine that he resented every detail in the Latin ritual.

In September, 867, the Emperor Michael III was murdered by Basil "the Macedonian", an Armenian groom whom he had married to his mistress, and raised to the place that Bardas had occupied until the summer of 866. The position of Photius, as a friend of Bardas, had been shaken by the Caesar's fall the year before. His enemies were now restored to favour, and on 3 November, ten days before the death of Pope Nicholas, Ignatius was returned to the Patriarchate. Meanwhile, at Rome

---

[1] Nicetas, *Vita Ignatii*, in PG 105, c. 537; Bury, E.R.E., p. 203.

[2] Metrophanes of Smyrna in a letter to Manuel the Patrician, cited by H-L, IV, i, 448, from Mansi, xvi, c. 418, in the acts of the council of Constantinople in 869. This letter has probably been doctored, but this particular detail, out of accord with the general picture drawn by the Ignatian partisans who assembled our sources, seems certainly genuine.

[3] PG 101, c. 949–51.

Louis II was master of the situation without a battle, and promptly installed Hadrian II, a more compliant Pope from the point of view of Frankish policy.

Hadrian must have been a married man, for a great uproar arose in Rome in 868,[1] when Eleutherius, the brother of Anastasius the Librarian, first abducted, and then murdered, the wife and daughter of the Pope. It is small wonder that some supporters of Nicholas, especially Formosus, regarded him with some distrust. In January, 868, he received Cyril and Methodius, whom Nicholas had invited to Rome, possibly in the interests of his Bulgarian policy. At first they were universally welcomed, for they brought the relics of St Clement. Mass was celebrated in Slavonic at several Roman basilicas. Formosus, who still hoped to return to Bulgaria, ordained some of their disciples. Later their influential German adversaries arrived and accused them of heresy. Formosus, who was particular about the *filioque*, then deserted them, but Anastasius the Librarian, who read Greek, and found Cyril a mine of information, did his best to defend their Orthodoxy. His influence, however, was diminished by his brother's scandalous crimes. Between the two parties Hadrian hesitated. He did not send Formosus back to Bulgaria, or appoint the deacon Marinus,[2] who was the second choice of Boris, to be archbishop in that country. On the other hand, he did not send Cyril or Methodius, or any of their disciples, to introduce the Slavonic liturgy. He waited for a final settlement of outstanding issues between Rome and Constantinople. Meanwhile King Boris lost his patience, and approached the Patriarch Ignatius.

Ignatius gave him a sympathetic reception. He was neither so powerful nor so papalist as they believed at Rome, where they trusted too much in the reports of his exiled partisans,[3] who had fled thither in the time of Pope Nicholas. Photius had many admirers, who accepted Ignatius unwillingly, because

---

[1] See *Premiers temps*, pp. 247-9.
[2] Anastasius, Life of Hadrian in PL 128, c. 1395-6.
[3] For instance, the *Libellus* of Theognostus, Mansi, xvi, c. 296-301.

political circumstances left them no choice. At the council held at Constantinople in October, 869, after a significant delay, only twelve bishops at first attended. The Roman legates, in accordance with their instructions, asked them to sign a *libellus* on the lines of the famous formula of Hormisdas, accepted by the bishops of Illyricum in 515–18, "the Catholic faith is always kept inviolate in the apostolic see".[1] So they would accept the verdict of Nicholas I in the cause of Photius, as their spiritual ancestors had accepted the verdict of Rome in the cause of Acacius, Euphemius, and Macedonius. But at that time, it will be remembered, the Roman formula was subscribed reluctantly, if at all. In 869 Rome's prestige was not so high as in 518, when Latin influence was strong in Illyricum, and the memory of the *Tome* of St Leo was still young. The emperor's representative at the council, a lay minister called Baianes, objected that the decisions of Rome required confirmation by five Patriarchates. This was the normal Eastern doctrine, for even Theodore the Studite, who laid exceptional stress on appeals to Rome, regarded them as an emergency measure, to be used when the "fivefold strength of the church",[2] the five Patriarchs acting jointly, could not reach agreement. In Eastern treatises the five Patriarchates correspond to the five senses.[3]

According to Anastasius the Librarian, the government used underhand means to recover possession of all copies of the *libellus* that had been signed.[4] It seems probable, though it is nowhere stated, that other bishops who joined the council never signed it at all, for after this controversy numbers slowly rose from twenty-two to sixty-six, and then to a hundred and

[1] *Supra*, p. 39.

[2] PG 99, c. 1417; but cf. also his appeal to Jerusalem, ibid., c. 1161, cited *supra*, p. 93, n. 3.

[3] Even Anastasius the Librarian uses this comparison, culled from his Greek learning, in his defence of the oecumenical authority of this "Eighth Council", PL 129, c. 16.

[4] PL 129, c. 9–24. Eventually every copy except the one belonging to Anastasius himself, who was in Constantinople on other business, was stolen by Dalmatian pirates, who also stole the council's acts. It does not necessarily follow that this robbery was arranged by the government, as Anastasius supposed.

three. Photius was allowed to appear, but refused to speak, protesting in silence against the papal claim to judge him unheard at Rome. For the avoidance of future controversies, canons were passed against lay interference in episcopal elections. The use of these canons in the investiture controversy of the eleventh century was mainly responsible for the return of this council, never confirmed by Rome,[1] and repudiated by Pope John VIII in 879,[2] to the Western lists of Oecumenical Councils.

Meanwhile King Boris of Bulgaria, impatient at the delays of Hadrian II, was changing his mind about the relative advantages of Greek and Latin Christianity. At the very end of the council his ambassadors were introduced, and asked the fathers to decide whether their country belonged to the Roman or to the Byzantine Patriarchate.[3] The old boundaries, fixed at Chalcedon, divided Thrace from the Prefecture of Illyricum along a line that split Bulgaria in half. The boundaries of 732, confirmed by the usage of the eighth and ninth centuries, assigned the coastal dioceses around Bulgaria, from Dalmatia to the mouth of the Danube, to the Patriarchate of Constantinople. Against this Rome could claim recent occupation and present possession; but the Byzantines could point out that they had baptized King Boris. Many Christians of their rite had lived in the country in the last hundred years. Much of Bulgaria was in Thrace, and so had always been in the Byzantine Patriarchate. The legates of the other Patriarchs were invited to arbitrate, and at a special session without the Roman legates, who refused to consider the matter, Bulgaria was assigned to the Patriarchate of Constantinople.

Ignatius immediately consecrated an archbishop and several bishops for Bulgaria. If the Roman legates expected that gratitude for Roman patronage would make him support their claims, they might profitably have reflected on his corres-

---

[1] See F. Dvornik, *L'oecumenicité du huitième concile* (869–70) in *Bulletin de la classe des lettres*, Académie royale de Belgique, xxiv, Brussels, 1938, pp. 445–87, and *Photian Schism*, pp. 309–30.
[2] *Infra*, p. 126.
[3] See Anastasius in his life of Pope Hadrian, PL 128, c. 1391–6.

pondence with Rome [1] in the matter of Gregory Asbestas. Accident had made him appear as a Roman partisan, but like every loyal Byzantine he resented Roman interference in Bulgaria.

In an effort to retrieve something from this disaster Hadrian II sent Methodius back to Moravia (Cyril had lately died in the odour of sanctity) with full authority to command his German opponents, and with metropolitan jurisdiction in an immense archdiocese, centred in the old Latin see of Sirmium, a few miles above Belgrade. [2] This was to include all the inland parts of the old Prefecture of Illyricum, and so, on paper at least, half of Bulgaria. The Pope probably hoped that if the Slavonic churches in Moravia and Croatia could be strongly established, they would soon draw away the Serbs, and then the Bulgarians, from the Greek episcopate in Bulgaria to the Slavonic version of the Roman liturgy. He reckoned without the Germans, who had increased their influence in Moravia in the absence of Methodius. Their patron Svatopulk, who soon overthrew Rastislav, the older patron of the Slavs, handed Methodius over to the Bishop of Salzburg, who kept him in prison for two years. When he was released in 873 a new Pope, John VIII, ordered him not to use the Slavonic liturgy. [3] It was more important to appease Germans than to win Bulgarians. He and his missionaries disobeyed; they lingered in outlying parts of Moravia, where Svatopulk was not so powerful. They won protection from chiefs in Croatia, and even in Poland. Disavowed by the Pope, and at odds with the Latin and German clergy, Methodius remembered that he was a Greek.

Meanwhile the Greek hierarchy strengthened their hold on Bulgaria; and the position of Ignatius at Constantinople was improved by a reconciliation with Photius, who returned to court as tutor to the young princes. In the world of learning he had no rival. On the death of Ignatius in October, 877, he quietly resumed the Patriarchate, though a small party re-

---

[1] *Supra*, pp. 108–11.
[2] See F. Dvornik, *Les Slaves, Byzance, et Rome*, p. 207.   [3] Jaffé, 2978.

mained irreconcilably opposed to him, under the leadership of Stylianos, Archbishop of Neo-Caesarea. From 877 to 886 the power of Photius in church and state was at its height. Basil, despite his early enmity, leaned upon him more and more even in political matters.

At Rome the death of Louis II in 875 left Italy without any resident central authority. The only possibility of aid against the ravages of the Moors lay in the Byzantine fleet, which had co-operated with Louis II, despite some misunderstandings, since 867. In 876–80 Byzantine land forces occupied Benevento and much of Campania, as well as their usual strongholds in the far south.[1] Pope John VIII could not afford to quarrel with Byzantium. Moreover, he had lately had a great deal of trouble with Formosus, who probably aspired to the papacy on the death of Hadrian II in 872. At the Easter synod of 876 he excommunicated him and other members of the circle of Nicholas I.[2] A reaction was taking place in Rome against the Frankish tendencies of the last few years. Though Charles the Bald, King of the West Franks, was crowned emperor at Rome at Christmas, 875, he was not encouraged to remain in Italy. Carloman, who came from Germany to take the place of Louis II, was rejected. Even Anastasius the Librarian became a partisan of peace with the Greeks.

Photius saw in this a return to Leo IV and Benedict III. He was prepared to be diplomatic, and resigned all claims to Bulgaria. Elated by this concession of the main point at issue, John VIII sent legates to absolve and instal him. The "Photian" Council of Constantinople in 879–80 was attended by no less than three hundred and eighty-three bishops, in marked contrast with the poor attendance at the "Ignatian" Council ten years earlier. Most of these were ardent admirers of Photius, and many of them had been consecrated by him during his first Patriarchate. They insisted on the validity of his consecrations and ordinations, and refused to condemn the Byzantine custom of raising lay officials to the episcopate.

---

[1] Gay, pp. 109–28.
[2] See Jaffé, 3040, and *Premiers temps*, pp. 269–72.

They regarded him as Patriarch already, apart from any decision that might be made by John VIII.

The few extreme Ignatians, like Stylianos of Neo-Caesarea, who still refused to recognize Photius, were anathematized with the assent of the papal legates, who also agreed to cancel the council of 869, never properly confirmed by Hadrian II, since the acts were lost on the way back to Rome. The letters of John VIII to Photius, admitting him to communion if he gave way over Bulgaria, were revised in this sense either before or during the council. The effect of these alterations was to transform them into a kind of apology for the Roman church. In future, the council decided, the old Rome and the new would not receive exiles from one another. They would recognize the force of one another's excommunications. In a final session all additions to the creed were condemned, without any particular mention of the *filioque*. The Bulgarian question was again referred to the emperor, who this time decided in favour of Rome.[1]

All contemporary evidence shows that John VIII accepted these decisions, and died in communion with the church of Constantinople.[2] The story that he repudiated his legates, after sending Marinus, the next Pope, on a mission of investigation, bears every sign of being a later fabrication, devised when it was necessary to clear Rome of all suspicion of having consented to an anathema on the *filioque*. The Pope gave way for the sake of Bulgaria. For the sake of Bulgaria he removed the ban that he himself had placed on the Slavonic liturgy at the instigation of the German and Moravian opponents of Metho-

[1] The Greek acts are in Mansi, xvii, c. 373–524. See E. Amann, *L'époque carolingienne*, p. 492. Their authenticity was long disputed, but is now no longer open to any serious doubt. In the later Greek tradition as given by Theodore Balsamon in PG 137, c. 1003, 1085, the councils of 861 and 879 are both oecumenical.

[2] The decisive texts are to be found in the writings of Photius himself in PG 102, c. 380–1 and c. 820. For discussions see V. Grumel, *Y-eut-il un second schisme de Photius?* in *Revue des sciences philosophiques et théologiques*, vol. xxii, Paris, 1933, pp. 432–57, and *La liquidation de la querelle Photienne*, in EO, xxxiii (1934), pp. 257–88, and F. Dvornik, *Le second schisme de Photius*, B, viii (1933), pp. 425–74, *Études sur Photius*, B, xi (1936), pp. 1–10, and *Photian Schism*, pp. 202–19.

dius.[1] The Bulgarian dioceses were removed from the lists of
the Byzantine Patriarchate,[2] but the embassy which King
Boris sent to Rome bore only a polite message of greeting. He
liked his Greek bishops, and had no anxiety for a change.

Yet in the course of the next few years a change came, very
much on the lines that John VIII intended, without the co-
operation of Rome. In 882 Methodius paid a visit to Constantinople.[3] Photius welcomed him as an old friend, and
received from him the gift of some Slavonic liturgical books.
He left behind at least one disciple to study in the city, and to
impart to Greek priests a knowledge of the Slavonic language
and liturgy. This "school of Slavonic studies" was the last and
best contribution of Photius to the development of the Eastern
church. In 884 it became a refuge for Slavonic priests from
Moravia, who were sold as slaves at Venice by the order of
Svatopulk, but bought by the Byzantine ambassador, who
knew that Photius would be interested in them. In the previous
year Methodius had died, and his missionaries were being
scattered in the more remote parts of Bohemia, Croatia, and
Poland, as in the former time of troubles from 871 to 880.
Pope Stephen V repudiated them in 885.[4] Many went straight
to Bulgaria, which soon became the promised land of Slavonic
Christianity. The use of the Slavonic liturgy was universal by
896, but this time it was the liturgy of St John Chrysostom,
written in Cyrillic [5] script, that is obviously based on Greek.

Slavonic missions continued in Bohemia until the twelfth
century, and left behind powerful memories that were revived
by reformers at the end of the Middle Ages.[6] In Croatia the
Glagolitic version of the Roman Mass, forbidden at the Council
of Spalato in 924,[7] except where priests knew no Latin, survives

---

[1] PL 126, c. 904-6 (to Svatopulk), c. 928-9 (to Methodius).
[2] Gay, p. 124.   [3] First Bulgarian Empire, p. 124.
[4] PL 129, c. 801-4, a letter to Svatopulk, taking the German point of
view on the *filioque*.
[5] For the difference between Cyrillic and Glagolitic see the note *infra*,
pp. 128-30.
[6] John IX (898-900) again favoured them. See E. Amann in *D.T.C.*,
8, 1, c. 616, and *infra*, p. 130.
[7] Jaffé, 3571-2, and *infra*, p. 134.

in a few parishes to the present day. But Roman patronage of the Slavonic liturgy was intermittent and uncertain, because vernacular liturgies were not her idiom. The Byzantines were accustomed to them.

Photius was interested in missions to the Slavs, not only outside the empire, but on the northern shores of the Black Sea, where Greek missionaries had long used the vernacular languages of the Avars, Khazars, and Abasgi.[1] Photius had no particular desire to extend his own Patriarchate beyond the *Oecumene*, the sphere of Byzantine civilization and good manners, though he wished to see barbarous tribes receive the gospel from the right quarters. In 926–7 a Bulgarian Patriarchate was established with the goodwill of Constantinople, and very possibly with the blessing of Rome.[2] In this we may see a fulfilment of the promises made in 877–9. The Bulgarians got what they wanted, an autocephalous church. Except for two unhappy intervals of Byzantine and Turkish conquest, they have been autocephalous ever since.

NOTE ON THE SLAVONIC ALPHABETS

There are two Old Slavonic alphabets, the Glagolitic, used by the few Slavonic Roman Catholics of Croatia and Istria, who have the Roman Mass in Old Slavonic; and the Cyrillic, used by all the Orthodox Slavs and the Ukrainian Uniate Roman Catholics, who follow the liturgy of St John Chrysostom. The Cyrillic alphabet is obviously based on the Greek, with a few extra letters. The Glagolitic has a much greater appearance of originality. As Glagolitic manuscripts and inscriptions of the early Middle Ages have been found in Serbia and Bulgaria, it has been argued that this is the older script, and that Cyrillic is a later simplification under Greek in-

---

[1] Russian missionaries went on translating the liturgy into new dialects from the fourteenth to the twentieth century. See *Birkbeck and the Russian Church*, ed. A. Riley, London, 1917, pp. 210–14; *St Sergius, Builder of Russia*, by N. Zernov, London, 1939, p. 109; S. Bolshakoff, *The Foreign Missions of the Russian Orthodox Church*, London, 1944.

[2] See *infra*, p. 134.

fluence. But Sir Ellis Minns,[1] followed by Professor S. Runciman in his *History of the First Bulgarian Empire*, argues convincingly that Cyrillic is the alphabet that Cyril himself invented before he went to Moravia. Some of the supplementary letters are ligatures, some are modified from the Greek and some derived from the Hebrew, a language that he knew well enough to put a Hebrew pun into a sermon; finally, some letters seem due to sheer caprice. But "when he arrived in Moravia he found that an alphabet so closely akin to Greek met with

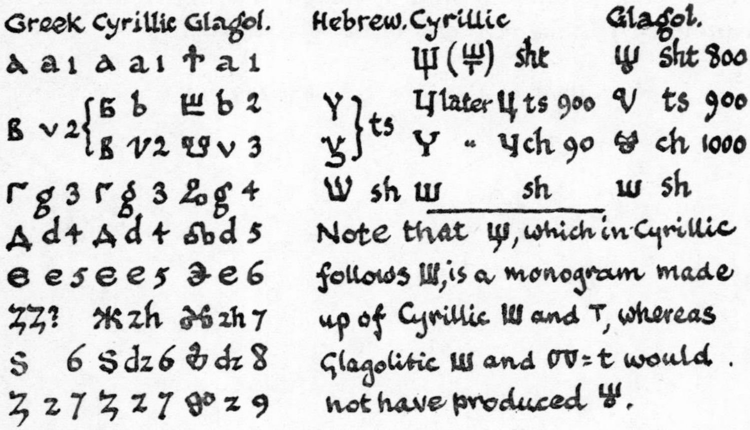

powerful opposition; so he disguised it, reversing most of the Greek letters, but retaining most of the invented letters, and he tidied it up into a vague uniformity with a free use of loops".[2] So he obtained Glagolitic, an alphabet that looked like nothing on earth. His disciples indeed claimed that it came to him by revelation from heaven. The two alphabets were then used side by side, Cyrillic triumphing by its superior simplicity and usefulness for the instruction of Greeks in the school at Constantinople, except among the Croats, who wished to avoid any taint of Greek influence.

The diagram above gives: (*a*) the first nine Cyrillic letters,

[1] "St Cyril really knew Hebrew", in *Mélanges publiés en l'honneur de M. Paul Boyer*, Paris, 1925, cited by S. Runciman, op. cit., pp. 297–9.

[2] S. Runciman, ibid. This is in subtanstial agreement with J. B. Bury, E.R.E., p. 398.

all derived from the Greek, either unmodified and agreeing with the Greek in numerical values, or modified and not used for numbers, confronted with the corresponding Glagolitic letters with their independent numbers; and (b) the four later letters which may go back to Hebrew, clearly belonging to both alphabets, but with different numerical values.

For the diagram and this explanation I am indebted to Sir Ellis Minns.

Information on the subsequent history of the Slavonic liturgy in Croatia, Dalmatia, and Bohemia may be found in C. Korolevsky, *Living languages in Catholic worship*.[1]

[1] Eng. trans. by D. Attwater, London, 1957, pp. 84–90.

II

ROME AND CONSTANTINOPLE
IN THE TENTH CENTURY

THE SETTLEMENT of 879–80 had adversaries in the East
and in the West: in the East among the implacable opponents
of Photius, the Studites and their allies, who had always been
unwilling to recognize Patriarchs chosen from civilian hierarchy;
and in the West among the champions of the *filioque*, especially
Formosus. But between the two oppositions the connection was
accidental rather than essential. Photius again retired from the
Patriarchate in 886 for political, not ecclesiastical reasons. The
new emperor, Leo VI, called the "philosopher" for his learned
interests in theology, law, and military science, was a pupil of
Photius; but he feared the overwhelming influence of his
master, and replaced him by his own younger brother, Prince
Stephen, another pupil, whom Photius had himself ordained
deacon. In a letter to Pope Stephen V, Leo insisted that the
Patriarch's retirement was voluntary. Although such explanations are commonly regarded with scepticism, this one may be
true, for on any calculation it is difficult to make him less than
seventy in 886.[1]

Stylianos of Neo-Caesarea and the other extreme Ignatians
were naturally unwilling to accept his successor, a royal
Patriarch of seventeen, whose orders were tainted by the im-
position of the intruder's hands. They consulted Pope Stephen
V, who would not judge without more information.[2] When

[1] A. Papadopoulos Kerameus in *BZ*, viii (1899), p. 658, cited (incorrectly)
by Bury, E.R.E., p. 186.
[2] PL 129, c. 795–6; Mansi, xvi, c. 437–8.

Formosus himself succeeded Stephen in 891, he may have given them more support,[1] but a later Pope, John IX, writing to Stylianos and his friends in 899,[2] told them that the whole Roman church recognized the Patriarchs Ignatius, Photius, Stephen, and Antony (the successor of Stephen) in that order. In this he claimed to be in the tradition of Nicholas, John VIII, and Stephen V. He respected the decisions of 879–80, but tried at the same time to avoid condemning the decisions of 862–3 and 869, to which Stylianos and his friends were devoted. On these terms East and West, Ignatians and Photians were reconciled, according to the life of St Antony Cauleas.[3] From a passage in the *Clerotogion* of Philotheus,[4] assigned by Bury to this year, it has been inferred that a permanent papal embassy was re-established in Constantinople.

Troubles continued during the Patriarchate of Nicholas Mysticus, another bureaucrat ("Mysticus" simply means "the private secretary"), a foster-brother of Leo, and a pupil of Photius. He wielded great political influence from 901 to 925, corresponding freely with the King of Bulgaria, Lombard, and Armenian princes, and even Moorish emirs, as well as with monks and missionaries, Popes and Patriarchs.[5] Like Photius, he grew too powerful for Leo VI, his rival in learning. When in 906 he refused communion to the emperor, who had un-canonically contracted a fourth marriage to secure the legitimacy of his only son, Constantine Porphyrogenitus, Leo appealed to the other Patriarchs, especially Pope Sergius III, who had not the same objections to the re-marriage of widowers.[6] A council of legates from all the Patriarchates in February, 907, dispensed the emperor as a special case. After this Nicholas

---

[1] See V. Grumel, *La liquidation de la querelle Photienne*, in EO, xxxiii (1934), pp. 257–88, but also F. Dvornik in B, viii (1933), pp. 460–9.

[2] Mansi, xvi, c. 458.

[3] PG 106, c. 191, quoted by J. M. Hussey, *Ch. and Learning*, pp. 135–6.

[4] Incorporated in the *De ceremoniis* of Constantine Porphyrogenitus as bk. ii, c. 2, PG 112, c. 1341. But Dvornik in *Photian Schism*, pp. 267–70, gives reasons for suspecting an interpolation. He thinks the reference is to the council of 907.

[5] His letters are in PG 111, c. 27–392.

[6] See Eutychius of Alexandria, *Annales*, Latin trans. in PG 111, c. 1144–5.

Mysticus went into exile, and a monk named Euthymius,[1] who seems to have had some connection with the tradition of opposition to bureaucratic Patriarchs,[2] took his place. But Byzantine opinion continued hostile to fourth marriages. Euthymius himself, though he allowed the legitimacy of the young prince, refused to crown the empress. Sergius III resented Byzantine criticism of the *filioque*, probably at this time, for in July, 909, his admonitions to shoot arrows against the errors of the Greeks in the doctrine of the Trinity were quoted in the north of France at the council of Trosly.[3] The effect of his intervention was rather to loosen the ties between the Byzantine monks and Rome. When in 912 the emperor died, Nicholas Mysticus returned, and according to his partisans Euthymius was much maltreated. But in the next year it became necessary to accept Constantine Porphyrogenitus as the one legitimate representative of the Macedonian house. Nicholas had the wisdom to make peace with Euthymius, and in a *Tome of Union*, accepted by both parties in 920, conditions for second and third marriages were laid down on a sliding scale. Older men with more children were subjected to heavier penances.[4] In future, fourth marriages were absolutely forbidden, but the legitimacy of Constantine Porphyrogenitus was allowed as a special case, and the name of Euthymius was restored to the diptychs.

In 923 this settlement was approved by legates from Rome, who came to Constantinople on their way to Bulgaria. So the danger of a new schism was avoided, for Nicholas on his return had removed the name of Sergius III from the diptychs, and spoken hard words about Western laxity in the matter of second, third, and fourth marriages.[5] In 923 relations between the Patriarchates were excellent, if they may be judged by a letter [6] of recommendation which Nicholas wrote for the

---

[1] See two articles by M. Jugie in EO, xvi (1913), pp. 388–95, 481–92, based on *Vita Euthymii*, ed. C. de Boor, Berlin, 1888.

[2] Vasiliev, p. 333.   [3] Mansi, xvi, c. 304.

[4] Mansi, xviii, c. 336–41.

[5] In a letter to Anastasius III, PG 111, c. 208–20.

[6] PG 111, c. 176–89.

Roman legates to carry to the King of Bulgaria. On their way back from Bulgaria to Rome they held a council at Spalato in 924, where the Dalmatian dioceses were restored to the Roman Patriarchate, and the Slavonic liturgy was forbidden, save under exceptional circumstances, as we have already seen.[1] This decision was opposed by Gregory, Bishop of Nona in Croatia, and had to be renewed at another Council of Spalato in 927; but we hear of no opposition from the Greeks, and it seems reasonable to assume that the transfer of Dalmatian dioceses from Constantinople to Rome was the direct result of the conversations in 923. More mystery surrounds the establishment of the Bulgarian Patriarchate, which was recognized at Constantinople in 927.[2] Pope John X certainly sent an imperial crown to the Tsar Simeon of Bulgaria in 926. According to a letter of King Kalojan, a later Bulgarian sovereign, to Pope Innocent III in 1202,[3] he also sent a "patriarchal benediction". At that time the Bulgarians clearly believed that Rome, as well as Constantinople, recognized their Patriarchate. Mr Runciman thinks it improbable that so active a Pope as John X would have made so great a concession. The matter may appear in a different light if we consider the fortunes of the settlement of 879–80 in Italy.

John VIII, its original author, had much trouble with Formosus from the very beginning of his pontificate. It is very probable that this trouble ended only in his death. According to the author of the *Annales Fuldenses*,[4] he was first poisoned, and then beaten to death with hammers, by "those who desired his high position as well as his treasure". His successor, Marinus (882–4), immediately removed the anathema on Formosus.[5] He was a personal enemy of the Emperor Basil, and it is possible, though not certain, that he was regarded as an anti-Pope in Constantinople. Afterwards the validity of his election

---

[1] *Supra*, p. 127.

[2] *First Bulgarian Empire*, pp. 174, 182. Cf. also E. Amann and A. Dumas, *L'église au pouvoir des laiques*, Paris, 1940, p. 433 and note. But E. Honigmann in *Studies in Slavic Church History* in B, xvii (1945), p. 137, would defer this recognition until 932.

[3] PL 215, c. 287, 290, and *infra*, p. 172.

[4] MGH sgus, Hanover, 1891, p. 109.   [5] *Premiers temps*, p. 284.

was impugned, on the ground that he had been Bishop of
Caere before he was translated to Rome. Hadrian III (884–5),
on the other hand, sent a "systatic letter" to Photius, who seems
to have regarded him as the immediate successor of his friend
Pope John.[1] Stephen V (885–91) certainly recognized Photius
as the lawful Patriarch at the time of his second retirement in
886.[2] Formosus (891–6) was recognized in Constantinople,[3]
in spite of the fact that opposition to his election was wide-
spread in Rome. Like Marinus, he was already a bishop.
Some time previously he had taken an oath not to seek the
papacy. As Pope he offended Italian parties by his alliance
with the German Arnulf, King of the East Franks, whom he
summoned to his aid in 893,[4] and crowned in 896 as Holy
Roman Emperor. After his death his body was exhumed and
condemned to an excommunicate's lot at the grim "cadaverous
council" of 897. Bitter strife between rival parties followed until
the triumph of Sergius III [5] in 904. He belonged to the party
who denied all validity to the ordinations and consecrations of
Formosus.[6] John IX (898–900), on the other hand, tried to discriminate between his lawful and unlawful acts, as he tried to
combine the attitudes of Nicholas I and John VIII towards
Photius. Christopher (903–4) is accused of heresy by a Byzantine author of the eleventh century [7] on the ground that he put

---

[1] Photius, *De Spiritus Sancti Mystagogia*, PG 102, c. 380–2. See J. Hergenröther's note *loc. cit.*

[2] *Supra*, p. 131.

[3] V. Grumel maintained in EO, xxxiii (1934), cited *supra*, p. 126, n. 2,
that the Byzantines broke with Formosus c. 892–3. See Flodoard's *History of
Rheims* in PL 135, c. 267.

[4] Jaffé, 3486.

[5] He was first elected in 898. See his epitaph in H-L, IV, ii, 729.

[6] They were defended by Auxilius and others in treatises which may be
found in PL 129, c. 1053–1112, and elsewhere. See *Premiers temps*, pp.
313–14. The Latin writings against Formosus have perished, but echoes
may be found in three Greek tracts of the Middle Ages, printed by J.
Hergenröther in *Monumenta Graeca ad Photium . . . pertinentia*, Regensburg,
1869, esp. pp. 160, 167–8, 179. (I owe this reference to Fr. Alexis van der
Mensbrugghe.) In the legends of the Russian "Old Believers" Formosus is
an heresiarch, whose body was mutilated and insulted because he was the
first to make the sign of the cross with the wrong number of fingers. See
A. P. Stanley, *The Eastern Church*, London, 1862, p. 397.

[7] In J. Hergenröther, ibid., p. 161; see A. Michel, *Humbert und Kerullarios*,
Paderborn, 1924–30, vol. i, pp. 21–2, but cf. *supra*, p. 133.

ECCLESIASTICAL ITALY IN THE TENTH CENTURY

the *filioque* into his "systatic letter" to Nicholas Mysticus.
Sergius deposed him in 904 and made him a monk.

After 904 the situation in Rome became more stable. For
nearly seventy years power was in the hands of one family.[1]
The Senator Theophylact, his wife Theodora, his daughter
Marozia, and his grandson Alberic were not at all in favour
with the ecclesiastical historians of later generations. They may
not have been so black as they were painted. The contribution
of this local dynasty to the history of papacy was to preserve
its political independence in an age of disorder in Italy. They
did so by holding at arm's length intruders from the north who
might come to Rome to claim the imperial crown of Charles
the Great. During the time of their power they crowned only
two Roman Emperors: Berengar of Friuli in 915, who came to
rescue Rome from the Moors; and Otto of Saxony, who came
from Germany and forced himself upon John XII in 962. They
preferred the more distant protection of Byzantium. John XII
even dated his acts by the regnal years of the Byzantine
emperor.[2]

We have already seen how Sergius III and John X (914–28)
maintained good relations with Constantinople, despite the
mistake of Sergius in supporting Leo VI against Nicholas
Mysticus in the matter of fourth marriages. In their time
Rome was within the sphere of influence of the Byzantine
empire in Italy. There is therefore nothing incredible in the
idea of a new boundary agreement between the Patriarchates
in 923 on the basis of the settlement of 879–80. Whether the
agreement was made or not, western Illyricum returned to
Rome and eastern Illyricum (Bulgaria) became autonomous.
The organization of two Byzantine provinces around the
metropolitan sees of Reggio and St Severina in Calabria,
about 900 [3] does not seem to have been the subject of any
protest from Rome, though Gay believed that some of their

---

[1] *Premiers temps*, pp. 308–27.

[2] Gay, p. 223, citing PL 133, c. 1025. The custom had been dropped by
Hadrian I in 781 (*supra*, p. 103), and its revival may imply a gesture of
loyalty to the true and original Roman Empire.

[3] Gay, pp. 185–91.

dioceses had Latin bishops, while others occupied territory that had once belonged to Latin sees before the devastation of Calabria by the Moors. In the middle of the tenth century Greek monks from Sicily spread their monasteries and churches beyond Calabria up the coast of Campania towards Rome.[1]

In 933 the real ruler of Rome was Alberic, Prince of the Romans, who kept under lock and key his half-brother, Pope John XI, described by the semi-official *Liber Pontificalis* [2] as the son of Sergius III and Marozia. In that year he sent four legates to Constantinople to assist in the consecration of the Patriarch Theophylact, the young son of the co-emperor, Romanus Lecapenus. Theophylact was not only under age, but a eunuch, who grew up into a disreputable character.[3] His election was vigorously opposed by the monks in the tradition of the Studites, and probably by the respectable officials who had admired Photius and Nicholas Mysticus. It did less harm to the Byzantine church than might have been expected, for the disgruntled took refuge on Mount Athos,[4] which began to be "the holy mountain" during the Patriarchate of Theophylact. But the part played by Rome helped to shatter her old alliance with the Studites. The next Patriarch, Polyeuctes (956–70), was a warm champion of Athonite monasticism, but his proceedings in Apulia [5] were viewed with alarm in the West.

In the middle of the tenth century the influence of the Byzantine church in East and West was at its height. According to the contemporary testimony of the Patriarch Eutychius of Alexandria,[6] the name of the Patriarch of Constantinople

---

[1] See the long study in Gay, pp. 254–86.

[2] ii, 243; see *Premiers temps*, p. 316.

[3] See John Scylitzes in the chronicle of George Cedrenus, CB, pt. ii, pp. 332–3; PG 122, c. 68. Two admirable cartoons of him, from the fourteenth century MSS. of Scylitzes in the National Library at Madrid, are reproduced in R. Byron, *The Byzantine Achievement*, London, 1929, p. 250; and H. Peirce and R. Tylor, *Byzantine Art*.

[4] See P. Meyer, *Die Haupturkunden für die Geschichte der Athosklöster*, Leipzig, 1894; Kirsopp Lake, *The Early Days of Monasticism on Mount Athos*, Oxford, 1909.

[5] Gay, p. 352.

[6] PG 111, c. 1156, in Latin translation. His continuator, Yahya of Antioch, agrees, PO, xviii, 5, pp. 710–11, and says that no Pope of Rome was commemorated from 685 to 999, for want of information.

appeared in the diptychs at Jerusalem and Alexandria in 937 for the first time since the Arab conquest. In 944 the Byzantine armies recaptured Edessa, and in 969 Antioch. In that year there was a schism in the Armenian church between the pure Monophysites and a party suspected of Chalcedonian tendencies. Ever since 860 Armenian princes had been in correspondence with Constantinople,[1] and the many Armenian settlers and soldiers who lived in the empire communicated in the Orthodox churches. Georgians came constantly to the capital, and founded one of the very early monasteries, Iviron, on Mount Athos.[2] The missions to Russia that began in the time of Photius had converted the Grand Princess Olga by the middle of the tenth century. Similar Slavonic missions continued in Poland and Bohemia, and among the Slav subjects of the Magyars in Hungary. In Italy the *Oecumene* extended as far as Rome. In 968 a new Byzantine province, with five new dioceses, was formed in Calabria and Apulia, probably at the expense of the Latin churches.[3] In 972 the Byzantines occupied Bulgaria, where the empire and Patriarchate had collapsed before a Russian invasion in 969. They advanced their own frontier to the Danube, and attempted to annex the Bulgarian church to the Patriarchate of Constantinople, retaining the Slavonic liturgy.[4]

But already these moves were provoking counter-moves. Otto of Saxony, who came to Rome from Germany in 962 and compelled Pope John XII unwillingly to bestow on him an imperial crown, was urged by his north Italian friends, especially Bishop Liudprand of Cremona, to defend the Latin churches in south Italy against Byzantine aggression. The Byzantines, on the other hand, resented his assumption of the imperial title, and his claim to purge the Augean stables of the church of Rome. In 972 there was a reconciliation in a marriage

---

[1] E.g. the letters of Photius, PG 102, c. 703–15; and Nicholas Mysticus, PG 111, c. 362–6; M. Ormanian, *The Armenian Church*, pp. 47–9.

[2] See A. Riley, *Athos*, London, 1887, pp. 133–5; and R. M. Dawkins, *The Monks of Athos*, pp. 196–8.

[3] Gay, pp. 352–3.

[4] *First Bulgarian Empire*, pp. 215–16, 255–6.

treaty between his son Otto and the Byzantine princess Theophano; but this led to fresh trouble, since Otto II and his Greek wife spent more time in Italy. Otto aspired to conquer the "Western regions" of the Roman empire, Apulia, Sicily, and Calabria.

In 974 the rival emperors supported rival Popes.[1] Boniface VII, the candidate of the Crescentii, who represented (through the female line) the family of Theophylact and Theodora, was obliged to take refuge at Constantinople. His rival, Benedict VII, the nominee of the German party and of Otto II, revenged himself upon the Byzantines by reviving the Roman claims in Bulgaria. According to the Bulgarian tradition [2] he, like John X before him, sent an imperial crown and "Patriarchal benediction" to the Tsar Samuel, who in Western Macedonia preserved the traditions of the Bulgarian empire. Samuel certainly revived the Bulgarian Patriarchate in about 980,[3] with or without the approval of Rome, and continued to resist Byzantine arms until he was finally defeated by Basil II, the "Bulgar-Slayer", in 1014.

In 983, on the death of Otto II, Pope Boniface returned to Rome with Byzantine support, and succeeded in getting rid of his rival, the immediate successor of Benedict. Next year he was killed by other adversaries, but his patron, John Crescentius, remained in power, and probably in alliance with the Byzantine empire, from 983 to 995. Until 991 the Byzantine princess Theophano ruled in Germany and northern Italy as regent for her young son Otto III, who had the beginnings of a Byzantine education from a Calabrian Greek, John Philagathos, afterwards Bishop of Cremona. In these years the conversion of the Grand Prince Vladimir of Russia in 988–9 enhanced the prestige of the Byzantine church. According to the Russian tradition,[4] he had to choose between Islam, the

---

[1] Gay, pp. 387–8; cf. Michel, i, pp. 11–12.
[2] PL, 215, c. 287, a letter to Innocent III in 1202; cf. *supra*, p. 134.
[3] *First Bulgarian Empire*, pp. 220, 226.
[4] See the quotations from the *Codex Colbertinus* in G. Schlumberger, *L'épopée Byzantine à la fin du dixième siècle*, 2nd ed., Paris, 1925, pp. 632–4; and F. Dvornik, *The Making of Central and Eastern Europe*, London, 1949, pp. 169–70.

religion of the "Black Bulgars" on the middle Volga; Judaism, patronized by the Khazars on the Don; and the two forms of Christianity, Latin and Byzantine. Certainly his grandmother Olga had tried to obtain missionaries from Germany.[1] The foundation of a Latin see at Prague [2] in 976, and of German missions in Poland and Hungary,[3] shows that the German church was beginning to take an active interest in the spiritual destinies of eastern Europe. Of late M. Jugie [4] has propounded a theory that Russian Christianity was as much Latin as Greek until 1051. This drastic reversal of tradition does not seem to be supported by sufficient evidence. At Novgorod, which is much nearer the Baltic end of the trade route than Kiev, the early architectural monuments are Byzantine of a very fine kind. It is clear that Bohemian Christianity was as much Slavonic as Latin at this time. Through Bohemia as well as Russia Byzantine cultural and artistic influences spread north and west towards Sweden, Denmark, and England.

In 996 the half-Byzantine Western emperor, Otto III, imposed upon the Roman church its first German Pope, his young cousin, Bruno of Carinthia (Gregory V). The Crescentii rebelled against him and set up John Philagathos as an anti-Pope. Dr Michel [5] has shown that he was recognized at Constantinople. Otto III turned fiercely on his old tutor, who was seized by the partisans of Gregory V and cruelly mutilated, despite the intercession of St Nilus, the Calabrian saint of Rossano, who founded the Greek monastery of Grotto-ferrata, not many miles from Rome.[6] When Gregory died in 999, Otto found him a successor in Gerbert of Aurillac, who had been Archbishop of Rheims. Gerbert so far had chiefly distinguished

---

[1] Dvornik, op. cit., pp. 68–70.   [2] Ibid., pp. 77–83.
[3] Ibid., pp. 105–67.
[4] In *Les origines Romaines de l'église Russe*, EO, xxxvi (1937), pp. 257–70. See also his *Schisme Byzantin*, pp. 172–86, but cf. V. Laurent in EO, xxxviii (1939), pp. 279–95, and F. Dvornik, op. cit., pp. 167–70.
[5] Op. cit., i, p. 16. See also P. E. Schramm, *Neun Briefe des Byzantinischen Gesandten Leo von seiner Reise zu Otto III*, in BZ, xxv (1925), pp. 89–105, for further evidence of Byzantine support.
[6] See the life of St Nilus in PG 120, especially c. 147–52.

L

himself by bitter invective against the Roman church [1] from the point of view of the movement of ascetic reform that was at this time arising beyond the Alps, especially at Cluny in Burgundy, but also in other centres in Germany, France, and England. He took the title of Silvester II, in memory of Silvester, the Pope of the *Donation of Constantine*. The choice was probably significant of a new stress on the universal mission of the elder Rome. But Otto III, the new Constantine, was seeking a bride from Byzantium at the time of his death in 1002. His own sympathies might have led him to seek a reconciliation with Basil II.

After his death the Crescentii recovered their power. In their eyes Rome was still the old capital of the Roman empire. [2] The Roman emperor was Basil II, the great "Bulgar-slayer". Pope John XVIII (1003–9) was commemorated in the diptychs at Constantinople and Antioch. [3] In Byzantine eyes the Pope was still the first of the Patriarchs, a court of appeal in differences between the church and the court, or between parties in the Byzantine church. [4] The prestige of the Roman church was still a positive asset in Byzantine diplomatic relations with the Western world. But in an age of confusion, not every Pope in possession of Rome was recognized in Byzantium. Between 972 and 1009 Boniface VII, John XV, John XVI (Philagathus), and John XVIII were in the Byzantine diptychs, but other Popes were not, because they were rivals of a Pope already recognized, like Benedict VII, John XIV, and Gregory V, or because their accession was never notified, for political reasons, or for want of an opportunity. Experience of Roman politics made the Byzantines increasingly cautious about Popes who might not succeed in establishing themselves. This may be the real reason for the absence of Sergius IV (1009–12) from Byzantine diptychs. He was elected while John XVIII was

---

[1] See Gay, p. 308, citing the Acts of the Council of Rheims in MGH ss, iii, p. 671; cf. also E. Amann and A. Dumas. Op. cit., pp. 68–73.

[2] See V. Grumel, *La question Romaine avant 1054*, in *REB*, x (1953), pp. 5–23.

[3] See Peter of Antioch to Michael Cerularius in 1054, PG 120, c. 800.

[4] As in 899, 906, 923, *supra*, pp. 132–4, and in 933, *supra*, p. 138.

still alive.[1] Afterwards, when the absence of his name was noticed, he was confused with Sergius III, who defended the *filioque*, and with Benedict VIII (1012–24), who belonged to the German party.[2] But Sergius IV was the choice of the Crescentii.

[1] John XVIII retired into the monastery of St Paul in May, 1009. See *Lib. Pont.*, ii, p. 266.

[2] In the Munich text of Nicetas Chartophylax, MSS gr. Monac. 256, fol. 444a, cited in Michel, i, p. 20 (c. 1100) and in the three (? earlier) *Opuscula de origine schismatic*, printed in J. Hergenröther, *Monumenta Graeca . . . ad Photium . . . pertinentia*, pp. 160–1, 168–9, 179. In these Pope Sergius appears as the author of a "systatic letter" to the Patriarch Sergius II (1000–18), including the *filioque*.

12

THE ROMAN QUESTION

THE ROMAN question for the Byzantines was the problem of
maintaining good relations between the Roman church and the
Roman empire. Distance, and the difficulty of communications,
made it impossible to consider maintaining a permanent
garrison in the old capital. A Pope under direct Byzantine
control was likely to be repudiated by some of the Roman
factions. But the Byzantines relied on the Italian Greeks and
on Latin parties favourable to a Byzantine alliance, to maintain
in power a Roman Patriarch who would not be the subject of a
barbarian king. The instability of Roman politics made this
difficult. Friction continued between Latins and Greeks on such
minor matters as Saturday fasting, the length of Lent, liturgical
uses in penitential seasons, and the eating of things strangled.
The question of celibacy was for the present dormant, since many
Latin priests, and some bishops, lived in matrimony.[1] A more
important question for the moment was the boundary line of
the two Patriarchates, especially in Apulia. A dispute "about
some sees" is assigned to the time of the Patriarch Sergius
(1000–18),[2] and this is most probably connected with a revolt
of the Apulian Lombards, led by Meles, a Lombard of Bari,
before 1011.

Meles found allies in Norman soldiers of fortune returning
from a pilgrimage to Palestine, and also in the house of Tusculum, who in 1012–14 drove the Crescentii from Rome, and in
1014 bestowed the imperial crown on Henry II of Germany, a

---

[1] See *supra*, pp. 84, 118, and the life of St Nilus in PG 120, c. 129–32.
[2] By Nicetas Chartophylax (c. 1100) in what seems to be the oldest
version of his treatise, dependent on a source before 1028, in PG 120,
c. 717–19. See *Photian Schism*, p. 394.

king of genuine piety, whose followers insisted on singing the
Nicene creed at his coronation, probably in the longer version,
with the *filioque*, although our informant, an eyewitness, is careful not to commit himself to any statement that the custom
continued henceforth.[1] (The use of the creed at feasts was still a
controversial point.)

Henry II and Pope Benedict VIII were certainly found
fighting against the Greeks in the south. In 1022 at the council
of Pavia they began to take certain measures towards the en-
forcement of the neglected rules of celibacy.[2] But by that time
the catapan Basil Boiannes had defeated Meles, and Byzantine
power, supported by a strong emperor, who had lately completed the conquest of Bulgaria, showed signs of revival in Italy
as well. In 1024 Count Romanus of Tusculum, who had long
been Senator of Rome, succeeded his brother Pope Benedict
as John XIX. He received ambassadors from the Byzantine
emperor and Patriarch, who proposed, according to Raoul
Glaber, this cautious formula:

> that with the consent of the Roman pontiff the church of Con-
> stantinople in her sphere (*in suo orbe*), as Rome in the world (*in
> universo*), might be called and accounted universal.[3]

This was intended to cover a certain primacy in the Roman see,
but also a disclaimer of any title to interfere within the empire
proper, including Byzantine Apulia. The Pope was inclined to
concur, but a storm of protest reached him from over the Alps.
William, Abbot of St Benignus at Dijon, produced the
counter-formula:

> Although it may be that the power of the Roman empire, which
> once upon a time flourished monarchically in the whole world, is
> now wielded in diverse places and lands by innumerable sceptres,
> the power to bind and loose in heaven and earth belongs to the
> *magisterium* of Peter.

[1] Berno of Reichenau, *Libellus de officio missae*, PL 142, c. 1060–1. See
M. Lequien in PG 94, c. 224–6 (on St John of Damascus) and Bernard
de Rubeis in PG 142, c. 203–5 on George of Cyprus, for the inference that
the *filioque* was introduced at this time.

[2] See H-L, IV, ii, 919–20.

[3] PL 142, c. 671. See also Hugh of Flavigny in PL 154, c. 240–1.

The days of reforming Popes were not yet. William assumes that the Greeks "have obtained by asking the things which we have heard". He could only express a demand, a desire

> That in other matters, as is fitting in a universal bishop, you should act with more vigour for the discipline and correction of the holy and apostolic church, and be in Christ eternally and joyously strong.

We have no Byzantine account of this affair, and it is possible that on other issues the Pope resisted Byzantine demands, since his name was not in the *synodicon* in 1025, and there is no evidence that he was ever in the Byzantine diptychs.[1] In 1027 he crowned another German, Conrad II, who in the next year tried to make a matrimonial alliance with the imperial house, but this was broken off through the increasing instability of Byzantine politics.[2]

The death of Basil II in 1025 was a decisive turning-point. A man of austere life, who never married, he devoted himself to the tasks of government in an ascetic spirit, and concentrated all power and all responsibility in his own hands. Constantine VIII, who succeeded him, had remained in the background throughout his reign, and died in 1028, leaving two daughters, both of them elderly ladies. Zoe (1028–50) offended Byzantine traditions by her three successive marriages. Her first husband, Romanus Argyrus, divorced his wife for the purpose, and this damaged the prestige of the throne and of the church. Zoe and Romanus were not likely to favour a match between Conrad II and some younger Byzantine princess. Basil Boiannes was recalled in 1028, and in the next few years the Norman soldiers of Meles captured many Italian strongholds from the Greeks as well as from the Moors, and so became a power on the Italian coast, resented by the Lombards, the Moors, and the Greeks.

---

[1] Michel, ii, p. 25. Cf. ECQ, xi (1956), p. 308.

[2] According to the Franciscan chronicle of Erfurt (c. 1260), MGH ss, xxiv, p. 189, the Eastern church "withdrew from the obedience of the Apostolic see" in 1028, and this is repeated in another Erfurt chronicle, MGH ss, xxx, p. 189, but the chronology of these is very confused.

Meanwhile Conrad II was transforming the Western empire from an office or honour into a realm, a "collective term" for the three kingdoms of Germany, Burgundy, and northern Italy, an *imperium Romanum* whose political fulcrum lay beyond the Alps.[1] William of Dijon and Conrad II represent two aspects of the same movement. Both desired consolidation in the West under a Roman emperor or Pope. Neither had much confidence in John XIX or in his young nephew, Benedict IX, who continued the Tusculan succession in 1033. He failed in his political and military task of controlling the Roman factions, and his failure gave opportunities to the Western empire and to the ecclesiastical reformers. At the end of 1046 there were four possible Popes, Benedict IX, Silvester III, who had driven him from the city in 1044–5, Gregory VI, the priest John Gratian, in whose favour Benedict had for a time resigned his claim, and Clement II, Bishop Suidger of Bamberg, a Pope imposed by the emperor Henry III, on whose head he placed the imperial crown on Christmas day, 1046. None of these rivals was recognized by the Byzantines, who had neglected to come to terms with the Tusculan Popes since the death of Basil II. They now saw a succession of German Popes imposed on the Roman church by the other Roman empire.

These Popes were instruments of the political ambitions of Henry III, but they were also ecclesiastical reformers, who sought to break the power of the landed families over the local churches, including Rome, and to that end to enforce the ancient rules in such matters as simoniacal elections and the celibacy of bishops, priests, and deacons. Leo IX, the third of the German Popes (1048–54), was the most successful in enlisting the support of Italian reformers, such as Hildebrand and Peter Damiani, and Burgundians, such as Humbert of Moyenmoutier, Bishop of Silva Candida, whose allegiance was to the Roman church, not to the Roman empire, either in the Byzantine or in the Franconian sense. The Byzantines had reasons for objecting to the Germans, but also reasons for

[1] See G. Barraclough, *The Mediaeval Empire*, 1950, reprinted in *History in a Changing World*, Oxford, 1955, pp. 117–18.

believing that the activities of Leo IX could not safely be ignored. In 1050 he was holding councils on the borders of their territory. He was at Salerno, Siponto, and Amalfi, insisting on rules of clerical celibacy and Lenten fasting in direct contradiction to their traditions.[1] To the old frictions was now added a new dispute about the bread of the eucharist. The use of unleavened bread was not unknown in Eastern Christendom,[2] but there it was regarded as an Armenian custom, that could be connected not only with Jewish tendencies, but with Apollinarian errors.[3] In the West the custom was of some standing, but not apparently of great antiquity, perhaps not universal as yet.[4] The matter was in dispute first of all in Constantinople itself, where the Patriarch Michael Cerularius sought to impose in this the local use upon the Latin churches, who had hitherto been allowed to follow their own uses.[5]

Michael Cerularius had begun his career, like Photius, in the civil service, and retired to monastic life after a political setback in 1040.[6] Three years afterwards he emerged as Patriarch in 1043. While there is no reason to question the sincerity of his ecclesiastical patriotism, he was not a man of great learning.[7] His prejudices were those of a Byzantine layman, suspicious of foreign uses, Armenian, Jacobite, Latin, and doubly suspicious of the designs of Argyrus, the son of the rebellious Meles, who had lately entered the Byzantine service, and in 1051 was appointed governor of the Italian outposts.

Argyrus was a soldier of the Roman empire, but also a Lombard and a Latin. He had a project for a defensive alliance between the two Roman empires, Byzantine and German, to dislodge the Normans. In this alliance the Roman church would be the connecting link. But as Cerularius perceived,

---

[1] H-L, IV, ii, 1036–40.   [2] Michel, ii, pp. 116–18.
[3] See Peter of Antioch to Dominic of Grado in PG 120, c. 761–8, 777–8.
[4] See art. on *azymes* in *D.A.C.*, ii, c. 3254–60, by F. Cabrol.
[5] The quarrel began before 1051, while Argyrus was still in Constantinople. So Michael to Peter of Antioch, PG 120, c. 787–8, and for the date of Argyrus's presence, Lupus Protospatharius in PL 155, c. 135–6.
[6] Scylitzes in the *Compendium* of Cedrenus, PG 122, c. 263–4.
[7] See Peter of Antioch in PG 120, c. 797–8, and Michael Psellus as edited by Bréhier in *REG*, xvii (1904), pp. 68–9.

some delimitation of spheres of influence would be required, and the Italian dioceses of the Byzantine Patriarchate might well prove to be the price for Rome's assistance. He therefore stimulated a campaign of propaganda against the Latins, not only in the matter of unleavened bread, but of Lent and of things strangled.[1] On the other hand the Patriarch Peter of Antioch, with whom he had other differences,[2] wrote a "systatic letter" to Leo IX,[3] and in further correspondence with Dominic of Grado, an Italian bishop in touch with the East, attempted an eirenical discussion of eucharistic and other differences.[4] Michael Cerularius himself, on receiving fresh information as to the Pope's character, ability, and learning, changed his tune to this extent that he offered to place the Pope's name in the diptychs of all the churches of his Patriarchate if his own name was remembered in the church of Rome, but he did so in a manner that showed little deference to the Roman primacy.

His letter to the Pope,[5] with another letter from the emperor in pursuit of the project of alliance, was sent into Italy in the summer of 1053. But by the time these letters arrived the Pope was a prisoner in the hands of the Normans. Replies prepared in the Norman camp and in concert with Argyrus were not likely to meet with a friendly reception from Cerularius. One of the legates who brought them had, in all probability, the chief hand in their composition.[6] This was Humbert of Moyenmoutier, Bishop of Silva Candida, who had already composed in his own name a dialogue between a Roman and a Constantinopolitan [7] in reply to the "calumnies of the Greeks". The other legates were Frederick of Lorraine, chancellor of the

---

[1] In the letter of Leo of Ochrida to John of Trani, a Greek bishop in Italy (1053) in PG 120, c. 835–44, PL 143, c. 793–8, and the tract of Nicetas Stethatos in PG 120, c. 1011–22, PL 143, c. 974–84.
[2] See V. Grumel in *Le patriarchat et les patriarches d'Antioche*, EO, xxxiii (1934), pp. 140–1.
[3] In Michel, ii, pp. 446–57.
[4] PG 120, c. 751–82.
[5] This letter is known through references in the Pope's reply, PL 143, c. 773–7, and Michael's letter to Peter of Antioch, PG 120, c. 784.
[6] Michel, i, pp. 45–76.   [7] PL 143, c. 931–74.

Roman church, and Archbishop Peter of Amalfi, who had lately been driven from his see by a hostile party. The Pope commended him to the emperor as a true Roman,[1] but Michael Cerularius had another opinion.[2]

The legates left the Pope in January and arrived in Constantinople in April, 1054. They brought with them, besides the Papal letters, a memorandum from Jerusalem on the use of the churches there.[3] The Patriarch had heard from another quarter that the Pope was commemorated in the diptychs at Jerusalem and Alexandria, and that in these two churches the Patriarchs themselves sometimes celebrated the eucharist in unleavened bread.[4] He also knew that Peter of Antioch was in correspondence with the Pope, and might commemorate Leo IX in his diptychs.[5] An appeal to the other Patriarchs was a recognized mode of resolving differences between the church and the court. He had much reason to suspect, when he read the papal letters, that his deposition was in the wind, for his election was questioned, and he was accused of encroaching on the rights of the Eastern Patriarchs.[6] The legates treated him with scant respect, and he replied by rejecting their credentials. Then, or shortly afterwards, he denied that they came from the Pope, and treated them as emissaries of Argyrus.[7]

The emperor, Constantine Monomachus, received them with honour, but his own position was not very secure. The Patriarch was a popular figure, and the legates in their anger played into his hands. Had they been content to concentrate on the single charge that the Patriarch and his party denied that unleavened bread was properly "living bread", and therefore that a eucharist in *azymes* was a true liturgy,[8] they might have consolidated their support among those who were unwilling to

---

[1] PL 143, c. 780–1.   [2] PG 120, c. 785–6.
[3] Cited, PL 143, c. 951–2.   [4] PG 120, c. 789–90.
[5] Ibid., c. 787–8.   [6] PL 143, c. 774.
[7] In his *Synodal edict*, PG 120, c. 737–8, 741–2. See also his letters to Peter of Antioch, *idem*, c. 815–16, and (later), c. 784–5.
[8] The case is most clearly argued by Humbert in PL 143, c. 945–62, Even Peter of Antioch makes the point to Dominic of Grado, PG 120. c. 765–6, though in a later letter to Cerularius, *idem*, c. 813–14, he seems to think that *azymes* should be allowed for the sake of peace.

make any final breach with the West. But Humbert in controversy with Nicetas Stethatos, a Studite monk whom he engaged
in debate and induced to recant his attacks on the Latins,
dragged in other issues,[1] of Lenten observance and clerical
marriage, an ancient error that he identified with the heresy of
the Nicolaitanes, mentioned in the book of Revelation.[2] Moreover in the bull of deposition [3] that he placed on the altar of
Saint Sophia on 16 July, he added to his other charges against
the Patriarch and his personal adherents the excision (not
the omission) of the *filioque* from the Nicene creed.

Not all his charges applied to the whole Byzantine church,
and some of them were inferences [4] from the strong language
of Byzantine controversialists about the Latin eucharist and
the Latin ritual of baptism. Some, like the charge of "simony"
amount to little more than vituperation, but it may be true
that in the Byzantine church eunuchs were promoted to
ecclesiastical office, and that the baptism of sickly infants was
deferred until they and their mothers received communion on
the eighth day after their birth.[5] Much more important was the
question of married clergy (though this was stated as if priests
and deacons were allowed to marry, not only to continue in
matrimony), and the attack on the ancient form of the creed.
Yet the legates affirmed their complete satisfaction with "the
honourable and wise men" of this "most perfectly orthodox and
Christian city".[6] They seem to have supposed that the Patriarch's deposition was a question of time. He was at odds with
the court and must fall before long. They were called back to
meet him, but the prudent emperor advised them that this was
no time for a council. They left in haste as the Patriarch
published his edict.[7]

This was not an attack on the Roman church, but on three

---

[1] PL 143, c. 983–1000, especially c. 992–6 (Lent) and c. 996–7 (the
heresy of the Nicolaitanes).
[2] 2. 6.   [3] PL 143, c. 1002–4.
[4] E.g. the charge of rebaptizing Latins, of denying a sacrifice and baptism
outside the Greek church, of cursing the Mosaic law, and of refusing
communion to the cleanshaven.
[5] These points are enlarged upon by Humbert in PL 143, c. 973–4.
[6] PL 143, c. 1003.   [7] PG 120, c. 735–48.

unknown strangers and their preposterous anathemas. The influence of a moderating party in the synod may be suspected, for nothing is said about *azymes*, or (except in passing) on any question except the creed and the status of married clergy. The Byzantine church had not condemned the Roman, or the Roman the Byzantine. Leo IX was dead, and his death was known.[1] This did not prevent the legates from executing their mission, but it may well have made them anxious to return. Uncertainty about the position at Rome, where the next Pope might be a German, more opposed to the Byzantines,[2] or an Italian, opposed to the Germans, must have added to the obstacles in the way of a military alliance between the two empires.

In two letters to Peter of Antioch [3] Cerularius enlarged on the errors of the Latins, but in an interview at the height of the crisis with the Nestorian scholar, Ibn Butlan, he admitted the difficulties of his position, and did not attempt to deny that the legates came from the Pope.[4] Peter accepted the "official" view that the legates were emissaries of Argyrus, most probably because he wished to leave the door open for negotiations with the new Pope. He did not agree with Cerularius in his long list of Latin errors, and he criticized, politely but firmly, his views on church history.[5] Letters were also sent to the other Eastern Patriarchs, but nothing is known of their reactions to the crisis.[6]

The Patriarch of Constantinople had succeeded in parrying a dangerous attack on his own position by an appeal to popular feeling, but he was not yet out of danger. The Latin churches were probably open, though out of communion with him.[7] Next year the emperor Constantine gave place to the

---

[1] Michael Cerularius to Peter, PG 120, c. 783–4.
[2] The new Pope, Victor II, who did not arrive in Rome before the end of the year, had in fact opposed the Byzantine alliance. See *Schisme Byzantin*, p. 199, n. 4.
[3] PG 120, c. 781–6, 815–20. This order should be reversed.
[4] See R. Mayne, *East and West in 1054*, in *C.H.J.*, xi, pp. 140–1 and refs.
[5] PG 120, c. 795–816, especially c. 809, 813.
[6] *Idem*, c. 813–14.
[7] So it appears from the life of St Leo in PL 143, c. 499.

empress Theodora, whose position was stronger. She received a polite letter from Pope Victor II about tolls paid by Latin pilgrims.[1] The Patriarch's position continued to be difficult during her short reign and that of her adopted son, but in August 1057 his influence raised Isaac Comnenus to the throne, and for a year he was at the height of his power. In November 1058 Isaac turned against him. He was deposed for treason at a synod, after a long and eloquent arraignment by the philosopher Michael Psellus.[2] This contains no reference to the events of 1054, but in his funeral oration, delivered a few months later in another tone, the same philosopher pauses to congratulate the deceased Patriarch on his resistance to the Latins. Nothing however is said about *azymes*. The *filioque* was safer ground, on which all Byzantines agreed.[3]

Meanwhile in the West a great change was beginning. After the death of the emperor Henry III in 1056, the German imperial court lost control of the reforming movement. "In 1058 a great revolution in world history took place which even those most closely concerned had only dimly foreseen." [4] The moving spirit in this revolution was Humbert, who in the third book of his *Libri adversus simoniacos* [5] launched

> the first frontal attack on the whole position of laymen within the church, especially the ideas of royal theocracy which had held the field for centuries. The sacred character of the kingship was ignored, and for Humbert the king was a layman pure and simple.[6]

In this we may see a reaction against all the Western imitations of Byzantium since Charles the Great, and especially the *imperium Romanum* of the emperor Henry III. Henceforth the time had come when the Roman church would assert her

---

[1] In PL 149, c. 961–2, ascribed to Victor III. See *Eastern Schism*, p. 56, n. 2.

[2] Edited by L. Bréhier in *REG* xvi (1903), pp. 375–416, and xvii (1904), pp. 35–76.

[3] See *Eastern Schism*, p. 68, citing K. Sathas, *Bibliotheca Graeca medii aevi*, IV, Paris, 1874, pp. 348–9.

[4] G. Tellenbach, *Church, State, and Christian Society at the Time of the Investiture Contest*, translated by H. F. Bennett, Oxford, 1940, p. 111.

[5] PL 143, c. 1139–1212.   [6] Tellenbach, p. 109.

claims to the Western regions in terms of the *Donation of Constantine*.[1] Humbert had already made use of this in the struggle with Cerularius. He now employed it to bind the Norman chiefs, who had captured Leo IX in 1053, in close allegiance to the Papacy. At the synod of Melfi [2] in 1059 Robert Guiscard became Duke of Calabria and Apulia, "and hereafter of Sicily", "by the grace of God and St Peter". Richard of Aversa, another Norman, became Prince of Capua. They were the Pope's protectors, but also his vassals. They undertook to recover for Rome her regalian rights and her lost patrimonies, confiscated by the Isaurian emperors in 732. In practice they restored her Patriarchal authority in Calabria, Sicily, and the Terre d'Otranto, and in many places, though not in all, they replaced Greek bishops by Latins, who were naturally more willing to acknowledge their authority.

By 1071 the conquest of Apulia and Calabria was practically complete, though in isolated towns the local authorities maintained their allegiance to the Byzantines for many years, and in the independent cities of the Campanian coast imperial suzerainty was still recognized in the twelfth century. The Norman passion for conquest was not satiated, as they looked across the sea at other islands, Corfu and Cephallonia, and at the mainland of Apulia and Greece. There too were "patrimonies of St Peter", and provinces that had once received metropolitans from Rome. For the next fifty years Norman ambitions were intimately bound up with the revival of Roman claims upon Illyricum and Greece.

The papacy hoped to obtain satisfaction for these claims by negotiation. The weapon of conquest was held in reserve. On the two occasions when it was openly used, in 1082–4 and 1107–8, it was unsuccessful. The Normans could overwhelm Byzantine outposts, but not the Byzantine empire. On other occasions the Popes tried to combine peaceful persuasion with military pressure. When Hildebrand became Pope Gregory VII in 1073 he offered to come to Constantinople to preside over a

---

[1] It is quoted extensively in PL 143, c. 754–5.
[2] Gay, pp. 516–19, H-L, IV, ii, 1180–90.

General Council, but he would come with an army at his back, raised in the West, to deliver the Eastern Christians from the peril of the Turks.[1] This plan came to nothing at the time, for the Pope's attention was diverted to other problems in Italy and Germany, but it contained in germ the idea of the First Crusade.

The Byzantines had two defences against the Pope and his Norman allies. They might combine with the Germans, as they did in 1062, when the emperor Constantine Ducas recognized Bishop Cadalus of Parma as Pope Honorius II, "the Patriarch of Rome raised by the royal constitution over the universal church".[2] At the time this anti-Pope was supported by many Roman nobles, by the citizens of Amalfi, and by the dowager-empress Agnes, the widow of Henry III. The Byzantines may well have regarded him as the representative of the German party, with whom the negotiations interrupted in 1054 might be resumed. A letter of enquiry on the sense of the *filioque* from the Patriarch Constantine Leichudes (1059–64) was probably intended for his address, though Peter Damiani replied [3] on behalf of his rival, Alexander II, whose cause prevailed.

This did not encourage the Byzantines to support Guibert of Ravenna, who was set up as Pope Clement III by the supporters of the emperor Henry IV in 1080, though a letter from him to the Metropolitan Basil of Reggio shows that he expected support from his "holy brother the Patriarch of Constantinople", whose right to consecrate a metropolitan for Calabria is implicitly admitted.[4] The schism in the Western church impeded negotiations between Constantinople and the Roman re-

---

[1] See his letters in PL 148, c. 326, 329, or MGH, *Epistolae selectae*, ed. E. Caspar, t. ii. fasc. i, pp. 69–76.

[2] Letter in the narrative of Benzo of Asti in MGH, ss, xi, c. 617. See ibid., c. 622–3, Gay, p. 527, H-L, IV, ii, 1226, 1231, and F. Dölger, *Regesten der Kaiserkunden des Ostromischen Reiches*, vol. ii, Berlin, 1925, No. 952.

[3] In PL 145, c. 633–42, addressed to "Domno L., beatissimo patriarchae". Peter does not claim to have *seen* the letter of enquiry.

[4] Printed with other letters from British Museum MSS. add. 34060, by W. Holtzmann, with an introduction in *BZ*, xxviii (1928), pp. 59–60. Cf. also a letter to Clement III from the Metropolitan John of Kiev, discussing differences in a friendly way, in B. Leib, *Rome, Kiev, et Byzance*, Paris, 1924, pp. 34–41.

formers; but there was never any real chance that the two empires would join forces against the Popes of the Hildebrandine party. The first object of the Byzantines was to prevent the Normans from crossing over the straits of Brindisi and attacking Albania or the Ionian islands. They were not in a position to take the offensive in Italy. Therefore, Byzantine diplomacy, instead of co-operating with the Germans against Rome, rather sought to separate the Romans from the Normans.

This is especially obvious in the long career of Alexius Comnenus, a master diplomat, who reigned from 1081 to 1118. He began by repulsing a Norman invasion of Albania and Macedonia. He met a papal excommunication by forbidding Latin churches in Constantinople to offer eucharist in *azymes*.[1] But when in 1089 a more politic Pope, Urban II, with the leave of Roger of Sicily, the cautious brother of Robert Guiscard, removed his excommunication, he opened the Latin churches again, and advised the synod to place the Pope's name provisionally in the diptychs, since no "synodical judgment and examination" could be pleaded to justify its absence. The synod decided to ask the Pope for a "systatic letter". If it did not come within eighteen months "the position will be clarified with ecclesiastical accuracy". Meanwhile Jerusalem and Alexandria were to be consulted.[2]

The Patriarch had recently received a "systatic letter" from Jerusalem, enclosing a communication from Rome. His comments on this reveal his own attitude to the Roman question:

> There was a time when the Pope was the first among us, when he had the same sentiments and the same thoughts as we have. Now that he is of another mind, how can he be called the first? Let him present an identical confession, and receive the primacy, that faith may establish rank, not violence and tyranny. And indeed if he does not, he will never receive what he asks from us.[3]

He also insisted that "we will never offer in *azymes*, or receive

---

[1] See Gaufredus Malaterra, *Historia Sicula*, PL 149, c. 1192.

[2] See *BZ*, xxviii (1928), pp. 60–62.

[3] Quoted in V. Grumel, *Jerusalem entre Rome et Byzance*, in EO, xxxviii (1939), pp. 104–17. The date is not certain. Fr Grumel assigns it to 1089, but Simeon II became Patriarch of Jerusalem in 1085–6.

those who offer in *azymes*". Nevertheless in a letter to the Pope he assured him that the Latin churches of Constantinople had full liberty to follow their own uses. He named the Greek Archbishop of Rossano in Calabria as his reference, and asked that the metropolitan Basil might be restored to the see of Reggio. Of the *filioque* he said nothing directly, though he asked the Pope to clarify his attitude to the canons of the church.[1] From this we may gather that he was prepared to concede his rights in Calabria, now irretrievably lost to the empire. Basil of Reggio was not so willing to admit the claims of Urban II, whom he regarded as an anti-Pope. In a letter to the Patriarch, also found in the same collection of documents, he hotly protested against the proceedings of the Latins in Calabria. He pointed out that Urban was insisting on his Patriarchal rights in Illyricum, and enclosed a sympathetic letter from Clement III.[2]

A treatise by the Metropolitan Theophylact of Bulgaria [3] fills in the details of a Greek point of view. He made light of minor differences, and discussed the *filioque* reasonably, insisting on the necessity of a common symbol, but finding a justification for Latin theology in the poverty of the Latin language, that left them without words to distinguish between the communication of the Holy Spirit by the Father and the Son and the underlying cause of His being. If such views were common, it is hardly likely that the canonical grievances against the Latins, or even the question of *azymes*,[4] were the main obstacle to the progress of negotiations. What was required was a "systatic letter" confessing the faith in traditional and acceptable terms. But by dispatching such a letter the Pope might appear to submit himself to the judgment of his colleagues, the other Patriarchs. On such a point the reformed papacy was very sensitive.[5]

---

[1] In *BZ*, xxviii (1928), pp. 62–4.
[2] Ibid., pp. 59–60, 64–7.
[3] PG 126, c. 221–49.
[4] For the views of the Patriarch Simeon of Jerusalem on this question see B. Leib, *Deux inédits Byzantins sur les azymes au début du xii ème siècle*, in *Orientalia Christiana*, 9 (1924), Rome, pp. 213–39.
[5] F. Dvornik holds that Pope Gregory VII abandoned "the venerable custom" of making a profession of faith at his coronation. See *Photian Schism*, pp. 319, 327–8, 445–7.

M

In 1090 Byzantine ambassadors appeared before the Pope in Campania,[1] but there is no evidence that a "systatic letter" was ever sent, or that any formal, synodical judgment was at this time pronounced on the errors of the Latins. The Latin churches in Constantinople certainly remained open, and perhaps the Pope's name continued in the diptychs, while behind the scenes negotiations continued. At the Council of Piacenza in March, 1095, new ambassadors raised the question of military aid.[2] The Byzantines had lost their best recruiting grounds in the Anatolian highlands. They needed mercenaries to reinforce the Varangian guard, which at this time was mainly composed of English exiles. The matter was relevant to the hope of religious peace, for the Latin element in the Byzantine army was one of the factors that made the Latin churches in Constantinople politically important. With this hope in mind, and with his eyes on the Eastern Patriarchs, who were not as yet fully committed to either side in the dispute between Constantinople and Rome, the Pope preached a famous sermon on 27 November, 1095, at Clermont-Ferrand in France.

[1] *Chronicon Bernoldi*, PL 148, c. 1403.
[2] See S. Runciman, *History of the Crusades*, vol. i, Cambridge, 1951, pp. 104–5.

13

THE CRUSADES

THE FIRST CRUSADE was intended to demonstrate the value of Rome's friendship in military terms. In 1095 the Byzantines might still hesitate to commit themselves between Urban II and Clement III. The Pope sought to prove that he could command the allegiance of men of war in every part of Western Europe outside the empire. The hordes of pilgrims who set forth at his command proved this up to the hilt. Henceforth no Byzantine could doubt that the Pope was the real emperor of Western Christendom. But they were more like invaders than mercenaries. Anna Comnena remembers the alarms of her girlhood:

> For the whole West and all the barbarian tribes which dwell between the farther side of the Adriatic and the pillars of Hercules, had all migrated in a body and were marching into Asia through the intervening Europe . . . making the journey with all their households.[1]

Among the Crusaders were the Norman conquerors of Apulia and Sicily. Some of these had been in Greece before as invaders, and some like Bohemond, the son of Robert Guiscard, were rightly suspected of designs on the capital and the throne.[2]

The Pope had launched a mass movement too great for his control, but he did try to guide it through his very able legate, Bishop Adhemar of Le Puy, whose influence was greatest with the Provençals from the south of France, but less with the Normans and other detached adventurers. Adhemar's best friend, Raymond of Saint-Giles, Count of Toulouse and Mar-

[1] *Alexiad*, x, c. 5, p. 248 in Eng. trans. by E. A. S. Dawes, London, 1928.
[2] Ibid., p. 250.

quis of Provence, was, of all the Crusaders, the most inclined to
co-operate with the Byzantines, and it is reasonable to suppose
that the legate did his best for peace, but occasions of friction
multiplied. The emperor wanted soldiers to recover his lost provinces, but the most religious of the Crusaders were the most
anxious to press on at once to Jerusalem. They thought of the
Crusade as a great armed pilgrimage, to restore the Holy
Places to the possession of Latin Christians, as Sicily and Spain
were being recovered from the Moors. The more ambitious
sought principalities for themselves.

The conflict came to a head with the capture of Antioch in
June, 1098. This Patriarchal see had been in Byzantine possession from 969 to 1084. The Patriarch John, who had remained
in the city during the siege and suffered at the hands of the
Turks, was restored to his throne by the Crusaders. Adhemar
was on the best of terms with him, and with the Patriarch
Simeon of Jerusalem, who was by this time an exile in Cyprus.[1]
It was clearly part of his policy to maintain these Patriarchs in
their sees. The Greeks of Antioch, with their Patriarch, were
naturally loyal to the emperor Alexius. But he was not at hand,
and when the Crusaders were besieged by superior forces, he
did not come to their aid. Bohemond, the wily chieftain of his
Norman enemies, had himself captured the citadel, and
claimed Antioch as his personal possession. In his view Alexius
had failed to fulfil his obligations to the Crusaders, and his
rights lapsed.

The other Crusaders did not immediately agree. Raymond of
Saint-Giles, and probably Adhemar, defended the rights of the
emperor. But Adhemar died on 1 August, and almost immediately afterwards it became clear that some of Bohemond's
friends were agitating for the election of a Patriarch of the
Latin rite.[2] The position of the Patriarch John was bound up

[1] See Runciman, *Crusades*, i, p. 222, and letters in Simeon's name in
H. Hagenmeyer, *Die Kreuzzugsbriefe*, Innsbruck, 1901, pp. 141–2, 146–9;
PL 155, c. 469–70.
[2] See Runciman, *Crusades*, i, p. 253, for Peter Bartholomew's vision of
St Andrew and Adhemar, with counsel to this effect, two days after the
latter's death. As Adhemar expressed contrition for disbelief in Peter's

with the political question of the rights of Byzantium. In September Bohemond and other princes wrote a letter to the Pope in which they complained of heretics, "Greeks and Armenians, Syrians and Jacobites" whom they could not overcome.[1] They summoned him to come and occupy St Peter's chair at Antioch. Yet for the time being they remained in communion with the Patriarch. When a Provençal priest, Peter of Narbonne, was chosen to be bishop of the neighbouring city of Albara, "a Roman bishop in an oriental church, for its administration", he was brought to Antioch and consecrated there in October by the Patriarch John, in whose province he was.[2] The common worship of Greeks and Latins continued.[3]

In the same month at the Council of Bari the Greeks of Calabria and Sicily accepted the authority of the Roman Patriarchate and the orthodoxy of the Roman creed, on condition that they were allowed to retain their own uses, including the old version of the symbol, without the *filioque*.[4] If the treatise of St Anselm of Canterbury *On the Procession of the Holy Ghost, against the Greeks*, represents the line taken by the Latins at this Council, where he certainly took a prominent part, the Greeks were not pressed to say more than that the Latins were justified in making the addition in their own liturgies:

> For what church is there, extended over the amplitude of a single kingdom, that has not the power to ordain something in accordance with the right faith, that in the congregation of the people may be profitably said or sung? And how much more is it lawful for the Latins to set forth this in common, wherein all races and kingdoms, which use the Latin speech, are equally agreed.[5]

St Anselm defends with great ability the orthodoxy of the

---

earlier visions, it is not to be supposed that in his lifetime he had opposed the Patriarch John.

[1] Hagenmeyer, op. cit., pp. 161–5, from Fulcher of Chartres, *Historis Hierosolymitana*, Heidelberg, 1913, pp. 258–64.

[2] The evidence for this consecration is collected by H. Hagenmeyer in *Chronologie de la Ière Croisade, ROL*, vii (1899), pp. 324–5.

[3] See Albert of Aix in PL 166, c. 513.

[4] See B. Leib, *Rome, Kiev, et Byzance*, pp. 291–4.

[5] PL 158, c. 318.

filioque, but he had no objection to the continued use of the old Greek form, still used in Greek churches in Rome.[1]

If Adhemar had lived, and the concord of Greeks and Latins had continued at Antioch, the settlement reached at Bari might have proved a satisfactory basis for joint action in Syria and Palestine. But as the war between Greek and Latin bishops in Italy that had gone on intermittently since before 1011,[2] reached a satisfactory conclusion, another war began at the other end of the Mediterranean. Even if the Byzantines, like the Italian Greeks, could acquiesce in the Norman conquest of Sicily and Calabria, they could not allow the right of the Franks to establish a Latin prince and a Latin Patriarch in the Greek city of Antioch.

This came about through a close alliance between Bohemond and the new Papal legate, Daimbert, who arrived in Syria in September, 1099, with a fleet from his city, Pisa, after plundering the Ionian islands on the way. By this time Jerusalem had fallen, but the Patriarch Simeon did not return. He died in Cyprus as the city was liberated. No other Orthodox bishop had remained, or returned. The Latins took charge of the Holy Places, and occupied vacant churches and shrines with few hesitations. At Christmas, when Daimbert arrived, he was inevitably elected Patriarch. He consecrated bishops, not only for sees in his Patriarchate, but for Syrian sees accounted vacant, including Edessa and Tarsus.[3] Moreover he invested Bohemond with Antioch.[4] The Patriarch and the emperor were alike ignored. The Patriarch John perceived the utter impossibility of his own position, and soon retired to Constantinople. He was probably compromised in the emperor's eyes, for he resigned in October, 1100,[5] but his clergy were encouraged to

---

[1] Anselm's view contrasts with Humbert's, *supra*, p. 151.

[2] *Supra*, p. 144.

[3] Radolf of Caen, *Gesta Tancredi*, PL 155, c. 579.

[4] See Runciman, *Crusades*, i, pp. 305–6. This clears up the question of dates. Radolf says Easter, 1100.

[5] See V. Grumel, *Les Patriarchs Grecs d'Antioch du nom Jean*, in EO, xxxii (1933), pp. 295–6. His own account of his troubles survives in MSS 482 (117) in the library of St Catherine on Sinai, obtainable in microfilm from the Library of Congress, but hard to read.

elect a successor. Meanwhile at Antioch Bernard of Valence became Latin Patriarch.

In the eyes of Bohemond and Daimbert the Greeks and Syrians of Syria and Palestine were like the Italian Greeks of Calabria and Sicily, oriental Christians who had submitted to "the mother and mistress of all churches", Rome, or Jerusalem.[1] On this condition they kept their uses, but they had to accept Latin Metropolitans. In Sicily much ecclesiastical as well as civil power was concentrated in the count (afterwards the king) who claimed to be papal legate in all his dominions. Thereby the Byzantine unity of church and state was in a measure retained. To the Greeks the change meant little. In passing under a new civil authority they changed their Patriarchate, but they long continued to receive Greeks from Constantinople and Russians from Kiev in Palermo as in Jerusalem.

In Syria the position was more difficult. The submission of the Eastern Christians to their new governors was understood in a different sense by the two parties. The Latins believed that their subjects had submitted through them to Rome, but the Syrians saw their submission as analogous to their former allegiance to a Moslem government. The Latins were Christians, Chalcedonians, and up to a certain point, friends. They had not been condemned as heretics. But they could not break the bonds that bound the Greeks of Antioch and Jerusalem to other Greeks in Cyprus and Byzantium. Some of the Greeks and Orthodox Syrians in Antioch recognized Greek Patriarchs in exile. Many at Jerusalem resented the requirements of the Latin Patriarch, and some had thoughts of a rival.

In Latin eyes submission was open to Armenians and to Jacobites on the same conditions. They were less particular than the Greeks about ritual or even doctrine.[2] They were vague

[1] For Daimbert's views on the reverence due to Jerusalem see his letter to Bohemond in William of Tyre, PL 201, c. 457, and Runciman, *Crusades*, i, pp. 317–18.
[2] See a letter of Gregory VII to an Armenian in 1080, PL 148, c. 571–4; MGH, *Epistolae selectae*, t. ii, fasc. ii, pp. 510–14. He mentions only five oecumenical councils, omitting the sixth and seventh, and seems more anxious to approve the Armenian use of *azymes* than to blame "Who was crucified for us".

about the details of the early heresies, and appreciated military qualities in the Armenians of Cilicia, the Jacobites of Edessa, and the Maronites of Mount Lebanon, who made better soldiers than the Greeks or the Melkites of Palestine. Neither the Armenians nor the Jacobites had any strong bias against the Latins as they had against the Greeks from years of frontier warfare. They were ready to serve their princes, and this often involved some submission to the authority of the Latin Patriarch, who acted as minister of ecclesiastical affairs in the principality of Antioch. One Jacobite Patriarch in 1129 was consecrated in a Latin church in the presence of a Latin prince, but by the Maphrian or metropolitan of the East, who was the proper person to consecrate a Monophysite Patriarch of Antioch.[1]

Michael the Syrian, the Jacobite historian, says that the Latins did not raise questions of doctrine, but he himself has no doubt of their errors.[2] Armenians may have been less critical. They sometimes received communion from the Latin bishops, but they had no intention of separating themselves from their nation and its traditions. To check Latin influence among the Armenians of Cilicia and Edessa the northern and eastern Armenians set up a rival Catholicos at Aghthamar in 1114.[3] Yet Armenians of all parties continued to resort to Jerusalem, where they were hospitably received at the Armenian monasteries. Whatever arrangements particular Armenian communities might make with Latins and with Greeks, they did not break the fundamental solidarity of the Armenian church nation.

A Jacobite could say to the Greeks, "The Latins do not compel us to anathematize Severus".[4] The Latins were not learned in the Christological controversies, nor very intent on ritual issues that the Greeks were for ever reviving. They asked

---

[1] Bar-Hebraeus, *Chron. Eccles.*, i, c. 483–4.

[2] *Chronicle*, iii, p. 222.

[3] M. Ormanian, *The Church of Armenia*, p. 55. Gregory the Priest in *Bibliothèque historique Arménienne*, ed. E. Dulaurier, Paris, 1858–9, vol. ii, p. 329, tells of a Norman knight who had an Armenian confessor, and "in effect preferred the Armenians to the Franks".

[4] Theodore Bar-Vehbun in his dispute with Theorianus, PG 133, c. 297.

from all Eastern churches, without distinction, submission to the claims of the papacy as universal ordinary. Gradually this demand swallowed up every other. The Latins no longer objected to married clergy or to the omission of the *filioque* from the creed. These things were admitted in Calabria, and no doubt in Syria and Palestine. More gradually they became less insistent on their claims to the lost provinces. This was probably an issue in 1089, and certainly in 1112, when Pope Pascal II wrote to Alexius Comnenus:

> As for the metropolitans and provinces which were formerly attributed to the Apostolic See, they must return to their obedience and jurisdiction in order that the relations which, in the time of your predecessors, existed between the Old and the New Rome may be re-established, with the help of God, by the zeal of your highness; for it is impossible to establish an accord on the differences between Latins and Greeks, from the point of view of faith or usage, before the members are re-united to the head.

Here the return of particular provinces is a subordinate point. The most important demand is that the Patriarch of Constantinople

> should recognize the primacy of the Holy See, as that has been established by the religious prince Constantine, and confirmed by the consent of the Holy Councils.[1]

This clearly refers to a passage in *The Donation of Constantine*:

> And we ordain and decree that he shall have rule as well over the four principal sees, Antioch, Alexandria, Constantinople, and Jerusalem, as also over all the churches of God in all the world. And the pontiff who for the time being shall preside over that most holy Roman church shall be the highest and chief of all priests in the whole world, and according to his decision shall all matters be settled which shall be taken in hand for the service of God or the confirmation of the faith of Christians.[2]

If this was taken literally and translated into terms of practical policy the Eastern idea of a Patriarchate would lose most of its meaning. As the "universal episcopacy" of the Pope became more and more effective in the West, the question of Patriarchal

[1] PL 163, c. 388–9.   [2] Translated in Bettenson, p. 138.

boundaries grew less important. Less attention was paid to Illyricum, and more to the problem of Antioch.

On this point the Syrian Latins were always somewhat sensitive. According to William of Tyre, who reflects the Latin defence of their proceedings in the second half of the twelfth century,[1] the Patriarch John had peacefully retired, "seeing himself that he could not usefully preside as a Greek over Latins" . . . "just two years after" the Latin occupation began, that is, in June, 1100.[2] He himself had resigned, the see was vacant, and Bernard of Valence was therefore the lawful Patriarch. But the emperor Alexius insisted on a fresh election. Bohemond returned to the West to explain the position, and succeeded in convincing Pope Pascal II that the Byzantines were the real obstacle to the success of the Crusade. In 1107–8, under a banner blessed by the Pope, he made a daring raid into Albania and Macedonia. Alexius surrounded him and compelled him to surrender. He promised henceforth to rule in Antioch as a vassal of the empire, and to receive a Greek Patriarch elected in Constantinople.[3] But this promise was not fulfilled. He never returned to Syria, where his nephew Tancred stood firmly by Bernard. Alexius and his successors continued to press for the execution of this agreement, and the Latins continued to resist.

If the Latins could keep their hold on Antioch and transform it into a tradition, they might change the conception of a Patriarchate in the East. Alexandria and Constantinople might gradually be assimilated to Antioch and Jerusalem, not in liturgy and ritual, but in the manner of their subordination to the Pope. Daimbert indeed had dreams of independence, but after him the Latin Patriarchs of Jerusalem played only a minor part. The Latin Patriarchs of Antioch were no more independent than the primates of Germany and England, and not much more dignified than the honorary Patriarchs of Aquileia and Grado. If on the other hand the Greeks could recover Antioch,

[1] PL 201, c. 377. Cf. Ordericus Vitalis in PL 188, c. 775–6.
[2] "Lest two Patriarchs should occupy the same throne, against the sacred canons." So William of Tyre, *loc. cit.*
[3] The treaty is in *Alexiad*, Bk xiii, c. 12.

they would resume actual possession of three out of five Patriarchal sees. Their influence at Jerusalem would inevitably
increase, and they might hope to modify the attitude of Rome
towards the Eastern churches.

John Comnenus was received with royal honours in the city
in 1141, and his son Manuel in 1159. On each occasion promises
were given and received that a Greek Patriarch would be installed. Amaury de Limoges, who was Latin Patriarch from
1142 to 1196, put up a stubborn resistance. After 1153 he was
constantly at odds with the Prince of Antioch, but he had his
partisans among the barons. The Jacobites [1] favoured him out
of hatred to the Greeks and the Syrian Melkites. Yet the
necessities of the military situation drove the Franks into the
arms of the Byzantines in the absence of effective help from the
West, especially after the failure of the Second Crusade,
attributed by the French to Byzantine treachery. At last,
between 1164 and 1167 the Greek Patriarch Athanasius
arrived in Antioch. Manuel allied with the Latin king of
Jerusalem for the conquest of Egypt from the Moslems. The
liberation of the church of Alexandria must have been yearly
awaited. Meanwhile Byzantine influence in Italy made an
unexpected recovery. The Greek armies recovered Bari in 1151,
when the Byzantines and the Holy Roman emperor Conrad
III were allies against the Normans. From 1166 to 1173 they
occupied Ancona, this time as allies of Pope Alexander III and
the Lombard cities against the emperor Frederick Barbarossa.

Under these circumstances Manuel made a most extraordinary proposal that in the light of later history is bound to
appear more chimerical than at the time it actually was. He
was prepared to unite the church of Constantinople to the
church of Rome "in that status in which it is known to have
been of old time", if the Pope would recognize him as the only
lawful Roman emperor and restore the city of Rome to the
Roman empire. [2] At the time Byzantine subsidies were sus-

---

[1] Mich. Syr., iii, p. 332; *Chron. Eccles.*, i, c. 545–6.
[2] In Cardinal Boso's life of Alexander III in *Lib. Pont.*, ii, pp. 415,
419–20, there are two separate accounts of what F. Dölger, ii, No. 1480,
takes to be one embassy from Constantinople to Rome in 1167.

taining the resistance of several Lombard cities to the Germans. The sphere of Byzantine influence in Italy was steadily though rather superficially increasing. Manuel probably hoped to create a chain of dependent states there and in Syria. If Rome would come within the *Oecumene*, the Roman Pope could be his Oecumenical Patriarch.

Alexander III sent a reserved answer that this was "too deep and complex a matter". "The statutes of the holy fathers" forbade a swift decision. If he had come under Byzantine protection he would have mortally offended the Germans, and many of the Latins of the East. He could not afford to give such an opportunity to his enemies, the emperor Frederick Barbarossa and the imperialist anti-Pope, Pascal III. Neither could he afford at the moment to quarrel with Manuel. The mission that he sent to Constantinople in 1168 or 1169, did not raise territorial or ritual questions. The discussion was confined to three points; the commemoration of the Pope in the diptychs, the primacy of Rome, and appeals to Rome from Constantinople.[1]

The first was simply an admission of the Orthodoxy of the Roman church; the second and third must be taken together. The primacy of Rome had always been admitted at Byzantium, and at one time appeals to Rome had been a regular resort for Byzantine parties, though never very common. But in those days the Byzantines were free to reject a Roman decision, as they had rejected the verdict of Sergius III in favour of fourth marriages.[2] Rome was a convenient court of reference, an umpire at a distance from the capital, but in no serious sense a juridical superior of the Patriarchate. Appeals from the decision of a particular Patriarch might be made to all five, or to the Pope, or to the emperor, but the decision depended in the last resort upon public opinion. The Byzantine laity never developed a juridical idea of church authority, because they had always joined with their clergy in all kinds of ecclesiastical

[1] H-L, V, ii, 1051–2, from Leo Allatius, *De ecclesiae orientalis et occidentalis perpetua consensione*, Cologne, 1648, Bk. ii, c. xii, pp. 664–5.
[2] *Supra*, p. 132.

and theological activity. They had never played a passive part. They could not accept the primacy "as established by the religious prince Constantine",[1] unless the Pope became a member of their community.

If Rome could have returned to the Byzantine empire, the Papacy might have developed into a primacy of the *Oecumene*, while the Western kingdoms became "autocephalous churches", with their own primates, like Bulgaria and Serbia in later times. But if Rome remained right outside the empire, the Pope could not be acknowledged as the supreme judge of dogma without laying an axe to the very root of the Byzantine constitution, for dogma was the very basis of Byzantine life.

This objection was most forcibly put by the Patriarch Michael Anchialus (1169–77), who argued that subjection to the Turks was better than submission to the Pope:

> Let the Saracen be my lord in outward things, and let not the Italian agree with me in matters of the mind, for I do not become of one mind with the first, if I do obey him, but if I accept harmony in faith with the second, I shall have deserted my God, whom he, in embracing me, will drive away.[2]

This is not mere rhetoric, but a theory based on observed instances. Christian churches on Moslem territory suffered from material exactions, but kept their own traditions unimpaired. Eastern churches under the Latins in Calabria and Palestine retained their own liturgies, but lived under Latin metropolitans, and gradually became assimilated to the spirit of the Western discipline. This change might be unimportant or fundamental; it might be a necessary adaptation to circumstances or it might imply a change in dogma. On this question Byzantine opinions differed, and continued to differ for three hundred years more. Manuel long continued to hope that by negotiations with the Armenians and some of the Jacobites he might improve the position of the Greeks at Antioch and at

---

[1] *Supra*, p. 165.
[2] Leo Allatius, *De . . . ecclesiae . . . perpetua consensione*, bk. ii, c. 5, p. 558. See V. Grumel in EO, xxix (1930), pp. 358–61, and *Eastern Schism*, pp. 121–2.

Jerusalem, and so increase his bargaining power at Rome.[1] But the Greek Patriarch of Antioch was killed by an earthquake in 1170, and although the succession continued, the Latin Patriarch soon recovered his former ascendancy.[2] In 1176 the victory of the Lombards over Frederick Barbarossa made Byzantine aid far less necessary to the Pope and the other Italians, and the great disaster at Myriocephalon in Asia Minor, where Manuel was defeated by the Turks, destroyed Byzantine power to take the offensive not only in Italy, but in Syria and Palestine. The changed situation is revealed in a letter to Manuel from Frederick Barbarossa demanding submission not only to the Pope's authority (Frederick was now reconciled with Rome), but to the one Roman empire.[3] At the Third Lateran Council in 1179 Manuel was represented by Nicetas of Casola, near Otranto, but the opportunity for peace had passed.[4]

When Manuel died in 1180, mourned by William of Tyre,[5] who spoke for the wiser part of the Latins in Palestine, his policy of union by negotiation was already discredited by material failures. While his friends among the Jacobites and the Maronites of Mount Lebanon submitted to the Latin Patriarchs of Jerusalem and Antioch,[6] the Byzantines revolted against his widow, Mary of Antioch, a Latin by birth, and established his cousin, Andronicus Comnenus, as emperor in 1182. The Italians and other strangers suffered in the tumult,[7] and in the further turmoils that lasted for the next twenty years the ideas of Michael Anchialus prevailed over those of Manuel.

So far the Byzantines had been reluctant to call the *filioque* heresy in any absolute sense, even when they blamed severely

---

[1] See Dölger, ii, No. 1527, *Chron. Eccles.*, ii, c. 549–60, 575–90; H-L, V, ii, 1084–6; S. der Nersessian, *Armenia and the Byzantine Empire*, pp. 42–50.

[2] Mich. Syr., iii, pp. 332, 339.

[3] Cited in Vasiliev, p. 430. See Dölger, ii, No. 1528.

[4] Mansi, xxii, c. 237–8. For Nicetas (Nectarius) and his monastery. See K. Lake in JTS, v (1904), pp. 33–8.

[5] PL 201, c. 851.

[6] See *Idem*, c. 855–6, *Chron. Eccles.*, ii, c. 584, Mich. Syr., iii, pp. 382–8.

[7] See William of Tyre, PL 201, c. 857–62, for a contemporary impression by a Latin favourable to the Byzantine alliance.

any addition to the creed.[1] But their experience in the last hundred years told them that the West had a different doctrine of the church from their own. In retrospect the *filioque* was a symptom of this, an important and controversial addition to the common symbol made without common consultation, and also a sign of a different doctrine of the Trinity. These charges were not made in a hurry nor were they yet developed at all clearly. But the consciousness of grave divergence was real and not imaginary.

In the last years of the twelfth century both sides began to take up positions for a final conflict. In 1187 Saladin captured Jerusalem and expelled the Latin clergy. The Jacobites of the party of Michael the Syrian recovered their shrines from the Latinizing party of Theodore Bar-Vehbun.[2] The Holy Sepulchre was left to the Syrians, Greeks, and Georgians, who, according to one account,[3] had given Saladin some help. If so they may have been swayed by the news of the revolutions in Constantinople. Two years later, in 1189, Saladin guaranteed the freedom of the Greek and Syrian rites in Jerusalem in a treaty with the Byzantine emperor Isaac Angelus, though he would not allow the Syrian Orthodox in the church of Jerusalem to receive a Greek Patriarch from Constantinople.[4] Three out of four Eastern Patriarchates were linked in an anti-Latin attitude under the leadership of an aggressive claimant to the fourth, Theodore Balsamon, titular Patriarch of Antioch.

On the other hand the Latins occupied Cyprus in 1189, and set up a Latin hierarchy there in 1191.[5] The Greek bishops were not expelled, but made subject to the Latins, like the Maronites

---

[1] Photius is an important exception, but he wrote before the Latin church as a whole was resolved on the addition.

[2] This is implied in *Chron. Eccles.*, ii, c. 584, also in Mich. Syr., iii, p. 394.

[3] *The Coptic History of the Patriarchs of Alexandria*, cited by R. Grousset, *Histoire des Croisades*, vol. ii, pp. 811–12, and in my *Syrian Christians in Jerusalem, 1183–1283*, in ECQ, vii (1947), p. 47. See also Runciman, *Crusades*, ii, pp. 465–7.

[4] See Beha-ed-din, *Life of Saladin*, in *PPTS*, vol. XIII, pp. 334–5, cited in ECQ, vii (1947), pp. 47–9, Dölger, ii, 1584, 1591, 1593.

[5] See the bull of Celestine III in PL 206, c. 1147–8, and for the later history, Alexander IV, *Constitutio Cypriana* (1261), PG 140, c. 1533–60, and J. Hackett, *A History of the Orthodox Church in Cyprus*, London, 1901.

and the Armenians in Latin Syria. Pope Innocent III (1198–1216) corresponded with the Serbs and the Bulgarians, who had broken loose from Constantinople in 1186, with the Cilician Armenians,[1] and with the Alexandrian Melkites.[2] His negotiations with the Bulgarians [3] are especially interesting. The King of Bulgaria evidently wanted a Patriarch elected and consecrated in the country, like the Bulgarian Patriarchs of the tenth century. Innocent put him off with a primate, who must swear an oath of allegiance to the Roman see, attend Roman councils, and wear a pallium on certain festivals. On these conditions Bulgarian customs and the Slavonic liturgy might continue. The primate asked him for the holy chrism, which hitherto the Bulgarian church had received from Constantinople. Without this priests could not confirm, "the people would remain without the holy chrismation, and this would be a sin". It would be interesting to know how he replied, since at Constantinople he objected to priests' confirmations;[4] but his negotiations with Bulgaria were interrupted by the outbreak of a general war between Greeks and Latins, in which the Bulgarians found themselves after all on the Greek side. From 1204 to 1206 the Patriarch of Constantinople was a refugee on their territory, and naturally they received the chrism from him.

Innocent made essentially the same demands on all the Eastern churches. The Patriarch of Constantinople, like the primate of Bulgaria, must receive the pallium from Rome,[5] for all the churches in the world are in the Roman church, as "things creeping innumerable, both small and great beasts", are in "the great and wide sea".[6] From one point of view, indeed, the Roman church "is not the universal church, but a part of the universal church, the first indeed and principal part, as the head in the body". From another point of view "the

---

[1] PL 214, c. 775–80.
[2] A. Potthast, *Regesta Pontificum Romanorum*, vol. ii, Berlin, 1873, No. 1430 (1201).
[3] PL 214, c. 1112–15; 215, c. 277–98.
[4] PL 214, c. 772, and 215, c. 1352; *infra*, p. 189.
[5] PL 215, c. 259–60 (1203), c. 727–9 (1204).
[6] PL 214, c. 756–65, to the Patriarch John Camaterus of Constantinople (1199).

Roman church alone is universal, because she alone and uniquely by privilege of dignity is over the rest". The Fourth Lateran Council of 1215 defined the Papal primacy, that the church of Rome "by the disposition of God holds over all others the principality of ordinary power". After her there are four Patriarchs; Constantinople first, then Alexandria, Antioch, and Jerusalem.[1] In earlier years the Popes had maintained the superiority of the three Petrine sees, Rome, Alexandria, and Antioch, over the upstarts, Constantinople and Jerusalem.[2] Innocent could allow a precedence to Constantinople, since all the Patriarchal sees were under Rome.

Though the idea of universal episcopacy was not new, its application in practice was revolutionary, and, like most revolutions, defeated its own ends. When the Crusaders of the Fourth Crusade first captured Constantinople in 1203 the Byzantines were weary of turmoil and prepared to obey two emperors, whose primary task was to come to terms with the invaders. But when they discovered that these terms involved the complete submission of the Patriarch to the Pope,[3] and the independence of the Latin churches from all Byzantine authority, they rebelled against Venetian exactions and made one last struggle for freedom. The Latins in revenge sacked the city,[4] and established a Latin empire and a Latin Patriarchate. Even then some Greeks were willing to accept this revolution, if they might have a Greek Patriarch and Greek bishops of their own to represent them at a General Council that should "search the Scriptures" for a true basis of unity. When that was found they would rejoice to restore the Pope's name to the diptychs, and to hail him, like the other Patriarchs, "to Innocent, the Lord Pope of the Elder Rome, many years . . . , which is our witness that we do not desire to conquer, but rather would wish to be conquered, where it must be, if only we may draw the light

[1] Mansi, xxii, c. 990.

[2] So for instance did Gregory the Great in letters to Antioch and Alexandria, PL 77, c. 770–4, 843–4, 898–900; Nicholas I in his reply to the Bulgarians, PL 119, c. 1012; and even Leo IX to Michael Cerularius, PL 143, c. 774, and Peter of Antioch, c. 770–1.

[3] PL 215, c. 260–1 (Innocent to the Latin leaders).

[4] For a Greek account see Nicetas Choniates in PG 139, c. 967–1058.

N

together".[1] This letter represents the point of view of collabora-
tors, who wished to see a Latin and a Greek Patriarch ruling
together as at Antioch and at Jerusalem "where there are two
Patriarchs and one king".[2] Partisans were more aggressive,
according to the Fourth Lateran Council, where the Greeks
were accused of purifying altars that had been used by Latin
priests, and even of re-baptizing children who had received
baptism in the Latin manner.[3]

Innocent did very little to encourage collaboration. It is true
that he deplored the greed of the Venetians, who had diverted
the Fourth Crusade first to Zara and then to Constantinople,
and that on a suitable occasion he was willing to enlarge upon
the crimes of the Latins to Theodore Lascaris, the leader of the
Greek resistance.[4] But although he annulled the election [5] of
Thomas Morosini as Latin Patriarch, denying the right of the
Venetians to monopolize St Sophia as their share of the spoils,
he raised him to the office of his own motion, and gave him
very full instructions.[6] He was to wear the pallium on appointed
days and to convey it to other metropolitans, not only in the old
Patriarchate of Constantinople, but in Patras and other places
that in earlier times had been claimed for Rome. Provision
should be made for the Greek rite in Latin dioceses, but in
every place where Greeks and Latins were found together the
Latins must rule. Greek bishops who submitted need not be re-
consecrated, and they might retain their liturgy and other rites
until the apostolic see took further order, but they must take an
oath of fealty to Rome, and even then they might only rule
purely Greek dioceses. All fresh consecrations of bishops must
be in the Latin form that the Pope himself used for Greek
bishops in Italy.[7]

---

[1] This "letter of the citizens of Constantinople to Innocent III" is in
PG 140, c. 292–8. For the date (1211) and some of the circumstances see
Alice Gardner, *The Lascarids of Nicaea*, London, 1912, pp. 100–12.

[2] c. 297. See William of Tyre, PL 201, c. 377, of Antioch: "lest two
Patriarchs should occupy one and the same throne . . . against the sacred
canons".

[3] Mansi, xxii, c. 990.

[4] PL 215, c. 1372–5.   [5] PL 215, c. 515–16.

[6] PL 215, c. 727–9, 959–66.   [7] PL 215, c. 1353.

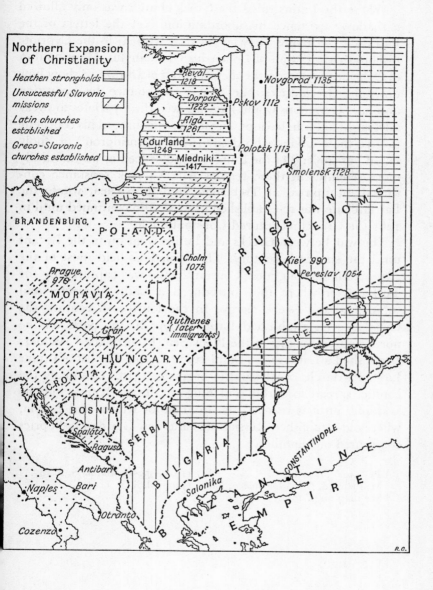

Northern Expansion
of Christianity

Heathen strongholds
Unsuccessful Slavonic
missions
Latin churches
established
Greco-Slavonic
churches established

Reval
1218
Dorpat
1222
Rigâ
1261
Courland
1249
Miedniki
1417

Novgorod 1135
Pskov 1112
Polotsk 1113
Smolensk 1128

PRUSSIA

BRANDENBURG
POLAND

Cholm
1075

RUSSIAN PRINCEDOMS

Kiev 990
Pereslav 1054

Prague
976
MORAVIA

Gran

Ruthenes
(later
immigrants)

THE STEPPES

HUNGARY

CROATIA

BOSNIA

SERBIA

Spalato
Ragusa

Antibari
Naples
Bari

BULGARIA

Salonika

CONSTANTINOPLE

BYZANTINE EMPIRE

Otranto

Cozenza

R.C.

Where the Latins ruled the Greek church was only allowed a shadowy existence in subordination. Yet the letters of the Patriarch Germanus II (who ruled at Nicaea) to the Cypriote bishops in 1223,[1] and of Demetrius Chomatenus, Metropolitan of Ochrida in 1222, to the metropolitan of Durazzo,[2] show how unwilling Greek ecclesiastics were to pronounce the separation absolute. Germanus would have allowed the Cypriotes to swear allegiance to Latin bishops. Demetrius encouraged his colleague to give those Latins who desired it the "antidoron" or "holy bread" at the end of the liturgy. Popular feeling was naturally more resentful in those regions where Greek resistance continued, in Epirus, at Trebizond, and at Nicaea, where the Patriarchate was re-established in 1208, and continued until in 1261 the Greeks recaptured Constantinople.

The war between Greeks and Latins went on in the Levant until the sixteenth century. The Venetians held most of the Aegean islands long after Constantinople was captured by the Turks. Everywhere they introduced a Latin hierarchy and subjugated the Greek clergy. In the fourteenth century the Genoese even established Latin bishops in the ports on the north and east coasts of the Black Sea. In 1219 the Crusaders established a Latin see at Damietta in Egypt. The list of titular Latin Patriarchs of Alexandria begins in 1310.[3] Gradually the conflict spread to Serbia and Bulgaria, Transylvania and the Ukraine, until it reached the frontiers of Russia and Latvia, where old-established Russian sees and new German bishoprics confronted one another.[4]

---

[1] PG 140, c. 601–14.   [2] PG 119, c. 959–60 and *infra*, p. 187.
[3] M. Lequien, *Oriens Christianus*, Paris, 1740, vol. iii, c. 1141–4.
[4] See map on p. 175.

14

THE NATURE OF THE SCHISM

WHAT MAY be called the traditional view of the schism between East and West is that it began with Photius, and reached a climax in the excommunication of the Patriarch Michael Cerularius by papal legates in 1054. But the researches initiated by A. Lãpôtre,[1] and completed by V. Grumel and F. Dvornik,[2] have proved that the settlement of 879–80 between Photius and Pope John VIII was accepted not only by the church of Constantinople, but by the greater part of the church of Rome. This settlement regulated relations between East and West in the tenth century, and remained authoritative in the West until the end of the eleventh.

If the significance of Photius has been misunderstood, the importance of Michael Cerularius has been exaggerated. In the light of the researches of M. Jules Gay,[3] Dr Michel,[4] and M. Jugie,[5] it is no longer possible to believe that a schism between Rome and Constantinople began in 1054. Michael Cerularius did not remove the Pope's name from the diptychs, for no Pope had been commemorated at St Sophia for some years. He closed the Latin churches, but they were open again before long. The exchange of mutual recriminations in Constantinople in 1054 [6] was less important for the relations of Greeks and Latins elsewhere than the Norman conquest of Apulia and

---

[1] *L'Europe et le Saint-Siège à l'époque carolingienne: le pape Jean VIII*, Paris, 1895.

[2] Cf. refs. *supra*, pp. 110–11, 123, 126, 132.

[3] *L'Italie méridionale*, pp. 484–500.

[4] *Humbert und Kerullarios, passim.*

[5] *Le schisme de Michel Cérulaire* in EO, xxxvi (1937), pp. 440–78, and *Schisme Byzantin*, pp. 150–70.

[6] *Supra*, pp. 149–52.

Calabria, the ratification of this by Rome in 1059,[1] and the later schisms between rival Greek and Latin Patriarchs at Antioch in 1100,[2] at Jerusalem after 1187,[3] and at Constantinople and Nicaea after 1204.[4] The general schism came slowly into being as schisms gradually formed in one Patriarchate after another.

Dr Adrian Fortescue, who in *The Orthodox Eastern Church* [5] presented a highly simplified picture of "the Cerularian schism", made some interesting admissions in 1917 in another book on *The Uniate Eastern Churches*,[6] on which he was engaged at the time of his death. It must be remembered that he was writing from the Roman Catholic point of view.

> To begin with, the matter of the schism of the East is not so simple as many people think. Indeed, it is very difficult to say when the Orthodox, outside Constantinople, became schismatics. . . . Probably for a long time none of them realized that a permanent state of schism between East and West had broken out. Hitherto they had been in communion with both the Pope of Rome and the Patriarch of Constantinople. They knew, of course, that these two were now quarrelling, but, presumably, they thought that this quarrel was no business of theirs. They, no doubt, hoped, that it would be made up in time; meanwhile they intended to keep out of it and to remain in communion with both.

As Dr Fortescue points out, the Eastern Patriarchs had done the same in the schism of 862–7 between Nicholas I and Photius. The action of their representatives at the Photian council of 867 was repudiated as unauthorized at the Ignatian council of 869.[7] He writes "the final test would be when they removed the name of the Pope from their diptychs. But we do not know when that happened". A mere absence proves nothing, for communications were often difficult, and always

---

[1] *Supra*, p. 154.   [2] *Supra*, pp. 162–7.
[3] *Supra*, p. 171.   [4] *Supra*, pp. 173–6.
[5] London, 1908, especially pp. 172–98.
[6] London, 1923, pp. 189–90.
[7] So Anastasius in PL 129, c. 45–6; cf. Bury, E.R.E., pp. 202–3. Better evidence of the neutrality of Jerusalem is provided by the *Itinerary of Bernard the Wise* (c. 867–70) in *Palestine Pilgrims' Text Society*, No. 23, vol. iii, 1893, pp. 3–11.

officially forbidden.[1] Moreover there are many other instances of schisms within Eastern and Western churches in which other churches did not feel obliged to take a side. In schisms between Popes and anti-Popes whole kingdoms sometimes stood aloof for a long time. As late as 1398–1403 the French church, with the moral support of the University of Paris, tried the experiment of a withdrawal of obedience from the anti-Pope at Avignon to induce him to come to terms with the Pope at Rome. The French did not join the Roman obedience, but hung suspended between the two contending parties.

In Western Europe schisms of this nature ceased after the Reformation. In the East they continue to this day: for instance the Bulgarian church, excommunicated by Constantinople from 1872 to 1945, yet remained in communion with Russia, Serbia, and Roumania. All the time Bulgarians who wished to join their own monastery on Mount Athos, where the Patriarch's authority was acknowledged, had only to abjure the schism in Constantinople.[2] After the first war individual Bulgarians were often admitted to communion in Greece, and Greeks in Bulgaria. Schisms in the Russian church do not divide the parties from the ancient Patriarchates, nor do they altogether divide them from one another. For some time the Russian church in London was used alternately by two communities, each acknowledging a different bishop. This was not modern tolerance, for the feeling between the parties ran high. But in their scale of values community in Orthodox dogma is more fundamental than any differences about ecclesiastical or civil polity. So in the Middle Ages those who believed that dogma in East and West was still fundamentally the same were prepared to receive Latins at the altar, despite differences about authority and ritual, and even about the form of the Nicene Creed.

In the eleventh and twelfth centuries no formal decision of the Eastern Patriarchs had yet pronounced judgment upon "the errors of the Latins". Though all Greeks agreed that the

---

[1] See *Schisme Byzantin*, p. 234, n. 2, for Moslem regulations against correspondence between the Eastern Patriarchs and bishops in Christian lands.

[2] M. Choukas, *Black Angels of Athos*, London, 1935, p. 307.

addition of the *filioque* to the creed was forbidden by the Council of Constantinople in 879–80, and ought never to have been made, it was another matter to pronounce the Latin doctrine heresy. In 1089 at Constantinople itself the synod answered an imperial enquiry:

> Not by a synodical judgment and examination was the Roman church erased from communion with ours, but as it seems, through our want of watchful care (ἀσυντηρήτως), the Pope's name was not commemorated in the holy diptychs.[1]

The same argument, that "this has never been decreed synodically", was used in 1190 and even later in defence of giving communion to Latins.

No one, so far as I know, has ever denied that the Patriarch Peter of Antioch was in communion with Rome and Constantinople in 1054. But the significance of his neutrality was missed so long as it was generally believed that Michael Cerularius began a new schism. In that case it would be merely an instance of "delayed action". L. Bréhier in *Le schisme oriental du XIème siècle* [2] assumed that the schism took effect at Antioch under the Patriarch Theodosius III, a political ally of Cerularius,[3] in 1057, and at Jerusalem and Alexandria either just before or just after. If however the Pope's name was removed from the diptychs in 1009 or 1012, Peter's neutral attitude is more likely to have been deliberately adopted in the hope of peace. In a letter to Michael Cerularius [4] he defended the commemoration of the Pope in the diptychs by the example of John of Antioch (997–1022) and Sergius of Constantinople (1000–19), who still commemorated Pope John XVIII in their diptychs in 1009, forty-five years before. To this defence he added two sentences, whose significance escaped comment until fresh attention was called to 1009:

In what manner the commemoration was afterwards excised,

---

[1] *BZ*, xxviii (1928), pp. 60–1, in W. Holtzmann's article cited *supra*, pp. 155, n. 4, 156

[2] Paris, 1899, pp. 237–41.

[3] But see V. Grumel, *Les Patriarches d'Antioche (969–1084)* in EO, xxxiii (1934), pp. 142–4.

[4] PG 120, c. 799–800.

and for what reason, I am in ignorance. And so long as I remain in this state about these things, I do not wish to take further action in the matter of the Pope's commemoration.

These sentences seem to me to imply that Sergius II of Constantinople had omitted the commemoration of the Pope's name without any formal consultation of the other Patriarchs. Patriarchs of Antioch who came from Constantinople may have followed his example, but Peter did not feel himself obliged to do so. Most of his subjects were Syrian Christians, like the chronicler Yahya of Antioch, who wrote *Annales* in Arabic in continuation of those written in the tenth century by Said Ibn Batriq (the Patriarch Eutychius of Alexandria).[1]

These Syrian Melkites had their own distinctive traditions and would not automatically follow a lead from Constantinople. Theodosius III, the second successor of Peter, writing to the King of Georgia, threatened him with an appeal to his four colleagues, the other four Patriarchs.[2] It seems clear that in 1060 Rome was still regarded as a senior Patriarchate in the church of Antioch. Roman Catholic historians very easily over-estimate the influence of Constantinople among the Orthodox churches of the Middle East, partly because they unconsciously assimilate the position of the Oecumenical Patriarch in Eastern Christendom to that of the Pope in the West, but also because they exaggerate the Greek and Byzantine character of the Melkites in Syria. Because in modern times the Syrian Ortho-dox, and Roman Catholic Melkites whose ancestors were Orthodox, use Greek or Arabic in their liturgy, they imagine that all Christians of Syriac liturgy in the Middle Ages must belong to one or other of the heretical churches, Nestorian, Jacobite, Maronite. But in Palestine most Syrian Christians were Melkites of Orthodox dogma.[3] Many of their Syriac

---

[1] Arabic edition of both, ed. P. L. Cheikho and others, 2 vols., Beirut and Paris, 1909–12. Two parts of Yahya have appeared in PO, xviii, 5, and xxiii, 3; and Eutychius in Latin in PG 111, c. 903–1156.

[2] See the life of St George the Hagiorite in *Analecta Bollandiana*, xxxvi (1917), Brussels and Paris, 1922, p. 115, quoted by V. Grumel in EO, xxxiii (1934), pp. 142–4.

[3] For Palestinian Syriac see F. C. Burkitt in JTS, ii (1901), pp. 183–5. See my own articles, *Syrian Christians in Palestine in the Middle Ages*, in ECQ,

liturgical manuscripts are known. The Jacobites had bishops in Jerusalem from the seventh or eighth century, but they did not rank as Patriarchs.[1] There were no Maronites out of the Lebanon, and very few Nestorians in Western Syria or Palestine.

The Orthodox community in Jerusalem consisted of Syrians, Greeks, Latins, and Georgians. Dr Michel has investigated references in Latin and Greek chronicles, and finds no conclusive evidence of a schism between Rome and Jerusalem before 1054,[2] nor can I discover any more between 1054 and the First Crusade. The assumption that Jerusalem and Alexandria followed Constantinople into schism with Rome rests on evidence of their continued communion with the Byzantines, not on any record of their breach with the West. Unfortunately no complete pilgrim narrative or description of the Holy Places can safely be assigned to this period,[3] but pilgrimages from the West continued, and the few references to them in Latin chronicles do not point to any breach between the Latin churches and monasteries in Jerusalem and the Greek Patriarchate.[4] The Patriarch Euthymius was in Constantinople in 1082-3, when he was employed by the emperor Alexius in negotiations with the Normans, possibly because he was acceptable to both sides.[5] His successor, Simeon II, also appeared at a Byzantine council, and, as we have seen, referred correspondence with Rome to the Patriarch of Constantinople.[6] Yet he was on good terms with the Crusaders, and sent them supplies from Cyprus at the time of the siege of Antioch. They evidently

---

vi (1945-6), pp. 363-72; and on *Syriac and Arabic in the church of Jerusalem* in CQR, cxlv (1947-8), pp. 230-40.

[1] See the list of Jacobite sees by E. Rey in *ROL*, viii (1901), p. 150, and Mich. Syr., iii, p. 493.

[2] *Humbert und Kerullarios*, ii, pp. 24-40.

[3] Possibilities are the very brief *Qualiter sita est Jerusalem*, in *PPTS*, vol. iii, pp. 12-14, and another anonymous narrative in *PPTS*, vol. vi, pp. 1-5.

[4] E.g. Lambert of Hersfeld in PL 146, c. 1081-5 (1064); see Vasiliev, p. 398.

[5] Dölger, ii, No. 1087, *Eastern Schism*, p. 69.

[6] *Supra*, pp. 136-7. For the council, condemning Leo of Chalcedon, see Dölger, ii, Nos. 1128-9 (1085-6), V. Grumel in EO, xxxviii (1939), p. 116 (1092).

regarded him as the lawful ruler of the church of Jerusalem, and based the claims of their Latin Patriarchs to their place in the succession on lawful election to a vacant see after the death of Simeon in July, 1099.[1] They made no distinction between Patriarchs before and after some supposed general schism between East and West about 1054–8.

Moreover there is much evidence that the Orthodox Christians of Jerusalem acquiesced in this point of view. First of all a number of narratives, Latin, Armenian, and Russian, give accounts of the Easter vigil in the Holy Sepulchre in 1101 [2] and 1107.[3] From these it appears that Latins, Syrians, and Greek monks of the monastery of St Sabbas prayed together in their own languages, but the principal part in the service was taken by the Latin Patriarch in 1101, and by his representative, a Latin bishop, in 1107. References to special chapels for Georgians, Latins, and Syrians appear in the rule of St Sabbas under the Latin domination.[4] That the monks continued to receive pilgrims from Russia by way of Constantinople is clear from the very interesting narrative of the Abbot Daniel, who stayed with them in 1106–7 and visited all the Holy Places. He lays great stress on their excellent relations with the Latin King of Jerusalem. He himself accepted hospitality from the Latin monks and clergy, and refrained from any but the mildest criticism of their ritual. He thought they mumbled in church,[5] and once he lets out a depreciatory remark about unleavened bread.[6] But he is full of praise for the Latin king, and a passing reference to "where the Patriarch lives" [7] seems to show that

[1] See the list in PL 155, c. 1054, William of Tyre in PL 201, c. 448–51, and M. Lequien, *Oriens Christianus*, iii, c. 498–9.

[2] Three Latin accounts were printed by H. Hagenmeyer in Fulcher of Chartres, *Hist. Hier.*, pp. 831–7. In one of them, by Bartolf de Nangeio, the Latin Patriarch is "re-elected by all with common consent". See *The Chronicle of Matthew of Edessa*, ed. by E. Dulaurier in *Bibliothèque historique Armenienne*, vol. ii, pp. 233–4, and B. Leib, *Rome, Kiev, et Byzance*, pp. 246–50.

[3] By the Russian Abbot Daniel in *PPTS*, vol. iv, pp. 74–82, and in *Itineraires Russes*, Geneva, 1889, pp. 75–83.

[4] In a τύπος, ed. E. Kurtz in *BZ*, iii (1894), pp. 167–70.

[5] In *PPTS*, No. 6, p. 77.

[6] Ibid., p. 68.

[7] Ibid., p. 13. In some Russian MSS the past tense is found.

he regarded the Latin Patriarch as ruler of the church, at least *de facto*. Another Russian pilgrim who visited the monks of St Sabbas in 1173 recorded her reception by the Patriarch as well as by the king. On her way she had seen the emperor and the Patriarch of Constantinople.[1]

At about the same time a deed of sale refers to fields possessed by the Abbot and convent of St Sabbas as an endowment for masses on behalf of the Latin Queen Melisenda.[2] An inscription of 1169 [3] in the church of the Nativity at Bethlehem refers to the making of mosaics by the Syrian artist Ephrem in the reigns of the Emperor Manuel (of Byzantium) and King Amaury of Jerusalem. In a commemoration [4] of the second oecumenical Council of 381 the divinity of the Holy Ghost is defined in Eastern fashion. Moreover, the narrative of John Phocas in his *Description of the Holy Land*,[5] a very full account of the Greek and Syrian monasteries in 1185, describes in loving detail the gifts of the Emperor Manuel, his old master, to the church of the Holy Sepulchre and other churches in Palestine. He speaks respectfully of the Latin Bishop of Bethlehem, though he calls the Bishop of Ramleh an intruder. His evidence with regard to Manuel's personal generosity is supported by William of Tyre, who mourned in him one whose "generous benefactions all the churches of the saints declare".[6] William at least once went to stay with him on the business [7] of his own church of Tyre, as well as on diplomatic business for the King of Jerusalem.

A German writer of 1160–70, John of Wurzburg, puts the Greeks before the Latins in a list of nations who have places of worship at Jerusalem.[8] He sets the Ruthenians, who can only

---

[1] The Abbess Euphrosyne, Princess of Polotsk. She died in Jerusalem. Her narrative, translated into French by Mme B. de Khitrovo, is in *ROL*, iii (1895), pp. 32–5. For comment see R. Grousset, *Histoire des Croisades*, vol. i, Paris, 1934, pp. 312–13.

[2] PL 155, c. 1229; the date is established by another reference in a charter of King Amaury (1174), *idem*, c. 1235.

[3] H. Stern in B, xi (1936), pp. 100–52.

[4] Quoted in B, xiii (1938), p. 422.

[5] PG 133, c. 927–62; *PPTS*, No. 11, vol. v, is a bad translation.

[6] PL 201, c. 851.   [7] Ibid., c. 849–50.

[8] PL 155, c. 1088; Eng. trans. from another text in *PPTS*, No. 14, vol. v, p. 69; cf. a similar list of 1172 in Theodorich, *PPTS*, No. 17, ibid., p. 14.

be Russians, between the English and the Czechs, and the Armenians,[1] whom the Latins often treated as if they were Orthodox, between the Georgians and the Syrians. At the end are the heretical churches, Jacobites, Syri, (?) Nestorians, Indians, Egyptians, Copts, and "Capheturici", who may be Abyssinians [2] or more probably Tartars from the Assyrian (Nestorian) missions. This does not look as if the Greeks and Russians were considered heretical.

If the Greeks and Syrians in Jerusalem had been out of communion with the Franks we should expect to hear in pilgrim narratives of such scenes of discord as have been unhappily common in the Holy Places in modern times. That jealousies between Melkites and Armenians were not by any means unknown is only too clear from the narrative of Matthew of Edessa, who gives a dramatic picture of the *Dzrazadik*, the "erroneous Easter" of 1102, when the Easter fire descended from heaven in response to the supplications of the Armenians while "the inhabitants of Jerusalem" were engaged in a Palm Sunday procession.[3] I know of no such picture of an open clash between Greeks and Franks before 1187.

In the second half of the twelfth century Greek Patriarchs of Jerusalem appear in the proceedings of councils at Constantinople.[4] Later Orthodox controversialists[5] maintain that they represent the true succession from Simeon through a Patriarch Sabbas, who has been plausibly identified [6] with a metropolitan of Tyre, an eunuch, expelled from his see by the Turks, who came to Jerusalem as a refugee and took charge in the absence of the Patriarch, very probably in 1097. In 1107 he was present at a Byzantine synod under Nicholas III of Constan-

---

[1] See M. Ormanian, *The Armenian Church*, pp. 60–1, and *supra*, pp. 162–4.
[2] Theodorich has "Nubians".
[3] Op. cit. p. 251. See also *Mich. Syr.*, iii, p. 190.
[4] Nicetas Choniates, *Thesaurus Orthodoxae fidei*, PG 140, c. 1488, 180, 237, 257.
[5] Especially Dositheus, in his *History of the Patriarchs of Jerusalem* (in Greek), Bucharest, 1715, pp. 752, 1243.
[6] By E. Honigmann in *Studies in Slavic Church History*, in B, xvii (1945), pp. 152–3. The texts are PG 119, c. 908 on the translation of Patriarchs, and Nicephorus Callistus in PG 146, c. 1195–6.

tinople. But his name does not appear in diptychs made on Sinai, in territory controlled by the Sultan of Egypt, in about 1166, or in the metrical diptychs of St Sabbas, made at the end of the thirteenth century.[1] It is therefore likely that Nicholas, John, and Nicephorus, who do appear in these lists, and at councils in Constantinople in 1156, 1158, and 1166, were claimants whose pretensions to the see of Jerusalem were advanced in the course of the struggle for Antioch.

At Antioch on the other hand the line of Greek Patriarchs in exile commanded a considerable body of local support. This is especially evident in 1207–13, when Prince Bohemond IV restored the Greek Patriarch Simeon, despite the strongly expressed displeasure of Pope Innocent III.[2] By that time the Byzantine empire was in pieces. Simeon, who is not in the Greek lists,[3] was probably a local candidate. The schism in the church of Antioch was in the first place between the local Greeks and the local Latins, and in such a schism Latin noblemen could take the Greek side without conscious disloyalty to the Catholic church of the West, if circumstances made some concession to the Greek element in the principality a political necessity. This was a factor in 1164 and earlier,[4] but then the Byzantine alliance was as important. In 1207 the Greeks had no resources, and were no longer dangerous, but local Greeks could still be of use.[5]

The same Pope who objected to the reception of a Greek Patriarch at Antioch was prepared to recognize the Patriarch Nicholas of Alexandria, who ordained a Latin deacon with his consent.[6] He was represented at the Fourth Lateran Council in 1215. His church had been accustomed to give communion to Latin captives when the Patriarch Mark, in 1190, addressed a

---

[1] See F. E. Brightman, *Liturgies Eastern and Western*, Oxford, 1896, pp. lii, 501–2, and ECQ, vii (1947), p. 50 with refs.

[2] See PL 215, c. 1322, 1345; PL 216, c. 434.

[3] *Eastern Schism*, p. 96, n. 3.

[4] See the letters of Latin nobles to the King of France in PL 155, c. 1269, 1273, 1278 (1164).

[5] See A. Luchaire, *Innocent III; la question d'orient*, Paris, 1907, pp. 37–42, 50–2, and E. Rey in *ROL*, viii (1901), pp. 139, 147.

[6] Letters in Potthast, ii, Nos. 1430 (1201), 4365, 4726 (1212–13).

series of questions on this and other subjects to the canonist Theodore Balsamon, who was titular Patriarch of Antioch. On the matter of the communion to the Latins he replied as follows: [1]

> Because for many years the Western church has been divided in spiritual communion (πνευματίκης, κοινωνίαις) from the other four Patriarchs . . . and become alien to the Orthodox, for which reason the Pope is not mentioned in the relation of names . . . no Latins should be communicated unless they first declare that they will abstain from their doctrines and customs and be in subjection to the canons, and be made like unto the Orthodox.

According to Demetrius Chomatenus, who was Metropolitan of Ochrida in Macedonia in 1207–22, Balsamon's answer was criticized by many

> as showing too great harshness and bitterness, and an unjustifiable tone, in blaming the Latin forms and customs, "because all this", they said, "has never been decreed synodically nor have they ever been rejected as heretics, but both eat with us and pray with us".[2]

It is important to observe that neither party proposes to excommunicate Latins as such without examination. The discord is between those who would admit them unconditionally if they wish to come and those who insist on the strictest conformity to the diocesan regulations. I believe that these two standpoints can be traced back to the time of Michael Cerularius.

It has always been something of a mystery that in this Patriarch's quarrel with the Latin churches in Constantinople so much should be said about *azymes* and other liturgical uses. The tracts of Nicetas Stethatos [3] and Leo of Ochrida,[4] written in direct connection with the controversy, say nothing about the *filioque*. They are concerned with the use of leavened bread, Saturday fasting, and Lenten usages; the right days on which to celebrate the mass of the pre-sanctified gifts, and the wrongness of the Latin custom of omitting alleluia after Septuagesima.

---

[1] PG 138, c. 967–8. For the date see my own article in ECQ, vi (1945–6), p. 368.
[2] PG 119, c. 957–60.
[3] PG 120, c. 1011–22; PL 143, c. 974–84.
[4] PG 120, c. 835–44; PL 143, c. 793–8.

Nicetas has a little to say in defence of married clergy, and Leo of Ochrida against eating things strangled. Otherwise the whole of their argument has to do with *azymes* and Lent.

I think this concentration on liturgical issues can be explained if the Patriarch's first immediate object was to compel the Latins in his diocese either to conform to the diocesan regulations, especially in the matter of Lent or *azymes*, or to declare their opposition to received traditions. That the Latins desired to remain in his communion is clear from the example of Argyrus, whom he himself repelled four times from the altar.[1] In his second letter to Peter of Antioch, which was also sent to the other Eastern Patriarchs, he gives a longer list of Latin errors.[2] Latin monks eat suet; they shave; recite the Gloria in a form that reeks of Sabellianism; allow two brothers to marry two sisters; celebrate masses where the priest alone communicates. Not only do they add to the creed and fast on Saturdays; they put salt in the mouths of the baptized, and some say that they baptize with one immersion "in the name of the Father and of the Son and of the Holy Ghost", another sign of Sabellian fusion between the three persons of the Trinity. It is easy to see that Cerularius was quite sure that the Latins were heretics, and that he could prove it, by showing that they would not fast on the right days, and that they would use *azymes*. Peter of Antioch thought these barbarous customs wrong but not significant.[3]

The same issues arose again in 1089 between Nicholas III and Theophylact of Bulgaria,[4] and again in 1107-11, when a letter [5] of Bruno of Asti, Abbot of Monte Cassino, to the Benedictines of Constantinople warns them against the "soft persuasion" and "furious elocution" of "the bishop of the diocese and his clergy", who asked them "Is Christ divided in His body, that He is one in the sacrifice at Rome and another in the sacrifice at Constantinople?" "But", says Bruno,

---

[1] So he says in his letter to Peter of Antioch, PG 120, c. 788.
[2] PG 120, c. 789-94.
[3] PG 120, c. 763-78, to Dominic of Grado, c. 807-8, to Cerularius.
[4] *Supra*, p. 157.   [5] PL 165, c. 1085-90.

we truly hold, and from the heart firmly believe, that although the customs of the churches are distinct, nevertheless there is one faith, indissolubly united to the head, that is Christ: and that He himself is one and remains the same in His body.

The monks are told to plead the example of St Gregory the Great, who celebrated in the Latin fashion when he lived in Constantinople as *apocrisarius* in the time of the emperor Maurice. They are to claim toleration from their diocesan.

That Greek propaganda was not always unsuccessful is suggested by a much later letter [1] of Innocent III to the Latins of Constantinople in 1199 forbidding priests to confirm children according to the Eastern custom. This seems to show that some of them carried their conformity with the institutions of the local church to the extent of "taking chrism" from the Oecumenical Patriarchate. Peter the Venerable, Abbot of Cluny, writing in the reign of John Comnenus (1118–43), petitioned the Patriarch for the restoration of a closed Cluniac priory. In his letter he addressed him as "the venerable and great high-priest of God", and expressed his great desire "in you to venerate the blessed pontiffs of your city". [2] Thus he recognized him as the legitimate successor of all previous Patriarchs, with power to close and open even Latin churches.

Latin settlements in the empire were not confined to Constantinople. In 1164 the Abbot of St Mary in Adrianople and the Prior of the Hospital of St John in Constantinople acted as intermediaries between the emperor and the King of France. [3] The monastery of the Amalfitans on Mount Athos, flourishing in 1046, [4] was still in existence in 1196, [5] when the superior witnessed, in Latin, a deed of one of the other monasteries. Other evidence suggests that it was still there at the end of the century, when the Serbian monastery of Chilandiari was founded. In

---

[1] PL 214, c. 772.

[2] PL 189, c. 262. See *Eastern Schism*, p. 114.

[3] PL 155, c. 1275–7.

[4] P. Meyer, *Haupturkunden für . . . Athoskloster*, p. 157, a *typikon* of Constantine IX, allowing the monks to have a ship, not to be used for trade. I owe this reference to the late Professor R. M. Dawkins.

[5] A. N. Mouravieff, the Russian church historian, quoted in *The Christian Remembrancer*, xxii, Oxford, 1851, p. 338.

the remoter parts of the diocese of Durazzo priests of the Latin rite were still ordained by a Greek metropolitan after 1200.[1]

The survival of these Latin institutions in the Patriarchate of Constantinople is one among many signs that in the twelfth century there was as yet no clear line between Roman Catholics and Eastern Orthodox. Greeks and Syrians in Calabria, Sicily, and Palestine, who obeyed the Latin secular authorities, still received priests and pilgrims from Constantinople and from Russia.[2] Latins were still admitted to communion at Alexandria, Durazzo, and probably elsewhere. For a long time no clear distinction was made between Greeks who submitted to Rome, especially in Italy and Cyprus,[3] and Greeks of the independent churches. Even in the sixteenth and seventeenth centuries many Albanians and some Greeks crossed from their homelands to Italy, Sicily, and Corsica, and joined the existing churches of the Greek rite, or even founded new communities in union with Rome.[4] In the seventeenth and eighteenth centuries it would be possible to find instances of Latin missionaries received in Eastern churches, who accepted the bishops as their ordinaries and worked to bring them into union with Rome, especially perhaps in Syria and Palestine.[5] But at the same time converts from Roman error were rebaptized in Russia.

We cannot speak of "progressive estrangement" in the sense of an historical process that might be represented by a graph.[6] Place is more important than period. Schism at Antioch coincides in time with peace at Bari and at Jerusalem, war in Russia

---

[1] John of Citra, replying to Constantine Cabasilas, Metropolitan of Durazzo, in PG 119, c. 959–64.

[2] E.g. Nilos Doxipatres, who served first at Constantinople, then at Palermo, and then at Constantinople again. See V. Laurent in EO, xxxvi (1937), pp. 5–30. His book on *The Order of the Patriarchal Thrones* (1143) in PG 132, c. 1083–1114, is dedicated to King Roger of Sicily, but his point of view is Byzantine. For other anti-Latin controversialists among the Italian Greeks see K. Lake in JTS, v (1904), pp. 35, 39–40.

[3] For arguments used at Constantinople in 1412 against recognizing the Cypriotes as Orthodox see J. Hackett, *A History of the Orthodox Church in Cyprus*, pp. 142–9.

[4] A. Fortescue, *The Uniate Eastern Churches*, pp. 115–24, 169–70.

[5] Ibid., pp. 193, 197, see also Y. Congar in *L'église et les eglises*, vol. i, pp. 5–6.

[6] See R. Mayne in *C.H.J.*, xi (1954), p. 138.

with a relaxation of tension in Syria and Palestine. The constant
common factor is pressure from the West for submission to the
Roman primacy of jurisdiction. In the Latin states this was an
inevitable necessity, which might mean little more than any
other oath of allegiance to alien rulers, Frank, Turk, or Arab.
In many Greek islands the whole population was Uniate while
the Venetians ruled, but Orthodox when the Turks arrived. No
doubt some became and remained pro-Roman, but more had
never made a real submission. In Moslem lands on the other
hand the Roman primacy of jurisdiction might be more easily
admitted in theory, because it could never be exercised in
practice. In the Greek states the political arguments in favour
of Latin alliances, and therefore of submission to Rome, were
balanced by other political arguments against allowing the
Latin clergy and colonists to refer their disputes with the Greek
bishops and clergy to a Latin authority.

The primacy of Rome was seldom directly denied, in the
sense of "the primacy among her sisters, and the presidency in
the first place of honour at General Councils",[1] but the Latin
interpretation of the primacy in terms of jurisdiction revealed a
difference between East and West in the doctrine of the Church.
Attempts were made to relate this to the *filioque*, but these could
not penetrate to the heart of the matter while the distinctive
element in Latin theology was very little, if at all, understood in
the East. St Augustine was not translated into Greek before the
fourteenth century. His *De Civitate Dei* and his anti-Donatist
writings did much to determine the development of the
Western doctrine of the Church, as his anti-Pelagian writings
are the starting-point of all Western controversies on the nature
of grace. Grace is the connecting link between theology (in the
Byzantine sense of the doctrine of the Trinity) and ecclesiology,
the doctrine of the Church. The Eastern churches never had a
doctrine of created grace, of the gifts of God apart from the gift
of Himself to the baptized who are buried and risen with Christ
and live and reign in the Holy Spirit. Therefore they could

[1] So Nicetas of Nicomedia reported by Anselm of Havelberg in PL 188,
c. 1219 (1136).

never understand the idea of the vicar of Christ ruling His Church in His absence. They thought of their bishops not in the first place as rulers, but as high-priests in the presence of Christ and the Spirit, witnesses to the truth, and stewards of the mysteries of God. Bishops are therefore judges in matters of penitential discipline, but in their guardianship of the church's goods, and in the administration of ecclesiastical offices, they were normally subject to the supervision of the emperor.

This attitude was and is easily misunderstood by those whose chief concern was with church order. In the West the typical schism was over an episcopal succession, not on a point of doctrine. African Donatism did not raise any doctrinal question, and this was always remembered through the writings of St Augustine. Such schisms were not unknown in Eastern Christendom,[1] but there they were easily healed and commonly ignored by third parties and by the faithful laity.[2] So were Western schisms between Popes and anti-Popes before the reformation of the Roman church in the eleventh century.

This is the decisive turning-point when communion with the Roman church, and above all with the legitimate Pope, became the West's test of orthodoxy. This was not so in 1054, when the Papal legates themselves admitted "the perfect orthodoxy" of the court and city of Constantinople, though the Pope's name had been missing from the diptychs for some years,[3] but in 1089 the absence of the Pope's name was the decisive question.[4] Should this be mended, or perpetuated? On this hesitations had to be resolved, and the actions of the Latins at Antioch were probably decisive.[5] By 1108 they could not be reversed without a loss of face for all the Latins in the East. By that time the Roman see had acquired an undisputed pre-eminence in Western society. A rebuff for Rome would be a defeat for the entire West. But in 1054 Leo IX might still appear to be the emperor's agent.

This date owes much of its prestige to the convenience of

---

[1] E.g. between Photius and Ignatius, *supra*, p. 110, and Euthymius and Nicholas Mysticus, p. 133.

[2] *Supra*, pp. 178–9.   [3] *Supra*, p. 151.

[4] *Supra*, pp. 156–8, 180–1.   [5] *Supra*, pp. 162–3, 166–7.

historians, who were anxious to prepare and complete the schism between East and West before the reformation of the Western church, sometimes to throw the West's share of the blame on the Papacy before the reform. But the reform is the schism. It carried with it a revolution in the relationship between church and state. The Pope's claim to lordship as vicar of Christ in temporal and spiritual things implies that the Church is in charge of the world, and that political revolutions should be directed by ecclesiastical pronouncements. This claim was advanced, not by the German Popes in the reign of Henry III, but by Gregory VII and his successors, whose victory was assured only after the first Crusade. This victory brought a change in the whole conception of the Church.

In a certain sense the schism was political but Byzantine distaste for Papal pronouncements on political and military matters had theological roots. Many Byzantine politicians including most of the emperors, were prepared to compromise. Stubborn resistance came from the monks, the parish clergy, and the lower classes in town and country, who loved their part in the liturgy, and could not believe that the Latins had the same religion as themselves.

The theological difference between East and West is elusive and difficult to state, but it may be safe to say that the difference in the doctrine of the Trinity implies a different idea of personality in God,[1] and therefore of the personal action of the Holy Ghost in the Church and in the world. This underlies the difference in the doctrine of grace, which did not become explicit until the schism was an accomplished fact,[2] as also the West's need for a human focus and centre of authority in the Church.

This was felt before the need was effectively supplied. The reformed Papacy was first of all a vision of Rome seen in the northern seas and forests, interpreted by those who admired and envied the Caliphate of the Ommayads and the Abbasids.

---

[1] *Supra*, p. 74.
[2] In the Palamite controversy of the fourteenth century. See V. Lossky, *The Mystical theology of the Eastern Church*, Eng. trans., London, 1957.

Italy in the eleventh century was still a detached part of the Byzantine empire, but the new civilization of the Latin universities, of Paris in the twelfth century, is not Byzantine but Syrian, brought to the West through the schools of Spain, Jewish, Mozarabic, Moslem. The ultimate sources are the same, Greek, Hebrew, Babylonian, but the streams diverge before the rise of Islam, in the revolt of Syria against Greece and Rome. In this revolt the West was implicated from the very first. The discontents that troubled Egypt and Syria were also found in Italy and Africa. But for a long time the two Romes adhered to one another. When they quarrelled, they were reconciled. They fell apart only when German and Norman influence in Italy was strong enough to overpower the Greek element, when to a Neapolitan such as St Thomas Aquinas the loadstone of culture was no longer Calabria, but Paris.

TABLE OF EMPERORS,
PATRIARCHS OF CONSTANTINOPLE,
AND POPES

(Anti-Popes and Patriarchs restored to the throne, are italicized.)

EMPERORS.	PATRIARCHS.	POPES.
Marcian 450–7	Anatolius 449–58	Leo I 440–61
Leo I 457–74	Gennadius 458–71	Hilary 461–8 (Sardinian)
Leo II 474	Acacius 471–89	Simplicius 468–83
Zeno 474–5		
Basiliscus 475–7		
Zeno (again) 477–91	Fravitta 489–90	Felix III 483–92
Anastasius I 491–518	Euphemius 490–6	Gelasius I 492–6 (African)
	Macedonius II 496–511	Anastasius II 496–8
		Symmachus 498–514 (Sardinian)
		Laurentius 498, 501–7
	Timothy I 511–18	Hormisdas 514–23
Justin I 518–27	John II 518–20	
	Epiphanius 520–36	John I 523–6
Justinian I 527–65		Felix IV 526–30
		Boniface II 530–3 (Goth)
		Dioscorus 530 (Egyptian)
		John II 533–5
	Anthimus 536	Agapetus 535–6
	Menas 536–52	Silverius 536–7
		Vigilius 537–55
	Eutychius 552–65	Pelagius I 556–61
Justin II 565–78	John III 565–77	John III 561–74
Tiberius 574–82		Benedict I 575–9
	Eutychius 577–82	Pelagius II 579–90 (Goth)
Maurice 582–602	John IV 582–95	Gregory I 590–604 –
	Cyriacus 595–606	
Phocas 602–10		Sabinian 604–6
	Thomas I 607–10	Boniface III 607
		Boniface IV 608–15
Heraclius 610–41	Sergius 610–38	
		Deusdedit I 615–18
		Boniface V 619–25
		Honorius I 625–38
	Pyrrhus 638–41	Severinus 640
Constantine III 641		John IV 640–2 (Dalmatian)
Constans II 641–68	Paul II 641–52	Theodore I 642–9 (Palestinian)
	Pyrrhus 652	Martin I 649–53
	Peter 652–64	Eugenius I 654–7
	Thomas II 665–8	Vitalian 657–72

EMPERORS.	PATRIARCHS.	POPES.
Constantine IV 668–85	John V 668–74	Deusdedit II 672–6
	Constantine I 674–6	
	Theodore I 676–8	Domnus 676–8
	George I 678–83	Agatho 678–81 (Sicilian)
	Theodore I 683–6	Leo II 682–4 (Sicilian)
Justinian II 685–95		Benedict II 684–5
	Paul III 686–93	John V 685–6 (Syrian)
		Conon 686–7 (from Asia)
		Sergius I 687–701 (Syrian)
Leontius 695–8	Callinicus 693–705	
Tiberius III 698–705		John VI 701–5 (Greek)
Justinian II 705–11 (restored)	Cyrus 705–11	John VII 705–7 (Greek)
		Sisinnius 708 (Syrian)
Philippicus 711–13	John VI 711–15	Constantine 708–15 (Syrian)
Anastasius II 713–16	Germanus I 715–30	Gregory II 715–31
Theodosius III 716–17		
Leo III 717–40		
	Anastasius 730–54	Gregory III 731–41 (Syrian)
Constantine V 740–75		Zacharias 741–52 (Calabrian)
		Stephen II 752
	Constantine II 754–66	Stephen III 752–7
		Paul I 757–61
	Nicetas 766–80	*Constantine II* 767–8
		Stephen III 768–72 (Sicilian)
Leo IV 775–80		Hadrian I 772–95
Constantine VI 780–97	Paul IV 780–4	
Irene 780–95, 797–802	Tarasius 784–806	Leo III 795–816
Nicephorus I 802–11	Nicephorus 806–15	
Stauracius 811		
Michael I 811–13		
Leo V 813–20	Theodotus I 815–21	Stephen IV 816–7
Michael II 820–9	Antony I 821–32	Pascal I 817–24
Theophilus 829–42	John VII 832–43	Eugenius II 824–7
		Valentine 827
		Gregory IV 827–44
Michael III 842–67	Methodius 843–7	Sergius II 844–7
Theodora 842–56	Ignatius 847–58	Leo IV 847–55 (pro-Greek)
Bardas 856–66		Benedict III 855–8 (pro-Greek)
		Anastasius 855–8 (pro-Frank)
	Photius 858–67	Nicholas I 858–67 (pro-Frank)
Basil I 867–86	*Ignatius* 867–77	Hadrian II 867–72 (pro-Frank)
		John VIII 872–82
	Photius 877–86	Marinus 882–4
		Hadrian III 884–5
Leo VI 886–912	Stephen I 886–93	Stephen V 885–91

EMPERORS.	PATRIARCHS.	POPES.
	Antony II 893–901	Formosus 891–6
		Boniface VI 896
		Stephen VI 896–7 (anti-Formosus)
		Romanus 897
		Theodore II 897–8 (pro-Formosus)
		Sergius III 898 (anti-Formosus)
		John IX 898–900
	Nicholas Mysticus 901–6	Benedict IV 900–3
		Leo V 903 (pro-Formosus?)
		Christopher 903 (pro-Formosus?)
		Sergius III, restored, 904–11 (anti-Formosus)
	Euthymius 906–12	Anastasius III 911–13
Alexander 912–13	*Nicholas Mysticus* 912–25	Lando 913
		John X 914–28 (anti-Formosus)
Constantine VII 912–59		
Romanus I 919–44		
Christopher 921–31		
Stephen and Constantine 924–45	Stephen II 925–8	
	Tryphon 928–32	Leo VI 928–9 (House of Theophylact)
		Stephen VII 929–31 ,,
	Theophylact 933–56	John XI 931–6 ,,
		Leo VII 936–9 ,,
		Stephen VIII 939–42 ,,
		Marinus II 942–6 ,,
		Agapetus II 946–55 ,,
Romanus II 959–63	Polyeuctes 956–70	John XII 955–64 ,,
Basil II 963–1025		
Constantine VIII 963–1028		*Leo VIII* 963 (pro-German)
Nicephorus II 963–9		Benedict V 964 (anti-German)
John I Tzimisces 969–76	Basil I 970–4	John XIII 965–72
Basil II 963–1025		
Constantine VIII 963–1028	Antony II 974–9	Benedict VI 973–4 (pro-German)
		Boniface VII 974–85 (Crescentii)
	Nicholas II 979–91	Benedict VII 974–83 (pro-German)
		John XIV 983–4 (pro-German)
		John XV 985–96 (Crescentii)
	Sisinnius 995–1000	Gregory V 996–9 (German)
		John XVI 997–8 (Calabrian)

EMPERORS.	PATRIARCHS.	POPES.
	Sergius II 1000–19	Silvester II 999–1003 (French)
		John XVII 1003 (Crescentii)
		John XVIII 1003–9 (Crescentii)
		Sergius IV 1009–12 (Crescentii)
		Benedict VIII 1012–24 (Tusculan)
	Eustathius 1019–25	*Gregory VI* 1012–14 (Crescentii)
Zoe 1028–50	Alexius 1025–43	John XIX 1024–32 (Tusculan)
Theodora 1028–56		
Romanus III 1028–34		
Michael IV 1034–41		Benedict IX 1032–46 (Tusculan)
Michael V 1041–2	Michael Cerularius 1043–58	*Silvester III* 1044–6 (Crescentii)
Constantine IX 1042–55		Gregory VI 1045–6 (reform)
		Clement II 1046–7 (German)
		Damasus II 1048 (German)
		Leo IX 1048–54 (Lorraine)
Michael VI 1056–7		Victor II 1055–7 (German)
Isaac I 1057–9		Stephen IX 1057–8 (Lorraine)
Constantine X 1059–67	Constantine III 1059–64	*Benedict X* 1058–9 (Roman)
		Nicholas II 1058–61 (reform)
Michael VII 1067–78	John VIII 1064–75	*Honorius II* 1061–72 (empire)
Romanus IV 1067–71		Alexander II 1061–73 (reform)
Nicephorus III 1078–81	Cosmas I 1075–81	Gregory VII 1073–85 (reform)
Alexius I 1081–1118	Eustratius 1081–4	*Clement III* 1080–1100 (empire)
	Nicholas III 1084–1111	Victor III 1086–7 (reform)
		Urban II 1088–99 (reform)
		Pascal II 1099–1118 (reform)
		Theodore 1101–2 (empire)
		Albert 1102–5 (empire)
		Silvester IV 1105–11? (empire)
	John IX 1111–34	
John II 1118–43		Gelasius II 1118–19 (reform)
		Gregory VIII 1118–21 (empire)
		Calixtus II 1119–24 (reform, French)
		Celestine III 1121–2 (empire)
		Honorius II 1124–30
		Innocent II 1130–43 (reform)
	Leo Stypes 1134–43	*Anacletus* 1130–8 (Sicilian)
		Victor IV 1138 (Sicilian)
Manuel I 1143–80	Michael II 1143–6	Celestine II 1143–4
		Lucius II 1144–5
	Cosmas II 1146–7	Eugenius III 1145–53
	Nicholas IV 1147–51	

EMPERORS.	PATRIARCHS.	POPES.
	Theodotus II 1151–3	
	Neophytus I 1153–4	Anastasius IV 1153–4
	Constantine IV 1154–6	Hadrian IV 1154–9 (English)
	Luke Chrysoberges 1156–69	Alexander III 1159–81 (reform)
		Victor IV 1159–64 (empire)
		Pascal III 1164–8 (empire)
	Michael Anchialus 1169–76	*Calixtus* 1168–77 (empire)
	Chariton 1177–8	
	Theodosius I 1178–83	
Alexius II 1180–3		Lucius III 1181–5
Andronicus I 1183–5	Basil II 1183–7	
Isaac II 1185–95		Urban III 1185–7
	Nicetas II 1187–90	Gregory VIII 1187
	Leontius 1190–1	Clement III 1187–91
	Dositheus 1191–2	Celestine III 1191–8
Alexius III 1195–1203	George II 1192–9	
	John X Camaterus 1199–1206	Innocent III 1198–1216
Issac II (restored) and Alexius IV 1203–4		
Alexius V 1204		

PARTITION OF THE EMPIRE, 1204.

INDEX

ABASGIANS, 58, 114, 128
Acacius, Patriarch, 34–9, 122
Acephali, 35, 38, 40
Acoimeti, 35–7, 40, 43, 45, 93
Adhemar, 159–62
Agapetus, Pope, 46
Agatho, Pope, 65–6
Albania, 21, 55, 103, 112, 156, 166, 176, 190
Alexander III, Pope, 167–70
Alexandria, 23–7, 31–47, 59–61, 66, 70, 118, 138–9, 150, 167, 172, 176, 186–7
Alexius Comnenus, Emperor, 8, 16–17, 156–62, 165–6
Anastasius I, Emperor, 36–9, 55, 93
Anastasius, Patriarch, 88
Anastasius II, Pope, 36–7, 47, 66
Anna Comnena, 6, 8, 16–17, 159
Anselm, St, 161–2
Anthimus, Patriarch, 46
Antioch, 4, 9, 21, 23, 26–7, 30, 33–5, 38–40, 46–9, 53, 64–7, 110, 118, 138–9, 149–52, 160–7, 169–71, 178, 180–2
Aphthartodocetae, 28–9, 40–54, 69, 75
Apulia, 88, 102, 139–40, 144–6, 148–9, 154, 161–2, 167, 186–7, 192
Arians, 19, 24, 36, 56, 64, 114
Armenia, x, 3, 31–2, 40, 43, 52–68, 72–3, 84, 86, 114–17, 120, 132, 139, 148, 161–4, 169, 172, 185
Art: in general, vii, 4–5, 7–12, 18, 141, 184; the problem of representation, 28, 70–1, 76–93
Assyrians, 29, 31–2, 40, 52, 58–61, 67, 69, 71–3, 83, 92, 152, 182, 185
Athanasius the Camel-driver, Jacobite Patriarch, 59, 62
Athanasius, Patriarch of Antioch, 167, 170
Athanasius, St, Patriarch of Alexandria, 25, 28, 32–4, 53–4, 74
Athos, 12, 16, 138–9, 179, 189
Autocephalous churches, 31–2, 58, 128, 134, 140, 169
Azymes, 10, 68, 148–50, 156–7, 163, 187–9

Bardas, 109, 120
Bar-Hebraeus, 59, 67, 70, 164, 170
Basil I, Emperor, 120–2, 125–6, 134
Basil II, Emperor, 139, 142, 146–7
Basil, Metropolitan of Reggio, 155, 157
Basil Boiannes, 145–6
Benedict III, Pope, 107–9, 125
Benedict VII, Pope, 140, 142
Benedict VIII, Pope, 143, 145
Benedict IX, Pope, 147
Benedictines in the East, 72, 105, 188–9
Bogomiles, 75
Bohemia, 111–12, 114, 124, 127, 141, 185
Bohemond of Taranto, 159–63, 166
Bohemond IV of Antioch, 186
Boniface VII, Pope, 140, 142
Bruno of Asti, 188–9
Bulgarians, 55, 73, 114–34, 139–41, 172, 179

Calabria, 4, 85, 88, 94, 102–4, 137–8, 140–1, 149, 154–7, 161–5, 190
Charles the Great, Holy Roman Emperor, 103–5, 137, 153
Civil Service, 2–4, 13–16, 32, 87–8, 93–7, 109, 132–3, 148
Clement III, anti-Pope (Guibert of Ravenna), 155, 157, 159
Constans, Emperor, 3, 42, 56, 62–4
Constantine the Great, Emperor, 2, 20, 54, 56; see *Donation of Constantine*
Constantine IV, Emperor, 64–6
Constantine V, Emperor, 85, 94–5
Constantine VI, Emperor, 95–7
Constantine Ducas, Emperor, 155
Constantine Monomachus, Emperor, 149–52
Constantine Porphyrogenitus, Emperor, 3, 7, 55, 132–3
Constantine I, Patriarch, 66
Constantine Leichudes, Patriarch, 155
Constantine, Pope, 85

201